TIM ANDERSON

JAMES DITTUS

GAIL SHADWELL

COMMUNICATING WITH OTHERS

A GUIDE TO EFFECTIVE SPEAKING IN A COMPLEX WORLD

HAYDEN
HM
McNEIL

THIRD EDITION

Hayden-McNeil Sustainability

Hayden-McNeil's standard paper stock uses a minimum of 30% post-consumer waste. We offer higher % options by request, including a 100% recycled stock. Additionally, Hayden-McNeil Custom Digital provides authors with the opportunity to convert print products to a digital format. Hayden-McNeil is part of a larger sustainability initiative through Macmillan Higher Ed. Visit http://sustainability.macmillan.com to learn more.

Printed in the United States of America

10 9 8 7 6 5 4 3 2 1

ISBN 978-0-7380-7402-3

Hayden-McNeil Publishing
14903 Pilot Drive
Plymouth, MI 48170
www.hmpublishing.com

Dittus 7402-3 S15

TABLE OF CONTENTS

DEDICATION

For Whitney

ACKNOWLEDGMENT

This third edition of *Communicating with Others* represents a significant change in format from prior editions, but much of the content from prior editions remains. We therefore think it is important to recognize Marta Walz, who was an author for the first edition of the text and hence much of her contribution to the quality of the text remains. We would also like to thank Jamieson Credille for allowing us to use her outline as an example for all students. We greatly appreciate the work of Erin Southward, Elizabeth O'Keefe, and Heather Galanty of Hayden-McNeil for their significant help and support on this project. Finally, thank you to our family, friends, and colleagues who have contributed to this text in numerous ways, from suggestions for material to giving us the support to complete this project; we thank you all.

COMMUNICATING WITH OTHERS   A GUIDE TO EFFECTIVE SPEAKING IN A COMPLEX WORLD

HOW TO USE THIS BOOK

In addition to the main body of the text, there are several other sections designed to help you develop and improve your communication skills.

TRAQ YOUR UNDERSTANDING

First is the TRAQ column which will appear on the outside of every page. TRAQ stands for Thoughts, Reflections, Answers, and Questions and that is exactly what the column is for. In that space, you should answer the asked questions, note your own questions, and remark about thoughts and reflections you have as you read the material.

APPLYING THE FUNDAMENTALS

These separate sections of the text, inserted throughout many of the chapters, provide additional information and examples to help you see how this material applies in actually communication situations.

BEYOND THE FUNDAMENTALS

These sections provide material which goes beyond the basics of the fundamentals of communication. While this is more advanced material, being aware of these concepts and ideas will help you better understand the primary material, as well as give you a deeper understanding of the communication process.

BEYOND OUR PERSPECTIVE

The material in this book is based largely on the Western tradition of rhetorical studies which stems from the work of Aristotle and others in Ancient Greece. However, there are other perspectives on communication and its related concepts and these pieces help you see those other perspectives.

RESOURCES FOR BUILDING COMMUNICATION EFFECTIVENESS

These sections, at the end of certain chapters, provide worksheets to help you hone your communication skills and more effectively develop your speeches.

IN REVIEW

These sections, which will appear in the TRAQ Your Understanding column, will briefly summarize the key points in each section of the text. That will give you an opportunity to reflect on what you have just read and think about any questions you may still have about the material.

Throughout this book, you should use this column to answer the asked questions, note your own questions, and remark about thoughts and reflections you have as you read the material.

IN REVIEW
The supplemental sections in this book are...
- TRAQ Your Understanding
- Applying the Fundamentals
- Beyond the Fundamentals
- Beyond Our Perspective
- Resources for Building Communication Effectiveness
- In Review

Questions:

Reflections:

COMMUNICATING WITH OTHERS   A GUIDE TO EFFECTIVE SPEAKING IN A COMPLEX WORLD

CHAPTER 1

INTRODUCTION TO COMMUNICATION STUDIES

To some extent we are all the prisoners of stereotypes; we see each other in terms of distorted and oversimplified images.
Better communication in the realm of ideas, of the arts, and of science can help refashion these false images.
And by seeing more clearly we may act more wisely.

Chester Bliss Bowles

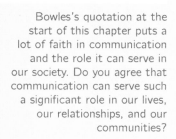

Throughout this book, you should use this column to answer the asked questions, note your own questions, and remark about thoughts and reflections you have as you read the material.

Bowles's quotation at the start of this chapter puts a lot of faith in communication and the role it can serve in our society. Do you agree that communication can serve such a significant role in our lives, our relationships, and our communities?

In order to be effective and successful when communicating a message,
it is important to understand exactly what communication is.

The title of this book is *Communicating with Others* and you are likely using it in a communication class. So, it is safe to assume that in this class you will be studying communication, but what is communication? Based on the context of your class, or your individual perceptions, you might answer simply, "public speaking." However, communication is more than public speaking. While communication does occur during presentations in classrooms and auditoriums, it also occurs in boardrooms and living rooms, across tables in coffee houses and conference rooms. It is not only the words you speak, but how you present them: your tone of voice, your eye contact, how you look, and how you act. In this opening chapter we will provide the framework for investigating many of these forms of communication.

COMMUNICATION DEFINED

So, communication is more than just public speaking; that still doesn't tell us exactly what it is. Everyone has a definition of communication, ranging from Tom Peters' whimsical definition that communication is everyone's panacea for everything, to Ralph Waldo Emerson's more philosophical approach that speech is power: speech is to persuade, to convert, to compel. But neither of those definitions serve our more practical purposes to help you hone your communication skills.

To better focus our discussion of how to improve your communication skills, we will define communication as **a transactive process in which people exchange and interpret symbolic messages in order to construct meaning with the intention of achieving some purpose.** This definition contains a few key ideas. First, communication is transactive, meaning the focus is not only on the speaker. We study communication from the perspective of all people involved. Second, communication is symbol based. That means we use words and behaviors to represent other objects, people, or ideas. Further, people use these symbols to construct meaning, and, because the words (and, in fact, the content of any message) are arbitrary symbols, that meaning is not inherent in the things we talk about or even in the symbols we use to talk about those things, but rather meaning is in the way people use and interpret those symbols. Finally, communication is purposeful, meaning that when we communicate a message we hope to achieve some goal and the measure of our success, then, can be how well we achieve that goal.

COMMUNICATION PRINCIPLES

Because each of these ideas further helps us understand exactly what communication is, we will explore each in more detail.

COMMUNICATION IS TRANSACTIVE

Since the middle of the twentieth century, scholars have been trying to figure out what the nature of communication is, and from those efforts have sprung several models of communication. The earliest models were linear models. These early, simple models sprang from the work of Claude Shannon and Warren Weaver in the late 1940s. As they were largely concerned with the development of technology for the transmission of messages, Shannon and Weaver's model included the equipment (i.e., a telephone) which would transmit the message. Simplifying the model to remove the technical elements, a linear model would look like this:

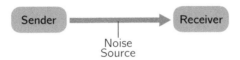

The basic idea is that there is someone (the sender) who wants to communicate some message, and who sends that message through a channel to another person (the receiver). Ideally, if the message is framed properly, the sender will respond as expected to the message. One thing that may prevent that is noise, any element that can negatively affect the effective transmission of the message.

When communication is linear, it implies that communication happens one way, and no feedback is expected. The military, for example, uses linear communication when superior officers give orders and expect them to be followed without question.

3

BEYOND THE FUNDAMENTALS ▬▬▬▬

THE LINEAR MODEL OF COMMUNICATION

This book is based largely on a transactional view of communication. The multi-variant nature of the transactional model makes it an excellent representation of communication as we understand it today. However, this is not the only model of communication, and, in fact, the transactional models of today are the result of theorists responding to perceived weaknesses in earlier models, particularly the linear models discussed in this chapter.

As noted, the linear model reflected the simplicity of the time it was developed, the late 1940s and 1950s, and in time, the linear model would be replaced by more complex models, like the transactive model. However, despite the simplicity of the linear model, knowledge of the linear model can make us more effective communicators, especially in particular settings. Much of the concern over the linear model was the role assigned to the receiver. This person was expected simply to be a passive recipient of the message and to respond appropriately without feedback, or any alternate agenda. We now know that is usually an unreasonable assumption. Because humans are cognitive beings, capable of thought and reason, each person will develop a unique personality and that means everyone will have a unique perspective on everything, including communicated messages. However, there are times when someone needs or wants to be sure that a message is responded to in exactly the way the person intends without question or feedback. Military generals, for example, need to know for the safety and security of all soldiers, that orders will be carried out exactly as intended. Also, some corporations are so concerned about a unified public image that they expect very particular actions from their employees. In both cases, the goals will best be achieved using a linear model of communication. However, analysis of the linear model shows that the independent thoughts of the receiver can limit the effectiveness of the model, so people who want to utilize a linear style of communication need to address that issue. They do that by trying to standardize the context and paradigm of the communicators and by establishing an acceptance of the assumptions of the linear model. To a great extent, that is what basic training, for example, is all about.

So, while most of your communication activities will be transactional in nature, an effective communicator understands other models and knows their strengths and limitations and works to establish a situation where the particular style of communication they would like to use is likely to be effective.

You should notice that this model is very simple. One element of that simplicity is that it assumes that only one person is communicating a message. The other is simply a passive receiver. While there are still vestiges of this approach today, as noted above in Beyond the Fundamentals, today communication scholars recognize receivers (the audience in public speaking, for example) have power and that communication is not just an action that one person performs on another with predictable results. At times, audiences may accept messages without thinking about the implications or may be swayed by a well-crafted message. Either way, this is the choice of the audience. They have the power to accept or reject your message, no matter how well-crafted or poorly constructed it is. In addition, audiences will communicate (often nonverbally) how they are exercising that power.

Instead, today communication is generally seen as a transaction, a process in which people engage each other in the simultaneous exchange of ideas and information. We take turns speaking and listening because we are polite, but we do not take turns communicating. While someone is speaking, another person is listening, nodding in agreement or rolling their eyes in disbelief, laughing at a joke or scowling in anger, all forms of feedback to the person speaking in that moment. We are all communicating, and our constant feedback not only gives a speaker the opportunity to influence a listener, but listeners can also influence speakers, leading them to feel more confident or uncomfortable. Listener feedback can lead a speaker to continue in a certain direction, change course, or give up completely. All people involved in the communication have power to affect the outcome. This is why we call communication transactional. A transactional model looks very different than a linear model, and may look something like this:

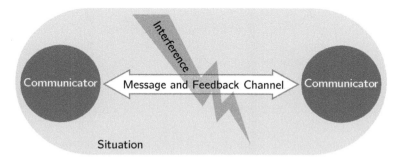

Notice now, there is not a sender and a receiver, but rather two people (it could be more) engaged in the simultaneous sharing of information. They both are sending messages and, now, also feedback, responses to prior messages. Finally, this model recognizes that communication occurs in context, which has a number of implications we will discuss in more detail shortly.

It is this view of communication as the simultaneous sharing of messages which will be the basis for our discussion of communication. This principle reinforces the idea that communication is not speaker-oriented. It is other-oriented. If we are to be effective communicators, we must consider all others participating in the communication. When we are speaking, we must consider the uniqueness and the power of our audience. When we are listening, we must carefully and thoughtfully attend to a speaker.

Seeing communication as a transaction implies that multiple messages are communicated at the same time. For example, in a group, everyone expresses their ideas and feelings as well as feedback about others' views both verbally and nonverbally and all those messages are communicated at the same time.

BEYOND OUR PERSPECTIVE

TRANSACTIVE COMMUNICATION AND CULTURE

In this chapter we discuss communication as a transactional process. As a result, communication is "other-centered." We attempt to understand the other person with whom we are communicating. We know that as individuals, we have different experiences and different filters through which we process information. This is true because of our unique experiences. At the same time, we all belong to certain cultures that help define us as both members of a group and as individuals. These cultures exist on an extremely large scale (i.e., different countries = different cultures) and on smaller scales as well, including groupings of race, ethnicity, age, gender, socioeconomic status, religion, sexual orientation, etc. All of these are considered "cultures," and while this text is meant to help you be an effective communicator in the larger culture of the United States, it is important to also understand that 1) cultures outside the U.S. have different ways of thinking, acting, and communicating which are equally valuable; 2) different cultures existing within the U.S. (sometimes referred to as "co-cultures") have different ways of thinking, acting, and communicating which are equally valuable; and 3) to be an ethical and effective communicator, cultural differences must be respectfully acknowledged. An effective communicator expects cultural differences to exist, recognizes them as a significant element of the context in the transactive model, and takes them into consideration when attempting to create an effective and successful communication message.

COMMUNICATION IS CONTEXTUAL

One by-product of looking at communication as a transaction is that it forces us to acknowledge that communication occurs within a context. In other words, the effectiveness of communication is affected by the entire communication environment: ourselves, our audience, the channel, message, feedback, interference, and situation. Every one of these has the potential to affect the outcome of the communication. They do not operate independently. A class that begins at 7:00 a.m. (situation) can create internal interference (tiredness) in a student. The student may unintentionally send feedback by yawning. The teacher may interpret the yawns as boredom and experience decreased confidence or even anger. The teacher may then alter the message to win over the audience or to express anger, disappointment, or a loss of confidence.

Any seemingly small aspect of the communication environment can have a major impact on the outcome, so to prepare a presentation (or to communicate any message), we must study the entire communication environment, also known as the **rhetorical situation**. The ability to analyze and respond to the rhetorical situation is known as **rhetorical sensitivity**. Because of the interdependence of all elements in the environment, developing rhetorical sensitivity is crucial to becoming a more effective communicator. Without this ability, communicating successfully becomes largely a matter of luck.

To be effective, we must adapt our communication to the context in which we are communicating. For example, we would communicate differently in a formal interview than we would when talking with our friends.

COMMUNICATION IS SYMBOLIC

A symbol is a representation of another thing, not the thing itself. For example, a flag is a symbol of a country. Sometimes people may even think that the flag says something about the country. However, a flag is just a flag, a piece of cloth. It is not a country. Nor does it say anything particular about the country. But, a flag can stand for a country and come to represent particular traits about that country and its people. That happens as a country, a society, chooses to define a symbol in a particular way. Words are also symbols. They represent other things, but are not those things. We may think of a word in a particular way and transfer those feelings to the thing, but, in the end, the thing is the thing and the word merely a symbolic convenience to help us talk about it.

It is also important to be aware that the words that are chosen to represent things are largely arbitrary symbols. There is nothing that makes this:

a cow, except that is what someone decided to call it and everyone else, at least, implicitly agreed.

7

So, to summarize what can sometimes be a difficult concept to grasp, the thing pictured previously is just that thing; it is not a cow. "Cow" is the arbitrary symbol we have chosen to attach to that thing so we can talk about it.

This arbitrariness of the symbols means there is no inherent meaning in a word. The meaning of the word can change depending on where you are, when you are saying it, and to whom you're saying it. Meanings are not permanently tied to words. Words may represent ideas or actions considered good or bad, positive or negative, but they are not good or bad themselves. Words, like other tools, are considered amoral. They can be used to do good or bad, but the morality (or immorality) is in the action, or use, not in the word. Because they are amoral, because they don't have inherent meaning, people often demean the importance of words. "They're *just* words" or "Sticks and stones can break my bones, but words can never hurt me." The truth is that symbols, including words, can be extremely powerful (consider how someone might feel if someone else used the word/symbol "cow" to refer to a large person).

Symbols, like the flag of the United States, although they are arbitrary and amoral, contain a great deal of power. The flag is a powerful symbol when burned in protest, when draped over a coffin at a military funeral, or when raised during a time of crisis. The flag was a powerful symbol for so many people that in 2006, a constitutional amendment to protect the flag from desecration failed by only one vote. The flag evokes strong emotions, bringing people to tears or filling them with rage.

Clearly, symbols are powerful. This is also true of words. While not every word evokes the same emotion or the same level of emotion in people, we all have words that make us cringe: certain profane words, racial slurs, or even words that seem benign, like Democrat or Republican. What is important to remember is that the meaning is drawn from how we view the symbol and therefore does not inherently refer to the object.

Just as a flag, as a symbol, can evoke strong feelings, so too can words.

MEANINGS ARE DETERMINED BY THE COMMUNICATORS

The power conveyed by words is ultimately found in people and the way they use and define words. For most words there are two definitions, denotative and connotative. The denotative definition (or denotation) is a literal, dictionary-type definition; it is something we can look up. However, if we insist, when we are misunderstood, on literal definitions, we show a shallow understanding of how communication works.

As communicators, we must be aware of the connotation as well. The connotative definition is a person's personal, more subjective definition. It is influenced by our experiences and therefore will be different from person to person. Although, when we hear the word "love," everyone will know what the word love means in a denotative sense, we will each describe it differently and have different expectations and explanations (connotations). As someone communicating a message, to insist that your receivers abandon the connotations they attach to the words you are using is unrealistic and impractical. Again, in a transactive sense, everyone has a role in the communication of a message and part of that is determining exactly what the message is, so the connotations of the audience or receiver is an important part of the context. Therefore, we must be open to the idea that even when we use understandable language, we will be misunderstood or possibly evoke strong emotional reactions. This is the power of language. Regardless of the "sticks and stones" mentality, we have all witnessed words used to build people up as well as to tear people down. Words are not good or bad. But as communicators, we are wielding powerful tools that leave us with a great responsibility, the responsibility to be accurate and respectful.

APPLYING THE FUNDAMENTALS

THE POWER OF LANGUAGE

We use words to communicate messages about what we see, think, and feel. But according to interpersonal communication scholar, Julia Wood, words not only describe our perceptions, but shape them. When we use a word to describe something we see, that word actually influences how we (and others) understand the very thing we are describing. For example, every time we speak, we make choices about which words will best capture the meaning we wish to transmit. Will you describe your new blue car as blue, ocean, azure, or teal? All of these descriptors would be considered neutral and non-judgmental, yet each one creates a different image in our mind—of both the car and the speaker using the words.

Wood argues that even neutral sounding words are loaded with value. The word "teacher" would be considered neutral; however, if society values a teacher there will be positive value attached to the word. Going further, consider the difference between the words teacher, educator, instructor, and professor. While any of these labels can be legitimately used to describe any teacher, the specific label chosen will shape your perception of the specific teacher being described. It follows that your behavior can be influenced by your perception; what is the appropriate level of respect for each of these labels? Some would argue that it is not the same, and therefore, the level of respect you display toward different teachers is influenced by the word being used to describe them.

9

Since meaning comes from how we use and interpret symbols, why can't we just ignore a message or word we see as an insult? Should we try to ignore such messages and words?

IN REVIEW
The approach to communication in this book sees communication as...

• Transactive
• Contextual
• Symbolic
• Purposeful

Questions:

Reflections:

While the previous examples may seem insignificant to some, they nonetheless have real impacts and apply to all our language choices. Consider the difference between labeling the same sexual behavior as either "free love" or "sluttish," or the same social behavior as "flirtatious" or "harassment." Consider, also, the difference in how you use language to describe race, ethnicity, gender, or any other group of people. Research exists to show that even if you are offended by language that degrades other people, it still influences how you see them in a negative way. The power of language is indeed great if we can be swayed by the very words we find offensive.

In response to this phenomenon, it is crucial that we increase our awareness over how our own language impacts us. As discussed in this chapter, language is amoral. Words are not good or bad, but they are powerful. However, the amount of power they have over us lessens as we increase our awareness of how they function. If we see the impact and make a conscious choice to reject or replace it, we can. But first we must see it. If we come to understand the way symbols really work, we need not be victims to the power of language.

COMMUNICATION IS PURPOSEFUL

Finally, the last key principle from our definition of communication is that communication is purposeful. We generally assume that people engage in communication behaviors for a reason. It may be as simple as getting your brother to pass you the roast at a family dinner, by saying "please pass the meat," or as complicated as a physics teacher trying to explain the third law of thermodynamics. Whether simple or complex, what is important to note is that you or the professor is communicating in the hope of achieving some result—you get your meat; the professor's students learn what they need to learn. It is rare that someone communicates for no apparent reason. Knowing that, we then have a way to evaluate the effectiveness of communication. If you are trying to achieve some purpose, your communication is successful if it leads to you accomplishing that purpose. It is important to note that this does not mean the responsibility for effective communication rests solely with the speaker. As noted before, in the transactive model everyone involved in a communication activity will play a role in how successful that communication is, but as a speaker you should consider all parts of the context as you construct your message in order to give yourself the best chance of achieving your goal, that is, of being successful.

WHY STUDY COMMUNICATION?

You may have already noticed that communication scholars envision communication as a much more complex endeavor than you had ever thought, and may be thinking to yourself: "I've gotten by so far in life, and have managed to communicate my ideas, goals, and desires; why do I need to understand communication any more deeply?" The answer may lie in Paul J. Meyer's simple observation that "communication—the human connection—is the key to personal and career success," and it is easy to see why mastering communication is important when we look at the skills we learn while studying communication and the benefits those skills can bring us.

Additionally, communication is consistently ranked as the most important skill set you can have on the job...whatever that job is. Also, your communication skills are linked to your level of happiness, your satisfaction in relationships, and your overall quality of life. So, why wouldn't you take this class? If nothing else, as English 101 and 102 help you write better papers for all your other classes, Speech 101 helps you prepare better presentations for all your other classes, but there are actually numerous skills you can learn in this class, skills that will benefit you throughout your life.

LEARNING TO COMMUNICATE EFFECTIVELY HELPS US HONE IMPORTANT SKILLS

If you take advantage of the opportunity your exploration of communication affords, there are many important skills that you can develop in this class. These will include:

An increased ability to construct effective messages. You will learn how to organize your thoughts so you can effectively express your desire and achieve your goals. When attempting to persuade others, you will be able to create compelling messages based in logic with the right amount of emotion. Developing these skills will help you communicate all messages, whether spoken or written.

Increased effectiveness in delivering a message. You will learn how to use your delivery to enhance your message and increase your effectiveness. You will also learn techniques for decreasing nervousness and have opportunities to grow more comfortable speaking in front of a group. You will have the opportunity to find your voice and make sure it is heard.

Increased proficiency in research and critical evaluation of evidence. You will find that, while you are entitled to your opinion, you often need the expertise of others to effectively communicate your message. You will learn how to find that information and critically evaluate its validity. You will find that those skills will help you not only develop effective speeches and write quality papers, but will also help you evaluate the numerous claims you encounter every day in advertisements, news stories, and blogs and chat rooms.

Increased ability to think quickly and critically. As you hone these skills, you will find that you are able to process information thoroughly and objectively, and to fashion a response, or determine how to use that information, more quickly. That will prepare you for the faster pace of life in the work world and other forums.

THE BENEFITS OF DEVELOPING THESE SKILLS

While it may seem either trite or overstated, developing these skills can improve our lives. Mastering these skills can improve our ability to interact with other people and that can reduce stress in our lives. Also, developing these skills will help you succeed in many facets of your life, including your future college classes, then your career.

Developing these skills can also equip a person to be a greater contributor to our social good. One of the greatest scholars whose work informs much of our understanding of communication is Aristotle. He provides the basis for many of the concepts presented in this text, including the modes of proof discussed several times in the text. Beyond that, most of the ideas of what makes for effective communication presented in this text have their roots in the original theories of Aristotle. Here, however, we are interested in one particular idea of Aristotle. In his book *Ars Rhetorica* (The Rhetoric), he discusses dialectical interaction as discussions designed to inquire about the world and determine what is true. All conversation can,

IN REVIEW

Studying communication can help you hone your skills of...

- Message construction
- Message delivery
- Gathering and evaluating evidence
- Thinking critically

Questions:

Reflections:

at some level, be considered a part of a similar, but much larger, social dialectic. Seen in this way, communication becomes an avenue for understanding our world and how it works and for changing the world, hopefully for the better. Arguably, all of us have a role to serve in those discussions and so learning the skills and then utilizing them allows us all to be better "citizens of the world," or to enter into what David Zarefsky calls "the public forum." However, we can come down from that very lofty ideal and identify some specific ways being better communicators serve a social role.

Zarefsky suggests we must use our communication skills to participate in the public forum. Do you agree? What do you think that means for us in the classroom? As speakers? As audience members? As members of society?

People have often applied Mark Twain's quotation about the weather, "everyone complains about it, but no one does anything about it," to many different social problems. Today, we all have to be willing to be the person who does something about our problems like poverty, environmental degradation, and widespread violence as a response to disagreement. Being that person starts with being a part of the conversations about the issues and how to address them. You will be more effective in that role if you have developed your communication skills. In addition, addressing many of these problems will require collaborative action. Developing your ability to interact with other people improves your collaborative skills and that, too, will equip you to be a part of this public forum. Finally, solving these problems will require open-minded discussion without judgment. The skills you develop, particular in evaluating research and developing persuasive messages, will help you critically evaluate all sides of an issue and that will help you participate in, and maybe even facilitate, these important discussions.

Hopefully, you can then use the information in this book to develop the skills that will enable you to be a part of the social conversations about many important issues that will occur during your lifetime. Ideally, you will also be able to use communication to improve your relationships with other people in many contexts, and perhaps even increase your knowledge of yourself. If you can contribute in that way, then communication can meet the promise that Rollo May sees for it, when he says "communication leads to community, that is, to understanding, intimacy and mutual valuing." On the other hand, maybe for you the skills development and the positive impact that can bring to your life will be the greatest benefit. Either way, set aside any false beliefs you might have about communication; decide which of these benefits is most important to you and make achieving that benefit your goal for this semester. Choose to become a better communicator.

SUMMARY

In this opening chapter you have seen what we think communication is and the implications of looking at communication in that way. You have also seen the benefits of studying communication. The information in this chapter provides a strong foundation for engaging the information and developing the skills which are discussed throughout the rest of this text.

BEYOND OUR PERSPECTIVE ━━━━━

OTHER APPROACHES TO RHETORIC

As noted in this chapter, much of our communication theory stems from the work of Aristotle. It is important to note that such a reliance on the works of Aristotle creates a certain bias in our study of communication and rhetoric, a bias toward the so-called Western world or tradition.

However, much of the world existed (and still exists) beyond the influence of Ancient Greece. Recently, communication theorists and scholars within the U.S. have been paying more attention to the communication history that occurred outside of traditional Western study. The field is expanding the boundaries of our current notion of communication history and the basis for our communication theories which may ultimately affect some of our assumptions about communication and the principles those assumptions seem to validate.

On one front we are acknowledging that Aristotle had important contemporaries who influenced the study and practice of communication within their own cultures, just as Aristotle did within his. In fact, scholars now note that ancient rhetorical practices took place in Mesopotamia, Egypt, Rhodes, and China, as well as within the ancient Jewish scriptures. In his text, Raymond Zeuschner describes the extensive written records of communication instructions found in both early Chinese and Japanese historical documents.

Zeuschner also highlights the influence of cultures with long-standing oral traditions, many of which did not maintain written records. In Native American or early African-American communities, speaking in front of groups and storytelling were key elements of the culture and influence of those traditions impact today's communication. Many would argue the power and style of speakers like Martin Luther King Jr., Malcolm X, and Jesse Jackson are rooted in the oral tradition of early African-American culture.

As communication scholars, it is important to be aware of the variety of styles and the range of history. When we pursue knowledge beyond our traditional base, we expand our potential to understand what comprises truly effective communication, and therefore you should seek to expand your knowledge of communication beyond what is simply presented in this text. That is the goal of these "Beyond Our Perspective" pieces, but there is so much more you can, and should, investigate on your own.

Has reading this chapter altered the way you think about communication? Why or why not?

CHAPTER 2

ETHICS AND PUBLIC SPEAKING

As communicators, we have ethical standards for both speaking and listening.

Clay Bennett/ © 1998 The Christian Science Monitor (www.CSMonitor.com)
Reprinted with permission.

Our ethical standards determine what are appropriate actions in different situations.

Maya Angelou once stated, "The needs of society determine its ethics." While a society sets certain ethical standards that its people try to uphold, there may be times that call for different actions. We may break "rules" in an emergency, if someone's life or safety is at risk. Angelou herself grew up in a violent and chaotic environment. She knew firsthand that ethical behavior, and ethics themselves, are living, growing, and changing. They often respond to the situation at hand. Public speaking is no different. As communicators, we have ethical standards for both speaking and listening that we attempt to uphold in most situations, and even before reading this chapter, you may be aware of some of those "rules."

Think about it this way: in certain situations we may want to say or do something, but a feeling inside or a "little voice" tells us not to. This "voice" is our ethical voice. When it comes to speaking, ethics are paramount to the process. They help us decide what the "right" thing to do is. As surprising as it may seem, remaining aware of our ethical voice can also help select appropriate topics, choose words and phrases that contribute to meaningful connections, and more. Additionally, audience ethics help cultivate a positive and supportive communication environment. Because of the profound power, as well as the practical benefits, this chapter will examine what ethics are, how ethics are important to the speaker, and how ethics are important to the audience.

DEFINING ETHICS

We often speak of ethics without being fully aware of what ethics are. The *Random House College Dictionary* gives a clear and concise definition: "The rules of conduct recognized in respect to a particular class of human actions or a particular group, culture, etc." In other words, groups of people decide what is right and wrong

Does society place too much emphasis on ethical behavior? Why or why not?

behavior in different situations. According to the definition, ethics are subjective. They differ between cultures and groups. Nevertheless, regardless of which cultures or groups we belong to, ethics serve the same purpose. They are spoken and unspoken rules that guide our actions. Ethics help us to determine the difference between what actions and thoughts are good/bad, right/wrong, or appropriate/inappropriate. For example, in a now famous episode of the sitcom *Seinfeld*, the main characters Jerry and Elaine encounter an ethical dilemma while visiting a friend with a newborn baby. Both Jerry and Elaine agree this friend happens to have, as Jerry calls it, "some ugly baby." The dilemma becomes how to respond. Our society sets honesty as a high ethical standard. However, the characters recognize there is a different ethical rule when it comes to discussing the appearance of children. They do not comment on the "ugliness" of the child because it would be *wrong*. This situation was written for humorous effect, but we naturally empathize with Jerry and Elaine because we've all encountered ethical dilemmas. Usually, though, we recognize the "rules" that guide us through these situations.

Not only do ethics help us in *Seinfeld*-like situations, but also in a public speaking setting. It is important to remember that because communication is a transaction, it is not just the speaker who has ethical duties, but also the audience. When it comes to communication, everyone takes part in the process and has ethical responsibilities.

People often say that "doctors" have credibility, and "used car salespeople" do not. Is there a connection between the perceived credibility of these occupations and the concept of ethics?

When we are faced with a decision, ethics serves as a guide to help us determine what is the proper course of action.

ETHICS AND THE SPEAKER

In various cultures, groups, or professions, there are expected behaviors that the members of a group must follow. These are called ethical codes, and they can be found anywhere. Doctors, lawyers, teachers, and firefighters all have ethical codes that guide their behavior and thoughts. When the codes are violated, there are typically negative consequences in terms of both a morally wrong action and a penalty for violating the code. For example, when doctors violate an ethical guideline, not only is there a possibility of harm or death to a patient, but they risk losing their medical license or even imprisonment. As with all other groups of people, speakers have an ethical code to follow.

What are some consequences of violating ethical codes as a student in a classroom?

As a parent?

As a consumer?

In other situations?

What would be some of the elements in your personal code of ethics?

APPLYING THE FUNDAMENTALS

EVEN COWBOYS HAVE A CODE TO LIVE BY

As discussed in this chapter, ethical codes provide the basis for making decisions about what is right and proper. Not surprisingly then, many professions have ethical codes. Doctors take the Hippocratic Oath. The American Institute of CPAs recently adopted new Codes of Professional Conduct. Lawyers, city managers, insurance agents, and even cowboys are expected to conduct themselves in ethical ways. Yes, there are ethical standards for cowboys. One of the most well-known codes was developed by Gene Autry, the famous singing cowboy. His Cowboy Code provided a basis for cowboys, and really anyone watching westerns in the middle of the twentieth century, with a basis for determining the proper course of action.

Gene Autry's Cowboy Code:

1. The Cowboy must never shoot first, hit a smaller man, or take unfair advantage.

2. He must never go back on his word, or a trust confided in him.

3. He must always tell the truth.

4. He must be gentle with children, the elderly, and animals.

5. He must not advocate or possess racially or religiously intolerant ideas.

6. He must help people in distress.

7. He must be a good worker.

8. He must keep himself clean in thought, speech, action, and personal habits.

9. He must respect women, parents, and his nation's laws.

10. The Cowboy is a patriot.

As you can see, like any code of ethics, this code simply lays out a list of acceptable behaviors, and knowing what is acceptable allows a person to make the ethically correct choice when making a decision. If you think about it, you probably even have a personal code of ethics. What are things you would do (or never do)? Thinking about that question allows you to examine your personal ethics.

ETHICAL SPEAKERS REALIZE THE DIFFERENCE BETWEEN THE LAW AND PRACTICE OF SPEECH

When living in the United States, we know the First Amendment of the Constitution guarantees certain basic rights, including freedom of speech. Legally, we have the right to say almost anything we want without fear of repercussion. However, there are exceptions. Freedom of speech doesn't allow you to run into a crowded theater and scream "Fire!" when there isn't one. Similarly, you will face legal prosecution if you stand up at an airport security checkpoint and scream, "I have a bomb!"

There are ethics involved in free speech. For example, it is both illegal and unethical to stand up at an airport security checkpoint and scream, "I have a bomb!"

These actions are illegal, violating a formal, written ethical code. Additionally, it is immoral, violating an unspoken code by manipulating people, playing on their fear and anxiety. It is important to keep this idea in mind: even when there will not be legal repercussions, there may still be a violation of an unwritten ethical code. We do have freedom of speech, but there are times when we don't exercise that right because we decide it's not appropriate in that moment or situation.

ETHICAL SPEAKERS UNDERSTAND THE POWER OF COMMUNICATION

We have all heard the saying, "The pen is mightier than the sword." Although we learned in Chapter 1 that words are amoral, we know they can be used in ways that are supportive or devastating to other people. They can be used as tools for building and growth or as weapons to tear down, ranging from the examples of feeling cheered up on a bad day by someone else's kind words to the destruction of a child's self-esteem by the constant negative feedback of peers or family, or the choice of particular word symbols which we know will create a particular meaning that can be hurtful or offensive to someone else.

What you say in your speeches has power as well. If a female student says during a speech that all men are sexist, what is the impact? It is possible that both men and women in the audience will be offended, but worse, there might be a shift in attitude where an audience actually begins to devalue the opinions of men. While there is the practical concern of not offending the audience, there is also the ethical concern of promoting an unfair stereotype. Even if the audience is entirely made up of women, degrading men as a group is an abuse of the power attached to language. The way we use language has the power to include or exclude people, and ethical standards for communicators insist upon people receiving fair respect, even if they are not in the room.

Is politically correct language a necessary response to the power of language?

In addition to the moral violation, as mentioned earlier, there is also the possibility of negative repercussions to the speaker for violation of the code. It is entirely possible for the audience to lose respect for the speaker. When refusing to follow an ethical perspective, we risk the loss of credibility and reduce the chance for achieving a true connection with the audience.

ETHICAL SPEAKERS PORTRAY *ETHOS*

One of Aristotle's rhetorical proofs is ethos. Ethos refers to the ethical aspects of a speaker (also known as credibility), claiming that in order for speakers to be effective, they must be ethical. The question then becomes, how do you, as a speaker, portray ethical behavior?

First, ethical speakers choose topics on which they are well informed. Aristotle called this "good sense." A heart surgeon has a good sense of how the heart works. A computer programmer has a good sense of how to "clean up" your computer's hard drive, and a film major has a good sense of what makes an effective horror film. As a speaker, when you have a good sense of the important elements of a game of hockey, and then choose that as your topic, you would be considered an ethical speaker. However, if you know very little about the game of cricket and make only a cursory attempt at research, this would be considered ethically inappropriate. It is an ethical violation to present yourself as an expert on a topic when you are not and it is inappropriate to waste the time of your audience when you are not knowledgeable on your own topic.

Who are some speakers you consider to be ethical?

Who are some speakers you consider to be unethical?

What makes these speakers ethical or unethical?

An ethical speaker who chooses to speak about hockey would understand important elements of the game; an unethical speaker would know very little about the game and would conduct insufficient research to become knowledgeable.

Second, Aristotle believed that speakers with ethos give truthful and accurate information, and thus possess and present "moral character." In a public speaking setting, there is a presumption of honesty. The audience assumes a speaker wouldn't distort information or knowingly use false information. If the audience cannot trust the speaker to be honest, there is no basis for communication. In addition to being honest and making certain of the accuracy of our own information before we present it, we can also cite research during a speech to reassure the audience that the information is credible. Being truthful and discussing information accurately helps promote the ethos of a speaker.

Third, Aristotle discussed the idea of "good will," explaining that ethical speakers speak to benefit their listeners. Again, because of the transactive nature of communication, we view speech giving as a relationship between the speaker and the audience. When an audience is willing to listen, they have collectively given something to the speaker. The speaker has received the time and attention of the audience. In return, the speaker owes it to the audience to give something back. It is important, then, that the topic of our speech has some impact and benefit to the audience. The benefit may be that by the end of the speech the audience will know how to save twenty dollars every time they go to the grocery store or they will have learned a new way of understanding the world in which we live. The point is the speech will have something to offer the audience. It will not be the purpose of the speaker to ignore the needs of the audience or worse, take advantage of them. Aristotle asserts that ethical speakers inform the audience of the benefit to them in the speech. In order for this to be possible, we must choose topics that actually benefit our listeners. The best interest of the audience should guide your topic selection, invention of the speech, and your delivery.

ETHICAL SPEAKERS RESPECT THE AUDIENCE

Have you ever felt like someone was "talking down" to you? Most people don't appreciate a condescending tone. As a speaker, it's important to respect the members of your audience. Respect includes a wide range of ideas. There is the obvious level of respect that asks us not to insult our audience with name-calling or false accusations. But respect can include the way in which we put together our message or the amount of time put into preparing. Being respectful can include the attempt to entertain and intrigue an audience, rather than boring them with too many surface level details or overly complex explanations. In addition, this guideline argues that threats or any other type of force or coercion is absolutely inappropriate. The right of the audience to make up their own minds must be acknowledged.

ETHICAL SPEAKERS TAKE RESPONSIBILITY FOR THE MESSAGE THEY SEND

Ideally, as speakers we are hoping that our message is received by the audience in the way we intend. Unfortunately, we may deliver the message in exactly the way we had hoped, but still we cannot control the way an audience receives our message. Additionally, we sometimes make mistakes in our delivery of the message. Either way, as the speaker, you are responsible for the message you send. Perhaps, in nervousness, we forget to cite our sources. It is possible that we use a term like "Indian giver" not realizing there is a racist history and connotation attached to that phrase. An ethical speaker understands that there are sometimes negative consequences for what has or hasn't been said and is willing to accept those consequences. It is

Do speakers need to satisfy all three elements of ethos in order to be considered ethical and credible?

If Aristotle were still alive, would he use the same criteria (good sense, goodwill, moral character) to judge ethos? If not, what would be specific criteria he would remove/add/adapt?

IN REVIEW
Ethical speakers...

- Realize the difference between the law and practice of speech
- Understand the power of communication
- Must have ethos
- Respect the audience
- Take responsibility for the message they send

Questions:

Reflections:

not appropriate or practical to insist that an audience should know what we meant. The ethical choice is to be accountable for your message. Attempt to understand the response of the audience and use that understanding as the starting place for renewed communication.

BEYOND THE FUNDAMENTALS

PLAGIARISM

As members of a college community, plagiarism is a term with which we are familiar. Grice and Skinner define plagiarism as "the unattributed use of another's ideas, words, or pattern of organization." Many simply think of it as submitting a paper purchased on the Internet. This is known as global plagiarism, or "stealing" an entire message and passing it off as your own. This form of plagiarism is a conscious decision.

But many cases of plagiarism occur unintentionally. Students are sometimes not aware that plagiarism includes not citing sources accurately, incorrect paraphrasing of ideas, or piecing together multiple pieces of information without distinguishing between what is research and what is original. As ethical speakers, we must realize the importance of sending a message that is our own and take steps to avoid plagiarizing.

Just as with other ethical violations, plagiarism is grounded in a lack of respect for other people and has consequences. In some cases the result is expulsion from a school or the loss of a job, as well as the loss of trust by people with whom you communicate.

Understanding that there are many ways to commit plagiarism, that plagiarism is a serious violation of the standards of academic integrity, and that there are serious consequences for plagiarizing, what would be some ways you could prevent plagiarism from even taking place?

ETHICS AND THE AUDIENCE

Many people, before they take a class in public speaking, assume the only two people who have to do something during a speech are the speaker and the teacher. This, however, is *not* the case. Audience members also have ethical guidelines to follow. Just as you are expected to cheer on the Cubs when you attend a baseball game at Wrigley Field, you are expected to take an active role in the communication process as an audience member in a public speaking class. The following are some basic ethical guidelines that audience members should follow.

ETHICAL AUDIENCES KNOW LISTENING IS AN ACTIVE PROCESS

As described in Chapter 11, there is a difference between hearing and listening. Hearing is the passive process of noise hitting your ears, whereas listening is much more involved. As an audience member, you must give the speaker proper respect by actively listening. You are *not* fulfilling your role by merely looking at someone while he or she speaks. Showing up and being quiet on speech days is not enough to meet your ethical obligation. The listening process is complex and sometimes challenging, but audiences respect the speaker by recognizing the different levels of listening and attempting to actively participate.

ETHICAL AUDIENCES FOCUS ON THE MESSAGE

Throughout this course, you will learn about the importance of having both strong content in a speech and effective delivery. As an audience member, however, you should strive to focus on what the speaker is saying, and not on their delivery. Speakers may have thick accents, stutter, or say "like" every other word, but that doesn't mean the content of their message is poor. Ethical audiences will look beyond nervousness, different dialects, or appearance. Audience members should strive to eliminate "noise" and focus on the message the speaker is attempting to send.

If you could construct an ethical code for communication, what qualities and/or behaviors would it include for speakers?

ETHICAL AUDIENCES WITHHOLD JUDGMENT

This guideline is often the most challenging. When we are sent a message that contradicts our own viewpoints, it is a common reaction to listen through a defensive filter or even to stop listening completely. However, as an ethical audience member we withhold judgment until the speaker is finished. There is always the possibility the speaker may offer something new about the topic that causes us to rethink our stance. Realize that there may be different ways to think about an issue or topic, and respect that fact instead of being closed to new ideas. In the end, the speaker may only reaffirm your belief. But remember, that should only happen in the end.

For audiences?

ETHICAL AUDIENCES ARE COURTEOUS AUDIENCE MEMBERS

As mentioned above, listening is an active process that involves much more than being quiet. Treating a speaker with respect involves recognizing the effort they are putting forth on your behalf. It is unethical for an audience to write, sleep, text message, and play games on their cell phones while someone is speaking. Additionally, don't interrupt the speaker, walk into the room during the middle of a speech, or roll your eyes. Just as a speaker may unintentionally send a negative message to the audience, the audience may send unintentional negative feedback.

Why would you include those specific guidelines?

Be aware of any gestures or behaviors that might be distracting to the person giving the speech. It is important to behave in a way that affords the speaker the appropriate amount of respect.

ETHICAL AUDIENCES REALIZE THERE ARE CONSEQUENCES FOR NOT LISTENING

Just as a speaker must be accountable for the message they send, listeners must be accountable for the choices they make. The consequences of poor listening as a student may include not capturing the necessary information to effectively complete an assignment or pass a quiz. When it comes to public speaking, the information missed might include almost anything, ranging from how to improve your study skills, to how to plan an exciting, but cost-effective vacation, to the proper steps in CPR for an emergency situation. Besides missing potentially important information, the consequences of poor listening extend to a possible negative impact on the speaker. If you are not giving appropriate feedback, the speaker doesn't have the opportunity to respond. Additionally, if the feedback is not respectful, damage may be done to the relationship between the speaker and audience. In a classroom, this may mean that when it is your turn to give your speech, it will be to a tougher audience. In the workplace, this may mean engendering hostility between yourself and a coworker. Just as language has power, so does the act of listening. There may be similar ethical violations of excluding voices or groups of people based on your listening response. As an audience member, it is important to realize the power attached to listening responsibly, and be accountable for the results attached to listening poorly.

SUMMARY

Ethics are a set of guidelines agreed upon by groups of people regarding what is appropriate or inappropriate behavior. All groups of people, including communication scholars, have established ethical codes to guide behavior and decision making within their groups. When it comes to communication, it is imperative that both speakers and audience members realize they have ethical guidelines, especially within the public speaking classroom. Ethics are not just important for one party of the process. Following these basic ethical guidelines can help ensure that every member of the class plays a part in making the communication environment a positive one.

IN REVIEW

Ethical audiences...

• Know listening is an active process

• Focus on the message

• Withhold judgment

• Are courteous audience members

• Realize there are consequences for not listening

Questions:

Reflections:

CHAPTER 3

COMMUNICATION APPREHENSION

Communication apprehension is a natural fear for many people.

Brian Gawalt, Cartoon from "Tongue Tied," *Cavalier Daily*, March 23, 2004. Used by permission.

Everyone will eventually have to make a public presentation and most people experience some level of nervousness when it is their turn. Understanding the basis for that nervousness can make us more effective speakers.

Jerry Seinfeld once joked that because the fear of death ranks fifth under public speaking, "That would mean at a funeral, people are five times more likely to want to be in the casket than giving the eulogy." If you experience anxiety at the thought of standing before a crowd to speak, you are not alone. The fear of public speaking is widespread. Nevertheless, there are ways of coping with and reducing what is known as communication apprehension. Because some aspects of nervousness can actually be beneficial for a speaker, this chapter is not meant to be a prescription for completely eliminating anxiety. Instead, we will take a closer look at the fear of public speaking, some causes, and strategies for building confidence in speech situations.

COMMUNICATION APPREHENSION

Whether you call it stage fright, anxiety, or anything else, communication apprehension is very simply the nervousness that people feel when they have to communicate. Some people feel highly anxious before giving a speech in class, but are perfectly comfortable talking to someone new at a party. Others can give fluent and articulate presentations at work, but panic over a simple wedding toast. There are many forms of communication apprehension, but for our purposes, we will focus predominately on the context of public speaking.

CAUSES OF APPREHENSION

Before dealing with the anxiety, it can be helpful to identify the cause. While people have different reasons for feeling nervous, there are generally four main causes of communication apprehension. Identifying the causes that have the most influence on you may help in choosing an appropriate coping strategy.

LACK OF EXPERIENCE IN A PUBLIC SPEAKING SETTING

For many students, this class is the first or second formal public speaking course they've taken. While classes in different subjects may have required presentations or reports, many teachers do not give the necessary instruction in public speaking. They expect you to get up and do it. Without experience or instruction, it is natural to feel nervous, but with more knowledge about what makes a successful presentation and more opportunities to practice your skills, you should experience a drop in communication apprehension.

Do you have any previous experiences with public speaking? Have those been positive or negative? Do you think those experiences influence how much apprehension you feel when having to give a speech?

BEING THE CENTER OF ATTENTION

As communicators, we do want an audience to focus on us and pay attention to our message. However, some people do not enjoy being the center of attention. They may feel added pressure to perform well or even imagine the audience is being critical. In any case, it feels uncomfortable to have everyone looking at you. It may help to remember communication is a transaction. Focusing on the needs of the audience may remove some of the stress and attention *you* are placing on yourself.

FEELING DIFFERENT

When you choose a topic, you are disclosing information about yourself. You may be letting the audience know about a person you admire, a hobby you have, or how you feel about a particular social issue. Part of the human experience is wanting to "fit in" and connect with others. Disclosing even slightly personal information risks exposing yourself as different from the members of your audience. Remember that your own experiences, ideas, interests, etc., add something unique to the speaking situation. While an audience may be hesitant about accepting differences, they are also intrigued by them. Using audience analysis, as discussed in Chapter 4, can help you make choices about how to deliver different ideas to your audience.

FEELING JUDGED

Another common cause of apprehension is the feeling that your audience is judging you. This is similar to "feeling different," but extends beyond highlighting individual differences or revealing personal information. It involves the fear that as a speaker, your audience is judging your competency and value. Speakers often worry they are being judged on not only their different viewpoints or experiences, but on appearance, delivery, the construction of the message, and more. In a classroom, the fact that a teacher is evaluating the speech and assigning a grade can amplify the intensity of the experience. In this case, it is important to remember that while we may view audiences as hostile and critical, they are more often supportive of the speaker, especially in a classroom situation. The other students are also required to give speeches and feel a sense of camaraderie. As for teachers, generally, they wish for their students to succeed.

Which of these causes of apprehension do you think is the most significant for you?

Many people feel anxiety about public speaking, but coping strategies and experience can help build confidence and reduce apprehension substantially.

COPING WITH COMMUNICATON APPREHENSION

There are some reasons to be nervous and those dynamics will always be present to some degree. We also know that everyone is likely to have to make a public presentation at some point in their life. So, how do we deal with the dynamics that underlie communication apprehension? If you ask people for advice you are likely to get answers which range from the silly ("imagine your audience in their underwear," advice the authors have never found to be useful) to meaningless platitudes ("just be confident in what you have to say." While that is easy to say and a good thing to do, if it were that simple, there would be no need for this chapter). Here we try to provide more meaningful advice based on three appropriate reactions: be willing to embrace the experience, actively engage the process, and understand human nature.

EMBRACE THE EXPERIENCE

By now it should be clear: speaking in public is a common activity which everyone is likely to have to experience at some point. So, put simply, get over it, face up to it, and accept that you are just one of many people who have to make presentations (and also one of many who would probably rather not make the presentation). There are several strategies that you can utilize which can raise your willingness to embrace the experience.

SET REALISTIC GOALS FOR SUCCESS

One common problem everyone has with the speaking process is that they tend to set unrealistic expectations for the event. They expect to be the best from the very start, but public speaking, like any skill, takes time to perfect and people are always improving. So, try to determine a reasonable definition of what "successful" means for you in regards to public speaking. Some students will say, "Success equals an 'A'." However, it is more reasonable to set goals that deal with your message and delivery, rather than the grade. Major League Baseball presents a good example of realistic goal setting. When a team goes on a ten game road trip, managers and players typically say, "If we win six games, this was a good trip." The same can be said for your speeches. Set goals for improvement, not perfection. The expectation of a perfect presentation adds to the level of stress. Instead, focus on something specific that you want to happen. For some people, getting through a seven-minute speech with only minor verbal fillers (like "um") may be an appropriate goal. For someone else, it could be getting through a speech without using notes. Other goals may include mastering the use of visual aids, following the outline without tangents, or making more direct connections to the specific audience. Set achievable goals for improvement. Reaching those goals and seeing real improvement can boost a speaker's confidence.

UNDERSTAND THE SIMILARITIES AND DIFFERENCES BETWEEN PUBLIC SPEAKING AND CONVERSATION

One of the reasons why people set unrealistic goals is because they don't understand the similarities and differences between conversation and public speaking. On the one hand, they focus on the similarities and think, "if I can talk to my friends, I can speak in public." That is a good start because it helps people see that they already have some skills which can help them succeed. On the other hand, sometimes focusing on the similarities blind people to the differences and they are then "freaked out" by how the actual experience differs from their expectations. In order to help you balance the confidence of being able to speak with others (even if only in conversation) with the need to understand the differences which will change the communicative experience when speaking in public, we offer a brief discussion of the similarities and differences between conversation and public speaking.

The most obvious similarity between conversation and public speaking is that they both involve the oral communication of a message, but there are more meaningful similarities, as well. The first of those is that in both public speaking and conversation we organize our thoughts logically. We attempt to give information in the order that makes the most sense and not jump back and forth too much between topics. Additionally, we adapt our messages to the audience. We ask for a favor in different ways when talking to different people. We tell a story differently to a friend than we do to a teacher. If we are skilled in conversation, we know that we approach issues and questions differently depending on the people involved. Similarly, in public speaking, we try to get to know our audience and tailor a message to that unique audience.

Another similarity is we tell stories for maximum impact. So, if it helps, think of public speaking as a different way of telling a story. Besides thinking about whether the message is organized (the plot), we think about the element of suspense, drama, humor, or other types of impact. What are we trying to achieve and what is the best way to go about it? Should we take a serious or light-hearted approach? Are we including unimportant or distracting information? The same strategies we use every day when telling stories in conversation are the strategies we want to incorporate into public speaking.

Finally, another similarity is we adapt to listener feedback. In conversation, if someone looks confused or disagrees, we modify our approach. We may answer questions or change our strategy and shift to Plan B. We do the same in public speaking. As suggested by the transactive communication model, we are aware of feedback and if we sense hostility, boredom, or confusion, we adapt.

29

While there is much in common, public speaking and conversation have differences as well. One difference is that public speeches should be more highly structured. In public speaking, you normally have a very specific amount of time in which to accomplish your goal. You also generally have a more complex message to communicate. This calls for more structure. You must determine in advance how much time is necessary for each portion of your speech and how much you can reasonably accomplish overall. Structure is also a method of increasing memory and understanding of the message for an audience.

Another difference is that public speaking generally calls for more formal language. Even if the audience is filled with people with whom you converse casually on a regular basis, there is an expectation that a speech should be special. You read in Chapter 1 that public speaking has become less formal over time, but when an entire audience has chosen to remain politely silent, they tend to expect something more special or elevated than ordinary conversation.

Finally, public speaking requires a different method of delivery. When speaking to a group, it is helpful to use a louder voice and straighter posture. Also, mannerisms that may not be noticeable in conversation will often stand out in a speech. More attention should be placed on reducing distracting mannerisms and verbal habits.

So, there are some things you have to do differently when presenting a speech which you wouldn't necessarily do in conversation. Recognizing these differences helps you be better prepared for the situation. However, you also should be aware that you have already honed many of the skills necessary for an effective speech just by talking to people every day. You should have confidence in those base skills and be prepared to use them to confront the unique challenges of public speaking.

VISUALIZE BEING SUCCESSFUL

Once you understand what to expect and you have used that to set realistic goals for your speech it becomes easier to visualize yourself being successful and that is an important element in overcoming communication apprehension. An abundance of research supports the idea that visualization impacts performance. Athletes use visualization to improve their play. Doctors urge patients to use visualization to facilitate a speedier and more complete recovery from illness.

Visualization is also a strategy that works for communicators. Begin the process of visualization when you receive your assignment. Find a quiet spot and when you feel relaxed, begin the process. Create a picture of yourself in your mind. See yourself in the room where you will speak, walking to the front of the room, and delivering your speech in an eloquent and relaxed style. Picture yourself doing all of this in a confident manner. Visualization can be the beginning of a desensitization process. Continue honing that vision as you work through the process of developing your speech and celebrate your successes along the way (a process we will look at in more depth in the next section).

Visualize success and then come to expect it. Reframing your expectations can lead to a positive **self-fulfilling prophecy**, the idea that we behave in ways that make our expectations a more likely outcome. For example, if we tell ourselves, "I'll never pass this class," we might put less effort into our work. It seems a waste of time to put too much effort into a class we are going to fail anyway. So we work less, behaving in a way that actually increases the likelihood of failing. On the other hand, self-fulfilling prophecies can work to bring positive instead of negative outcomes, so eliminate any negative expectations and replace them with positive ones and exploit the self-fulfilling prophecy to your benefit.

VIEW SPEECHMAKING AS A POSITIVE EXPERIENCE

One way you can help set and achieve realistic goals is to think about how you view the speech-making process. Don't think of it as a chore; think of it as a positive experience. When studying psychology, we learn that as humans, to a very large extent, we choose our own emotions. If we view public speaking as a threatening experience, we are more likely to feel nervous when speaking. But if we choose to reframe how we understand communication, we can change the way we feel in a public speaking setting.

When people describe how they feel before, during, or after they give a speech, they list many physical symptoms we associate with fear. For example, we may experience rapid heartbeat, sweaty palms, muscle tension, queasy stomach, or extremely high levels of energy. Interestingly enough, the symptoms are similar, or even identical, to those we experience when we are "excited" in a positive sense. These are the symptoms of adrenaline. If we love to ride roller coasters, we feel nervousness as the cart climbs its way to the first big drop. We experience a rush of emotion during, and even after, the ride. While some people fear roller coasters, others love them. They choose to accept the feelings and view them in a positive light. It is possible to do the same with public speaking. Often, if you ask speakers who claim they experience no nervousness at all, they will tell you that they get excited while giving a speech. They experience a "rush" or a "thrill" that is similar in feeling to the fear described by apprehensive speakers. They just understand it differently.

It may take time to change your attitude about public speaking, but make the decision and begin working on it. Speak about people you admire or topics that are of great importance to you personally. This is a chance to make a difference. Also, look at each speech as another step toward improvement as a communicator. It isn't easy to change your frame of mind, but it is possible. Do not fight to completely remove your physical symptoms; instead begin to understand them as a response to an opportunity filled with personal potential.

DO SOMETHING TO BOOST YOUR CONFIDENCE

Everything discussed above should help you respond differently when you are asked to give a speech. However, come speech day, you are still likely to feel some apprehension. As we will discuss later, that is actually okay, but you still need to control those feelings and the best way to do that is by boosting your confidence. Is there a song that makes you feel confident or happy? A ritual you perform that makes you feel better? An outfit that makes you feel good about yourself? A mantra that promotes a sense of calm? There are small actions you can take that will give you one quick boost of energy or confidence before giving a speech. Again, these are not substitutes for the real work of creating lasting comfort and confidence, but they can remind you to think positively.

What are some physical symptoms of extreme nervousness? Extreme excitement? Compare the two. What conclusions can you draw from that comparison?

Do you have any personal strategies to boost your confidence before you engage any challenging task? Could you use those before giving a speech?

ACTIVELY ENGAGE THE PROCESS

Once you have decided that you can handle the experience, that, in fact, you want to embrace the challenge of presenting an effective speech, the next step is to take the actions which are necessary to make that happen. In the coming chapters we will provide lots of information to help you do that, but here we identify some general tips to help you get started and reduce your apprehension about public speaking.

KNOW YOUR STRENGTHS AND WEAKNESSES AS A SPEAKER

You will have lots of choices to make as you develop a speech. As you make those choices, play to your strengths and avoid your weaknesses. Just as a football coach determines a game plan based on what his team does well, you can plan for success by knowing what you do well. Start by determining what you do well as a speaker. It can be easy to ignore the positive and focus on our weaknesses. However, while it is helpful to be aware of what needs work, it is equally important to identify your strengths. Again, we can use football as an example. If a team has a great running game and a poor passing game, they will work on passing, but their strategy in a game will rely more heavily on running. It follows that, as a speaker, we work on our weaknesses, but we play to our strengths. If you are a strong storyteller, incorporate narrative into your speech. If you are a strong joke-teller, incorporate humor. If you have graphic design skills, incorporate PowerPoint. Take an inventory of your assets and devise a strategy for incorporating them into your speaking. Focusing on what is positive can help you feel more confident about giving a speech.

Another strength you can exploit is your knowledge base. It is easier to feel confident if you have greater understanding about your topic. So, as you inventory your strengths, think about topics you know something about. If you are a bicycle mechanic, you might give a speech on how to keep your bicycle in proper working order. Speaking on a familiar topic is comforting for many people. Often a student will choose a topic because it seems "impressive" or even "easy," but it is easier to create a message and impress an audience when we feel like an expert on the topic. This is not to say that you should never choose new and challenging topics. If you have a sincere interest, choose that topic. Just start preparing early enough so that you feel like an expert before you give the speech.

PRACTICE YOUR SPEECH

After you inventory your strengths, you will want to exploit those as you move through the speech preparation process, a process we will look at in great detail in the coming chapters, so we won't discuss that much here. However, do be sure you start early because the process will take time and the more time you dedicate to the process, the better you will feel about it. In addition to beginning work early and expecting a positive outcome, it is important to actually practice presenting your speech once you have finished preparing it. This is simple advice that many people don't take. Often a speaker will run through a speech once, or not at all, before delivering it to an audience. Some speakers will run through the speech in their head, but not aloud. Practicing a speech out loud many times before the actual performance increases your confidence by making you more comfortable with the public speaking context.

APPLYING THE FUNDAMENTALS ▬▬▬

COMMUNICATION APPREHENSION ISN'T JUST PERFORMANCE ANXIETY

Speakers sometime feel nervous when they have to give a speech; we all know this to be true. The nervousness that many people associate with public speaking seems to be in regards to delivery or performance. However, there are other areas that can contribute to nervousness. O'Hair, Stewart, and Rubenstein go a little bit farther with their discussions of nervousness. According to these authors, nervousness is displayed not only in the performance phase, but also in the preparation phase of a speech. When a speaker has "preparation anxiety," they feel nervous when putting a speech together. Problems researching, worrying over how to best word main points and supporting points, concerns over if a speech will meet the time limit and other specific requirements are all examples of preparation anxiety. If you had a friend that had preparation anxiety, what tips would you give them to help them deal with the anxiety? Remember your pieces of advice, and compare them with what is mentioned in the later chapters that help you through the process of preparing a speech.

UNDERSTAND HUMAN NATURE

The last thing you can do to build your confidence is to understand how all humans react to stressful situations and use that information to be comfortable with, rather than concerned about, how you feel when engaging in public speaking.

REMEMBER EVERYONE EXPERIENCES NERVOUSNESS

As mentioned earlier, people consistently rank the fear of public speaking as their number one fear, so know that everyone is going to be nervous to some level when presenting a speech. Even experienced speakers will tell you they want to feel a little nervous when presenting a speech. That is how they know they are visualizing the situation properly, as discussed earlier. So, while the intensity of nervousness may vary, most people share this experience and you should not interpret nervousness as something that makes you different or deficient. It makes you human and there is nothing wrong with that.

Part of the problem that some people have with this particular strategy is that they don't think other speakers are nervous because they don't see signs of nervousness. However, what people are feeling is not necessarily what they show to the audience. Listeners can't see dry mouth or rapid heartbeat. They can't see sweaty palms or "butterflies" in our stomachs. Speakers often describe their shaking hands or wobbling knees much to the surprise of an audience. These speakers do feel nervousness, but they remember that feelings are not always observable, even when they are extremely intense. So, they work to control their nervousness and hide it from the audience. In time, you can learn to do the same. Finally, remember that we are often our own worst critic. The way we react to what we feel in a moment of nervousness is often far worse than it needs to be. You need to realize that you may be evaluating yourself in an overly critical way.

RECOGNIZE YOUR BODY'S REACTION TO STRESS

Being nervous will put you under some level of stress, and everyone experiences stress in a unique way. The challenge is to know how your body reacts to stress so you can properly respond to it. Know how your body, specifically, responds to stressful situations. For some symptoms, there are easy fixes. For example, if you know your mouth becomes dry while speaking, you can apply lip balm in advance and have a quick drink of water before taking your place in front of the audience. Other symptoms will exhibit themselves regardless, but having the expectation of rapid heartbeat or shaky hands decreases the surprise and fear that you might feel when they begin. Accept them as a natural part of public speaking.

One of the most important things to remember as you deal with nervousness and stress is to avoid causing what is called a "secondary disturbance." We increase the anxiety we are experiencing because we are not only worried about giving a speech, we are also worried about our worrying. So, our feelings of nervousness and stress can give us one more thing to worry about which adds to our anxiety about speaking which makes us more nervous, creating more stress and . . . well, you can see where this would lead. By accepting nervousness and controlling stress you can break that cycle of concern which can negatively affect your speech.

ACCEPT THE LENGTH OF THE PROCESS

You may have noticed that much of this section has focused on building confidence, not reducing nervousness. That is intentional, because the best way to reduce nervousness is to feel confident in a situation. However, you must recognize that building real, lasting confidence is a process that takes time. If you look hard enough, you can find quick fix remedies online that guarantee to rid you of your fear in 24 hours. However, the only way to truly overcome nervousness is to work at it. Your best bet is to understand the nature of stress, respond appropriately to it, and begin working on your project as soon as you can. Overcoming fear and crafting an effective message are both processes that take time. They are also processes that can influence each other. It is easier to build confidence if you are not procrastinating on your speech. Your work gives you a basis for that confidence.

However, it takes time and expecting a quicker fix can create another secondary disturbance. For example, much of the last minute advice you are often given before a speech offers only a brief remedy to communication apprehension. There are certain techniques we can use to calm ourselves quickly, for example, deep breathing. While this is helpful advice, it focuses on reducing nervousness rather than building confidence. The effects of that have less influence on long-range feelings than does a systematic long-term effort to build confidence. So, those moves aren't as effective. That lack of significant impact can make you worry that you are still too worried about the speech and that ends up impacting the quality of your communication. There is nothing wrong with these short-term fixes, but over time you need to embrace a longer term approach to building confidence and you have to recognize that does take time and that is okay.

By following the advice in this section and embracing the experience, engaging the process, and understanding human nature you can accept your reaction to public speaking as natural and develop appropriate and effective strategies for coping with any communication apprehension you are experiencing.

How do you react to stress? Do you have personal strategies for dealing with that? How could you apply those to public speaking?

34

BEYOND THE FUNDAMENTALS ▬▬▬

INTERPERSONAL COMMUNICATION APPREHENSION

While the focus of this chapter is geared towards communication apprehension and public speaking, there are also forms of communication apprehension that stem from interpersonal communication dynamics, specifically as written about by author Steven McCornack. While the root of the following types are more interpersonal, there are some key similarities and correlations to public speaking anxiety.

Situational Apprehension

This type of communication apprehension is present to the communicator, but only in certain situations. Interpersonally, you may find that you feel symptoms of anxiety when you are meeting someone for the first time, or when you have your yearly performance review at work. Outside of those instances, you may be more calm, cool, or collected. Situational apprehension can also happen in a public speaking setting. This specific situation of being a presenter to a larger audience is often just unique enough to many that when asked to be a speaker, many anxious thoughts and feelings begin to surface. The idea of being formally evaluated may fit into this as well, especially because evaluation in terms of a grade in class adds a unique twist to the situation.

Receiver Apprehension

This form of apprehension arises when a speaker feels apprehension when communicating to a specific receiver. For example, you may feel relatively comfortable and confident when speaking to your boss, but when you need to visit your professor to ask a question, you feel symptoms of anxiety. In a speech setting, an example of receiver apprehension would be speaking to a formal audience (one that is ethically obligated to remove distractions and focus on the speaker).

Trait Apprehension

Those that suffer from trait apprehension often feel such a high level of anxiety in any communication setting that they tend to withdraw themselves from contact, and this apprehension is seen as a personality trait. Sometimes, according to scholars, this form of apprehension is severe enough that to cope with it, a person may require counseling or prescription medication. Often counselors will recommend desensitization techniques to help cope with this type of anxiety. If you feel you have a personality that makes it difficult to interact with others, talk with your professor who may also be able to recommend some desensitization exercises. Remember, as noted frequently in this chapter, everyone has to communicate, so it is important that you take the steps you can to become more comfortable with that activity.

Regardless of the type of apprehension you may experience, McCornack believes that developing communication plans (what you want to say), plan actions (how you want to say it), and plan contingencies (how you will react to unforeseen influences) will all be helpful in dealing with situations where you may be prone to anxiety and reframing them so that you feel confident enough to share your message.

Three ways to build confidence in your abilities and reduce your feelings of communication apprehension are...

- Embrace the experience
- Actively engage the process
- Understand human nature

...and this chapter has suggested several strategies for achieving each of those goals.

Questions:

Reflections:

Based on everything presented in this chapter, why do you think that careful preparation and planning can reduce anxiety?

SUMMARY

Even though communication apprehension affects many people when it comes to public speaking, there are ways to cope with it. This chapter examined four main causes: lack of experience, discomfort from attention, feeling different, and feeling judged. Understanding the source and effects of nervousness can be helpful in responding to it. There are methods for coping with and reducing anxiety that include reframing your understanding of the experience, choosing appropriate topics, setting goals, visualization, practice, and more. In the end, we may experience apprehension in unique ways, but the experience itself is common. There are many strategies for managing nervousness, but they are all based in shifting your own attitude toward both anxiety and public speaking.

RESOURCES FOR BUILDING COMMUNICATION EFFECTIVENESS

PERSONAL REPORT OF COMMUNICATION APPREHENSION (PRCA-24)

The PRCA-24 is the instrument which is most widely used to measure communication apprehension. It is preferable above all earlier versions of the instrument (PRCA, PRCA10, PRCA-24B, etc.). It is highly reliable (alpha regularly >.90) and has very high predictive validity. It permits one to obtain sub-scores on the contexts of public speaking, dyadic interaction, small groups, and large groups. However, these scores are substantially less reliable than the total PRCA-24 scores because of the reduced number of items. People interested only in public speaking anxiety should consider using the PRPSA rather than the public speaking sub-score drawn from the PRCA-24. It is much more reliable for this purpose.

This instrument is composed of twenty-four statements concerning feelings about communicating with others. Please indicate the degree to which each statement applies to you by marking whether you: **Strongly Disagree = 1; Disagree = 2; are Neutral = 3; Agree = 4; Strongly Agree = 5**

_____   1. I dislike participating in group discussions.

_____   2. Generally, I am comfortable while participating in group discussions.

_____   3. I am tense and nervous while participating in group discussions.

_____   4. I like to get involved in group discussions.

_____   5. Engaging in a group discussion with new people makes me tense and nervous.

_____   6. I am calm and relaxed while participating in group discussions.

_____   7. Generally, I am nervous when I have to participate in a meeting.

_____   8. Usually, I am comfortable when I have to participate in a meeting.

_____   9. I am very calm and relaxed when I am called upon to express an opinion at a meeting.

_____   10. I am afraid to express myself at meetings.

_____   11. Communicating at meetings usually makes me uncomfortable.

_____   12. I am very relaxed when answering questions at a meeting.

_____   13. While participating in a conversation with a new acquaintance, I feel very nervous.

_____   14. I have no fear of speaking up in conversations.

_____   15. Ordinarily I am very tense and nervous in conversations.

_____   16. Ordinarily I am very calm and relaxed in conversations.

_____   17. While conversing with a new acquaintance, I feel very relaxed.

_____   18. I'm afraid to speak up in conversations.

_____   19. I have no fear of giving a speech.

_____ 20. Certain parts of my body feel very tense and rigid while giving a speech.

_____ 21. I feel relaxed while giving a speech.

_____ 22. My thoughts become confused and jumbled when I am giving a speech.

_____ 23. I face the prospect of giving a speech with confidence.

_____ 24. While giving a speech, I get so nervous I forget facts I really know.

SCORING

GROUP DISCUSSION
18 – (scores for items 2, 4, and 6) + (scores for items 1, 3, and 5)

MEETINGS
18 – (scores for items 8, 9, and 12) + (scores for items 7, 10, and 11)

INTERPERSONAL
18 – (scores for items 14, 16, and 17) + (scores for items 13, 15, and 18)

PUBLIC SPEAKING
18 – (scores for items 19, 21, and 23) + (scores for items 20, 22, and 24)

Group Discussion Score: _____   Meetings Score: _____

Interpersonal Score: _____   Public Speaking Score: _____

To obtain your total score for the PRCA,
simply add your sub-scores together. _____

Scores can range from 24–120. Scores below 51 represent people who have very low CA. Scores between 51–80 represent people with average CA. Scores above 80 represent people who have high levels of trait CA.

NORMS FOR THE PRCA-24
(Based on over 40,000 college students; data from over 3,000 non-student adults in a national sample provided virtually identical norms, within 0.20 for all scores.)

	Mean	Standard Deviation	High	Low
Total Score	65.6	15.3	>80	<51
Group	15.4	4.8	>20	<11
Meeting	16.4	4.2	>20	<13
Dyad (Interpersonal)	14.2	3.9	>18	<11
Public	19.3	5.1	>24	<14

Source
McCroskey, J. C. (1982). _An introduction to rhetorical communication_ (4th Ed). Englewood Cliffs, NJ: Prentice-Hall.

(Also available in more recent editions of this book, now published by Allyn and Bacon.)

CHAPTER 4

AUDIENCE ANALYSIS

If you don't know your audience, effectively communicating with its members becomes a matter of luck.

Analyze your audience before you begin speaking to create a message that is effective, targeted, and adapted.

Growing up, most children learn the practice of audience adaptation quickly. One style of communication works better with one parent than with the other—perhaps we whine for one parent and calmly present facts for another. In school, some teachers appreciate and use student suggestions; others punish students who make suggestions. We learn quickly who to approach, who not to approach, and how to formulate our requests or suggestions. These lessons transfer into speech making.

Author C. Kent Wright suggested that "To sway an audience, you must watch them as you speak." But more important is to watch your audience *before* you speak, to conduct a thorough audience analysis *before* you create your message, and to give careful thought to the rhetorical situation. If you don't know your audience, swaying them becomes a matter of luck, no matter how much time you've spent preparing and practicing. A speech that is wildly successful for one audience in one context will fail miserably with another.

Analysis and adaptation are crucial first steps in the speech-making process. After all, if you don't intend to have some connection with or influence over your audience, there is no point in giving a speech. Communication is other-centered and this chapter offers you suggestions for connecting with others.

AUDIENCE COMPOSITION

The composition of your audience is your first consideration. Who is in your audience? What do they have in common? How can you incorporate that information into your message? The question, "who is in your audience?" is asking for a breakdown of demographic information, or the characteristics shared by your audience that allows them to be categorized, for example, age, sex, and occupation. In this section, we list some of the major groupings you should consider, but by no means will this list be complete. It offers you a starting place.

Why is it important that speakers adapt their messages to the specific audience and context in which they will be presenting their speech?

AGE

The age of your audience may make a difference in how they hear your message. Even if it is in their best interest, a young audience may not be as interested in hearing about social security as an older audience who is nearing retirement. Understanding that doesn't mean you can't talk about social security, but you may need to think of strategies that draw in a younger audience, like incorporating humor or stressing immediate impacts. Senior citizens may not appreciate a speech on rap stars Eminem or Tupac unless you find a unique way to connect to them. While there are always exceptions, it's important to look to your specific audience and decide what information and what style will connect. For instance, research indicates that the Veteran Generation (today's seniors) is not as open to a casual style or very personal information about the speaker, while Generations X and Y are much more interested in personal anecdotes and a casual atmosphere.

SEX

While it might be difficult to connect a speech on conducting a makeover to many men (and some women), most topics apply to both sexes and all genders. At times, however, the speaker must remind the audience that the connection is there. It is possible, for example, for some men in the audience to tune out during a message about eating disorders or anorexia. It is helpful to remind all members of the audience that eating disorders and body image issues affect men as well as women and that the number of men affected is increasing. An even more effective strategy might be to stress that regardless of whether you struggle with these issues or not, you might be contributing to other people's struggles without realizing it, then give a speech explaining how. Or focus on the role that both men and women can play in recognizing symptoms in their friends and loved ones and giving strategies for how to respond, i.e., is there a place on campus to get information or take your friend to talk to someone? What are the right and wrong things to say to your friend if you suspect they might be affected (you might be surprised by some of this information)? Again, most topics can be focused in a way to appeal to all genders or sexes, but audiences often accept stereotypes that tell them what is or is not interesting. It's your job to break through the stereotypes and expand the audience's knowledge.

RACE/ETHNICITY

People of different ethnicities often have very different life experiences from one another. There are people for whom ethnicity plays a very small role in their life, but often, especially for people of color, race and ethnicity have profound impacts on the way they see the world. This impacts the way a message is heard. Please be aware, it is not the person's race that makes them see something differently; it is their experience. For example, in Peggy McIntosh's essay, "White Privilege," she makes the claim that people of color are often seen as a representation of their entire race instead of as an individual; i.e., if someone makes a mistake, it makes the entire race look bad ("Oh, *those people* are always late/lazy/rude/etc."). She argues that when Caucasian people make the same mistakes, they are only judged as individuals. An example might be that after the Oklahoma City Bombing, white terrorist Timothy McVeigh was judged as an individual, but after terrorist attacks on the World Trade Centers and the Pentagon on September 11, 2001, there was a widespread fear of the entire Muslim and Arabic communities in the U.S. and around the world. So for a student in the minority, there is often a different stress level attached to an experience that might be stress-free for others.

The race and ethnicity of your audience members affects their life experience and, as a result, the way they interpret your message as a speaker.

Because people of different cultural backgrounds don't always have the same experiences in the same situations, they often don't understand each other's reactions to the same messages. "Why are people so sensitive? You can't say anything without offending someone!" or "Why can't people see the importance of this issue? It's so easy to be respectful and make small changes; why won't they do it?" As communicators, it's important to consider these reactions and understand why they exist.

It is not the responsibility of white people alone or black people alone or Asian, Hispanic, or any other person alone to bridge that gap in understanding. It is the responsibility of all people to understand the audience with whom they are communicating. As a speaker, regardless of your cultural background, it is important for you to understand your audience and strive to connect with them.

OCCUPATION

There are many other demographic categories you could consider when analyzing your audience. Name at least three and explain how knowing something about that category could help you develop a more effective speech.

Does your audience work in offices or do they engage in physical labor outdoors? Is there danger inherent in their work situation? Does their job exist to sell a product or to better a community? Is the organization motivated by profit or charity-based? Artistic? Number-oriented? Quick-paced? If you are lucky enough to be speaking to an audience with a similar occupation or work experience, the answers to these questions can give you clues about what might be the best way to approach them. For audience members in a quick-paced, number-oriented occupation, you may want to get to the point quickly in a shorter presentation that clearly presents a bottom line. With a community not-for-profit, you will want to stress the social benefits of your idea.

You can see how these four demographic characteristics might influence your audience analysis. Other demographics work the same way. Consider income, education level, political affiliation, geographic location, religious affiliation, and any other common traits your audience might have.

The preceding demographics were listed individually, but they should be considered together. The fact that your audience is made up of college students is helpful, but college students at a college in the Midwest may have different experiences and worldviews than college students in Southern California. Students at a private four-year university may have different experiences and expectations from students at a public community college. The audience may share the trait of being students, but they are impacted also by the region in which they live, their socioeconomic status, and many other of their demographic characteristics. Don't rely on one trait—look for as many as you can reasonably determine. Then use that information to help construct and deliver your speech to meet the unique needs and concerns of your audience.

Obviously, some of the previous examples may seem stereotypical. In this case, that happens because we do not have a specific audience to analyze, so we rely on generalizations. However, when you are preparing your speech, you will hopefully have some specific information about your audience. Upon reviewing that information, a warning is in order. While it is useful to examine the common traits of audiences, be careful not to overgeneralize or rely on false stereotypes. Generalizations can be helpful, but they rarely hold true for all members of every group. Additionally, it can be easy to oversimplify. Remember that each member of your audience has unique experiences and perspectives. Take that into account. Use qualifiers with your statements; don't assume you know an audience better than they know themselves. And ultimately, recognize that people are complex. They deserve to be treated with respect and not reduced into caricatures.

BEYOND OUR PERSPECTIVE ▬

SPEAKING YOUR AUDIENCE'S "LANGUAGE"
Audience analysis can tell us so much about our audience and, if we use that information effectively, we have a good chance of connecting with them. As suggested throughout this chapter, knowledge of your audience helps you make every decision in the course of developing your speech, from topic selection to delivery style. Sometimes one of our greatest challenges in developing the message is stepping outside ourselves enough to look at the speech as others will see it. Even with a thorough audience analysis, it is still easiest to do what would work for *us*, not what will work for *others* (particularly the people in the audience). One area where this can be a significant issue is with language choice, particularly the decision about whether to use slang or jargon, and to what degree.

Why is it likely that you will engage in stereotyping if you only rely on a demographic analysis? How can you avoid that?

IN REVIEW
There are many possible demographic categories you could look at when analyzing your audience. Four examples discussed in this chapter are:

• Age

• Sex

• Race/Ethnicity

• Occupation

Questions:

Reflections:

In terms of being sure that you effectively tailor your speech to the audience, is there a meaningful difference between slang and jargon?

Slang refers to informal words or expressions that are generally not considered part of the formal language ("What up, Dawg?" or "That concert was off the hinges!"). The definition itself highlights one of the issues with slang. Speeches tend to be more formal occasions; therefore, informal language structures should be avoided. Some audiences will be more tolerant of informal language than others, so your audience analysis will let you know how far you can move away from formal language structures. The key with slang is to be sensitive to your audience. The issue is not how comfortable you are with informal language, but how comfortable they are. Even if you are comfortable using slang around your friends, you would want to use less of it in a formal speech setting. So, be sure not to undermine your credibility by using overly informal language.

Additionally, if you make the choice to speak using slang that is representative of the audience demographic, but not your own, you risk offending the audience. It is possible they will see you as insincere or patronizing.

An issue similar to the use of slang is the use of jargon. Jargon refers to language structures and words that are specific to a particular group of people. For example, when you watch *Grey's Anatomy* or *CSI*, the doctors and lawyers on those shows use language that is specific to the medical and legal professions. You might not know what they mean, but doctors and lawyers watching the show will know them. Jargon in each field does tend to have its own degree of formality, so the issue here is not so much one of comfort and credibility, but one of clarity. If your audience is not as familiar with the jargon associated with the topic area of your speech as you are, they may not understand your message. It is tempting to use the jargon because the words tend to be very efficient descriptors of the concept you are discussing. However, as efficient as the words may be, if they are not clear to the audience, your speech will not be effective. So, use your audience analysis to identify a vocabulary your audience will understand.

In a speech, words are the means by which we communicate our messages. Be sure to use language that will make your message credible and clear. Appropriate language choice is one of the primary keys to an effective speech and your audience analysis will help you to make effective choices.

Is it ever appropriate to use slang and/or jargon in a speech?

AUDIENCE TYPES

In addition to figuring out who is in your audience, it is important to know how they might feel about you and your topic. Sometimes doing the demographic analysis described above can help you move to the next step, a psychographic analysis. In this analysis you determine your audience type based on interest, knowledge, and attitudes. There are generally four types of audiences: Unaware, Indifferent, Favorable, and Unfavorable.

UNAWARE

An unaware audience is one who has little or no information on you or your topic. You may be speaking on modern-day slavery, which exists around the world, including very large numbers in the U.S. But because there is little media coverage, many audiences will be surprised to hear that slavery did not disappear with the passage of the fourteenth amendment. You may be speaking on the causes of civil unrest in the Ukraine and your audience may not know which part of the world you are talking about.

With unaware audiences, you may need to give more background information than you might with other audience types. Consider explaining why they may not have been aware of your information and why it is important. Sometimes just giving them the information is enough to make a difference.

INDIFFERENT

An indifferent audience may be aware of your topic and information, but they are not interested in learning more about it. Although the significance of a topic might be obvious to you, your audience may not share the same interest level. You might think it is crucial to be informed of local history, but your audience may be focused on the present and future, not caring about the past unless there is a direct impact to them. Your job is to show the direct impact to your audience. Some of the examples from earlier in the chapter apply here too. Why should a young audience care about social security? Why should an older audience care about hip-hop music? Why would an audience need to know how to correctly apply makeup or change the oil in their cars? Think of an answer and stress that answer throughout your speech. If you don't have an answer to why your audience should care, you might consider a new topic.

FAVORABLE

A favorable audience is one who is likely to agree with your point of view and/or support you as a speaker. Often, people assume this is the easiest audience to talk to, and in some ways it is. But to be truly effective, a slightly different style of speaking is required. While a favorable audience is likely to agree with you, they do not necessarily share your level of passion or commitment. They may agree with the point of view, but lack the confidence or conviction to express or act upon it. Your goal as a speaker is to increase the level of commitment of the audience, to leave them feeing something that lasts beyond the speech itself.

While all our speeches should be based in logic, the balance between logic, emotion, and source appeals should be reflected more toward the emotional end. Favorable audiences more readily accept emotional appeals, "extreme" examples, "bigger" delivery, and opposition attacks. The construction of the message can include a two-sided message as a way of inoculating audiences against counter-persuasion, but it is not absolutely necessary. It is often helpful to place the strongest portion of the message toward the end, building momentum throughout the speech, leaving the audience with the strongest sense of emotion.

Do not merely give the favorable audience information they already know. Seek information and examples that are likely unfamiliar to them. Stress the idea that the problem is likely bigger, more urgent, or has more far-reaching impacts than they have previously realized. Also remind them that the situation is not hopeless and they personally have the power to make a difference. Create a sense of personal power in the audience.

With which of these audience types do you think it is most difficult to be successful? Why?

IN REVIEW
The four common types of audiences are...

- Unaware
- Indifferent
- Favorable
- Unfavorable

Questions:

Reflections:

UNFAVORABLE

An unfavorable audience is often seen as the hardest to convince because they are predisposed to disagree with your information and claims. The biggest mistake speakers make is to ask an unfavorable audience to take giant leaps instead of baby steps. Leaps are for favorable audiences. With an unfavorable audience, your goal may not be to have them adopt all your views; your goal is only to weaken opposition, to question some of their current beliefs, or to reframe some of their current ideas. Your audience is only capable of giving you so much money, so much time, so much movement on an idea. If you ask for too much they will reject you. Set moderate goals. If a hunter has used guns safely for years, it is more reasonable to ask them to consider more thorough background checks for future gun purchases or bans on certain types of weapons rather than immediately asking them to give up their guns.

In addition to moderate goals, unfavorable audiences typically need more logical appeals to be convinced. Research, statistics, and citations are especially important. Attempt to find sources the audience already trusts. Frame the issue as relating to the audience directly whenever possible. Find local examples. A two-sided message is essential. You must refute opposing arguments, but you must do it in a gentle and respectful manner. Unfavorable audiences will not respond well to being insulted.

In terms of organization, it can be helpful to begin with a claim you think the audience is likely to accept. It can help establish some common ground. Additionally, once the audience rejects an idea from the speaker, it becomes easier to dismiss the following arguments. It is also a good idea to end with a strong idea the audience will likely relate to or accept.

As a speaker, you must work hard to earn credibility. Establish goodwill and common ground whenever possible. Emotional appeals are necessary, but use them with restraint. Emotion is more likely to backfire with an unfavorable audience and result in decreased credibility.

As you remember with the favorable audience, all members will not have your information or your level of commitment—there will be a range. The same is true with unfavorable audiences, or with any audience type. There is a range of attitude and information. Some people will be slightly uninformed and others will know absolutely nothing about your topic. Some will be mildly opposed to your point of view and others will never agree with you. And within an audience, you may have members of all four types. You may be required to come up with your best combination of strategies based on who is in your audience. In any case, audience analysis is crucial to succeed as a speaker.

APPLYING THE FUNDAMENTALS━━━

USING YOUR AUDIENCE ANALYSIS

Throughout this chapter, we have looked at many ways you can study your audience and identified the types of information you should gather. We have also mentioned some of the ways that information can help you construct an effective speech that will connect with your audience. Once a thorough audience analysis has been conducted, the following questions may help you decide how to use that analysis in constructing your speech. This is not a complete list of questions; it is meant to help you begin the process. Keep this list in mind as you move through the next several chapters and work through the process of developing your speech.

1. **Topic**: Is my audience interested in my topic? If not, how can I relate the topic to the audience? How can I stress the importance of my topic?

2. **Purpose**: Does my specific purpose make sense for my audience? What are they capable of "giving" in terms of time, money, interest level, attitude change, etc.?

3. **Content**: I cannot put everything about my topic into the speech. Have I chosen my content in terms of how it relates to the audience? Have I made sure not to merely repeat what the audience already knows? Do I have new and unique information? Have I made sure not to offend my audience or overwhelm them with information that is too complex for their background?

4. **Style**: Am I adopting an appropriate tone or mood for my audience and situation? Have I considered whether my audience/situation requires a more or less formal tone? Am I using enough/too much humor? Am I dressed appropriately?

Using your speech and your class as an audience (or some other audience, if your professor has created one as part of the assignment), discuss some strategies you might use to connect with your audience, particularly in the areas of Topic, Purpose, Content, and Style, to be most effective with the audience you will present to.

Are there other elements of the speech which you think could be more effective with a comprehensive knowledge of the audience?

SITUATIONAL ANALYSIS

The focus of this chapter is analyzing your audience, but the purpose of analysis is to effectively adapt your message to the specific rhetorical context. While you are making decisions about your message and delivery, it is also important to consider the rhetorical situation. All elements of the situation can affect how another person hears your message, so take some time to consider this as well.

How will the room affect your communication? Is it large or small? Will it require a louder voice or a larger visual aid? In a larger auditorium, you may need to be more animated and use slightly larger gestures. In a smaller room, you may need to be careful not to overpower your audience. Perhaps there are visual obstructions between you and your audience; you may need to determine where you can and cannot be seen. You may need to be aware of lighting and remain in a certain portion of the room or stage or risk becoming a mere silhouette. Arrive early and determine how your space may affect your message; make choices that will lessen interference between you and your audience.

Analyze the classroom space where you will present your speech. What opportunities are there for a more effective presentation? What challenges might the space present for what you want to do in your speech?

With technology being an integral part of many speakers' messages, it is also crucial to be aware of the technological capabilities of the setting. Does the room have the capability for PowerPoint or other computer graphics? Is there a projector or a large enough screen for your purpose? Is the lighting such that it will interfere with

IN REVIEW
When analyzing the rhetorical situation, you should consider...

- Size and design of the speaking space
- Technological capabilities
- Time of presentation
- Purpose for gathering
- Your relationship with the audience

Questions:

Reflections:

Can a speech truly be effective without a sense of audience? Why or why not?

how the audience will see the screen? Questions like these will be considered in the chapter on presentation aids, but should also be considered in your analysis stage. Many speakers prepare messages that they are not able to give without PowerPoint or overhead transparencies, etc. Find out in advance if your physical setting will support this strategy (and as suggested in Chapter 13, have a backup plan in case something goes wrong).

It is important to consider your setting beyond the physical constraints as well. How does your location or time impact the communication? An audience in a classroom might require a slightly more serious tone than the same audience in a bar on a Friday night. An evening presentation may require a different tone or length of time than a morning seminar. Consider, also, the reason the audience has gathered. Did they come to learn, to be entertained, or a little of both? Examine all elements of the communication environment and respond accordingly.

Another point of consideration for analysis and adaptation is your relationship with the audience. Have you had prior contact with this audience? If so, how is that likely to have affected their perception of you? The cliché is true: you only get one chance to make a first impression. There is no rewind. If your audience perceives you as having low credibility for any reason, you must think about ways to counteract that perception. Your speech is being filtered through every interaction you have ever had with your audience.

SUMMARY

As you have most likely gathered from the examples throughout the chapter, the analysis you conduct in preparation of your speech requires you to make choices in every step of the process. In fact, audience analysis is the first step of the process. Your audience influences your topic choice, your narrowing of the focus, your specific goal, content, length, organization, and style. In other words, it affects everything.

Communication is other-centered. In order to be effective as speakers, we must adapt to our audience. It is important to engage in a demographic analysis and find ways to incorporate information that connects to your audience into your speech. A psychographic analysis is also necessary; determine your audience's likely attitudes to your topic, purpose, or claims and present them in a way that is acceptable to the audience. Additionally, analyze the rhetorical situation; what is the context in which the speech is being given and how is that likely to affect the relationship between the speaker and audience? Use this information in every step of the speech-making process. Ultimately, our purpose as communicators is to connect with others, to share understanding and experiences. That will not happen if we do not know who they are.

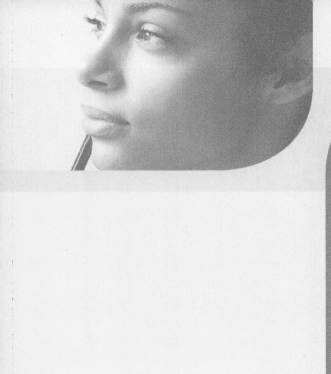

CHAPTER 5

PURPOSE

The first step in developing an effective speech is to determine your general purpose.

*Dwight Eisenhower understood the importance of focusing solely on his objective.
Effective speakers do the same thing, starting with having a clear sense
of what that objective is.*

Former President Dwight Eisenhower once noted that we succeed only when we
determine one primary objective, and then "make all other considerations bend to
that one objective." Eisenhower applied his description of success to life, war, or "in
anything else," and developing a speech certainly could be one of those "anything
else." Successful speakers are those that get the fullest possible response from their
audience. That is why, for example, some people find it daunting to speak to the
favorable audience we discussed in the last chapter. Because that audience is so
sympathetic to the speaker's position, the speaker should be able to get a very strong
reaction from the audience—anything else is not a complete success. That sets the
bar very high.

So, having analyzed the audience, the speaker is now confronted with the question,
what is the best reaction I can hope to get from my audience?

+ Will I be happy if my audience knows more than they did before the speech?

Or

+ Can I reasonably expect my audience to think or act in a particular way based
  on the information I provide?

Asking and answering those questions gets the speaker focused on the question
of purpose: in a broad sense, what do I hope to accomplish in this speech? If the
speaker seeks the first reaction from the audience, the speech will be informative;
if the speaker wants the second reaction and hopes to get the audience to think or
act in a particular way, the speech will be persuasive. Scholars generally identify
three general purposes. In addition to the speeches to persuade and the speeches to
inform, there is also the speech to inspire. Those speeches tend to be very unique, so
they are discussed separately and in great detail in Chapter 14.

At one level the distinction between persuasive and informative speeches is deceptively simple: informative speeches inform while persuasive speeches persuade. However, to some extent, informative and persuasive identify two ends of a spectrum and when speakers analyze their audience they generally find the best response they can get from the audience falls somewhere in between those two extremes, so many speeches will mix informative and persuasive strategies. Yet, before you can effectively mix those strategies you need to master the strategies and so your professor is likely to give you assignments which focus on one purpose or the other: either to persuade or inform. So, to help you respond to those assignments, this chapter will provide you detailed information about informative and persuasive speeches and then show how you can truly distinguish between those two purposes.

SPEECHES TO INFORM

The first purpose, to inform, is for a speech where the main goal is to transfer knowledge to your audience. It can be likened to teaching, where the goal is mainly to objectively present information. The students, or the audience, should learn something new, but not necessarily draw any conclusions from that knowledge. At times, speakers approach an informative speech as an opportunity to show off their own knowledge, but the true goal is to have the audience walk away sharing your knowledge, owning it themselves. Within this general purpose there are several types of informative speeches. The nature of the information being discussed determines what kind of speech will be given.

THE SPEECH OF DEFINITION

In this speech the speaker attempts to identify the essential qualities or properties of something. "I wish to inform my audience about the nature of hip-hop music" falls into the category of definition.

THE DESCRIPTIVE SPEECH

In these speeches the speaker does not necessarily attempt to explain the nature of the subject, but rather describes what the subject is. This is commonly used in speeches about events. For example, a speaker may say, "In my speech I will describe a traditional Chinese wedding."

Speeches of description, at first glance, may sound the same as a speech of definition. After all, when a speaker defines something, can't it also be said that the speaker is also describing that same thing? The answer is "no" because speeches of description function a bit differently. Instead of using your speech to discuss essential elements that make something what it is, a speech of description attempts to use a variety of details, imagery, etc., to help create a mental picture for the audience. A speech about the Illinois State Fair that discusses the fairgrounds and the fair activities would be considered a speech of description because it attempts to give a "virtual tour" and describe what the subject is.

THE COMPARISON AND CONTRAST SPEECH

This speech is closely related to the speeches of definition and description, but involve two subjects. In this speech, a speaker looks at the essences of two items and examines how they are similar and/or different. For example, a speaker might say, "I will explain to my audience how hip-hop music is different from rap music."

THE SPEECH OF EXPOSITION

This speech is perhaps the most common type of informative speech. Here the speaker explains some concept, process, or idea. This speech often differs from the speech of description because the subject of an expository speech is more theoretical or abstract and therefore the speaker cannot rely as heavily on the verbal imagery that is common in a speech of description. The speaker's goal in this kind of speech is to help the audience better understand the nature of the subject. While this may include definition, the speech will go beyond that to provide a more in-depth analysis of the subject. Examples of expository speeches would be speeches about computer-generated imagery in films, existentialism, or the Theory of Relativity.

Within the topic of hip-hop music, you could develop a number of different types of informative speeches.

THE SPEECH OF DEMONSTRATION

In this type of informative speech a speaker actually shows how to do something, like how to make a cake. These speeches tend to be a bit different than other informative speeches because the structure is driven by the steps in the process. As you will see in Chapter 8, organizing a speech can involve a series of complex decisions regarding how to group and present information which may not have an inherent structure. Generally, in demonstration speeches, the "groups" or main points are the steps in the process and what is included in that point is the information the audience needs to effectively complete that step. Thus, in many cases, demonstration speeches have more main points, but each point may be less developed. The audience can still follow along, however, because the speech progresses logically through whatever process the speaker is describing.

Explaining to your audience the step-by-step process of making a cake would be an example of a demonstration speech.

How could you address the following subject areas as an informative speech? As a persuasive speech?

Smoke detectors

Using Google for college-level research

Student loans

SPEECHES TO PERSUADE

The second general purpose is to persuade an audience, to convince them to accept a certain point of view as true or false, right or wrong, or to follow a specific plan of action. The goal is not only to provide information about your subject, but to use that information to build an argument which seeks to get the audience to think or act in a particular way. Usually, an audience will have to be informed before they can be persuaded, so a persuasive speech will include elements of informative speaking as well as argumentation.

PERSUASIONS OF FACT

The central idea in a persuasion of fact is an opinion which the speaker attempts to support as true throughout the body of the speech. It may seem odd to say that a persuasion of fact is based on an opinion because people tend to think of facts and opinions as two different things. However, when talking about persuasive speeches, they are used synonymously. Persuasive speaking involves convincing the audience to accept a particular outlook on an issue, which implies that there are other outlooks. So, if something were truly a verifiable fact there would be no disagreement and hence no need for persuasion. When there are different perspectives you can have your opinion (or way of looking at the situation) and somebody else can have another and your goal in the speech is to convince the audience they should accept your opinion as the right way to look at the situation.

PERSUASIONS OF VALUE

Similar to a persuasion of fact, in a persuasion of value the goal of the speaker is, again, to alter how the audience thinks. In this case, however, the focus is not on just the truth or validity of some opinion, but on the implied or explicit value statement contained in the central idea. In other words, a value claim makes a statement about the quality of the topic being discussed. So, the thesis: "Electric cars are the most viable alternative to conventional gasoline-powered engines" is a fact-based thesis,

IN REVIEW
The types of persuasive speeches are...

• Persuasions of fact

• Persuasions of value

• Persuasions of policy

Questions:

Reflections:

while the statement: "Preserving America's standard of living depends on reducing our dependency on foreign oil" is value based. Note that in the first example, the speaker makes no assertion about the relative worth of electric cars. The speaker may feel that developing electric cars is not necessarily a good thing, but still sees it as the only viable alternative to gasoline. In the second case, there are some implied value judgments: that the American way of life is a good thing and protecting it is important. This speaker doesn't care if electric cars (or any other alternative) are viable—this speaker sees the American way of life as a good thing that must be preserved.

PERSUASIONS OF POLICY

These types of persuasive speeches are noticeably different from the other two. Here the focus is on what action we should take. The central idea in a persuasion of policy focuses on convincing the audience that they should take some action, or support someone else who will, can, or should take an action. Extending the examples from the last paragraph, a persuasion of policy would argue something like, "I want to convince people to buy an electric car," or "The United States Government should develop incentives to encourage auto makers to develop low-cost electric cars." In the first example, the focus is on an action the audience can take directly. In the second case, assuming there are not a large number of senators and representatives in the audience, the focus is on an action others should take. However, even in that case, the speaker should get the audience actively involved in the issue by giving them steps they can take to support those who will actually implement the action. In this case, that could mean, for example, writing letters in support of legislation promoting low-cost electric cars.

APPLYING THE FUNDAMENTALS

ISSUES OF PURPOSE IN SPEECH CLASSES AND ELSEWHERE

The discussion of purpose in this chapter probably emphasizes the distinction between types of speeches more than may be necessary for speakers outside of a speech classroom. In the classroom, where the goal is to learn particular skills, professors separate the purposes of informing, persuading, and inspiring to more clearly identify expectations for particular speech assignments in a basic speech class.

However, in order to respond appropriately to those assignments, we must recognize that common speeches do not necessarily fit neatly into these three categories. Effective speakers will try to get as much as they can out of a speech situation and will choose the mix of informative, persuasive, and inspirational strategies accordingly. Typically, the audience will respond to the presentation, without thinking much about the mix. For example, campaigns meant to spread information to increase awareness about AIDS, smoking, breast cancer, or the dangers of driving while texting on your cell phone, all contain strong elements of both information and persuasion. Campaigns such as the "Vote or Die" campaign run during the 2004 presidential race certainly informed, persuaded, and inspired many people to become more active citizens by voting and convincing others to vote.

So, many speeches may contain elements of all three general purposes. However, in order to do that effectively, it can be helpful to learn what those various strategies are in separate assignments. As a result, speech teachers will somewhat artificially isolate the three general purposes for speech class assignments. What helps you respond to those assignments is to focus on the primary purpose of the speech, and identify a tone that responds well to that purpose. Do you want your audience to *know* something or *believe* something? Is the tone more objective and informational in nature or subjective and open to interpretation? The truth is we can make arguments either way on most topics, but in speech classes, we will divide the purposes, as mentioned above, in order to practice different skill sets. With informative speaking, we will practice explaining clearly, developing ideas, simplifying information, and connecting to the audience. With persuasive speaking, we will add the element of argumentation; we will practice developing complete arguments and avoiding logical fallacies. With inspirational speaking, we blend these skills and focus on a moment, using both our informative and persuasive strategies to commemorate special events.

While many speeches appropriately blend purposes, students in a speech class will need to be more aware of what distinguishes the purposes. Isolating the purposes can help in practicing the skill sets and, of course, responding to the instructor's assignment.

DISTINGUISHING BETWEEN SPEECHES

As noted at the start of this chapter, sometimes a speech will contain elements of both informative and persuasive speaking. In fact, it is often difficult to say that any one speech is purely informative or purely persuasive, (or even purely inspirational). For practicing different skill sets, your professor will likely separate categories, but the truth is most speeches contain some overlap in terms of their purpose.

In fact, some scholars argue that all communication is persuasive in nature. For example, arguably, there is a persuasive element in every conversation. When you answer an informational question in a job interview, you are answering in a way that is crafted to persuade your potential employer that you are knowledgeable, responsible, and desirable as an employee. Or, when you tell your significant other about a new restaurant, there is probably at least some implication that you would like to visit that restaurant. Similarly, speeches considered informative in nature may include some element of persuasion. For instance, in an informative speech about the musical genius of John Lennon, you will be persuading your audience that the topic is interesting and important, that your information is realistic and credible, and that you are competent to speak on the topic. In Chapter 14 you will see that a commemorative speech at a graduation (one of the speeches to inspire) not only seeks to inspire the graduates to go forth and do good deeds, but may also seek to persuade the more cynical members of the audience that their time has been well spent, that the future is a positive place, and that their ideas and their contributions will be meaningful.

How could you address the following subject areas as a persuasion of fact? A persuasion of value? A persuasion of policy?

Final exams

Zero tolerance for violence policies in schools

The Chicago Cubs

When you tell someone about a great coffee shop are you really just telling them about the shop, or are you suggesting you should go to the coffee shop? That is the thin line between informative and persuasive.

Is it possible to have a speech that is purely informative or purely persuasive?

If there is so much overlap, then how do we distinguish between an informative speech and a persuasive speech? Consider, again, the topic of electric cars. One speaker may choose as her focus: "In my speech I will help the audience understand how electric cars work." Another student may adopt a thesis that says: "You may not realize it, but electric cars are becoming a viable alternative to conventional gas-powered cars, and in this speech I will tell you how those kinds of cars work and describe some currently available electric cars." Yet another student could adopt as his thesis: "We are overly dependent on foreign oil and therefore must promote a switch to electric cars." The first speech is clearly informative while the third is clearly persuasive, but what about the speech that is, quite literally, in the middle? The focus seems to be on informing about electric cars and how they work, but there is the claim that "electric cars are a viable alternative to conventional gas-powered cars," and that seems like an opinion that the speaker needs to support, which would make the speech a persuasion of fact. So, which is it? The answer is the speech would be considered informative because the focus of that speech is not on convincing the audience to believe that statement. Rather, that statement is used to help the audience organize the information.

Like the topic of electric cars, many topics can be developed as either persuasive or informative speeches. In fact, sometimes the line between persuasive and informative is very thin. So, how can you be sure you are responding appropriately to your professor's assignments? The following factors can help you determine if your speech is informative or persuasive.

TOPICS IN INFORMATIVE AND PERSUASIVE SPEECHES

Informative speeches tend to deal with less controversial subjects (or focus on less controversial areas of that topic). For an informative speech to work the audience must be receptive to the information and not resistant to the message. With more controversial topics the audience is likely to be more defensive and demand a higher level of proof (see the later section on the role of evidence). The audience will also be more likely to argue with the speaker, even if the speaker isn't trying to make a specific argument. For these reasons, while informative speeches are possible on subjects like abortion, gun control, and euthanasia, they are less likely to be effective. Also, note, for example, how we examined the topic of electric cars earlier. Some facets of that topic area are likely to be more controversial than others. How such a car works is factual; the components of the engine and the car work in a particular way. When describing that process there is no controversy. There is also not likely to be much of an emotional reaction from the audience; we don't have strong social feelings about how a car works (contrast that with a topic like abortion, where the process could be described factually, but people are likely to attach value judgments to the nature of that process and those value judgments are likely to clash because different people look at the issue in different ways). While how an electric car works is not likely to be controversial, the decision to buy one may be (note here we are using the term "controversial" to refer to any situation where people are likely to have a difference of opinion). Some people may feel that it is important to protect the environment at all costs, whereas others may think that economics should also be considered. Also, some people feel the environmental benefits of electric cars are overrated because most electric cars have a limited range and so are not useful for the ways we use cars. These people would say we couldn't achieve the benefits promised by electric cars because people would still need to use gas-powered cars for longer trips. Others may respond to that by saying that short trips are the most polluting, so if we could at least replace gas cars for shorter trips we could still favorably impact the environment. As you can see, there are lots of things to think about if you were making the decision to buy an electric car, and so if you were to do a speech trying to show your audience the viability of those cars, you would have to do more than just provide information; you would also need to use that information to defend the position you were taking. When your chosen focus within a topic area (what we will refer to as your thesis in Chapter 7) demands that kind of effort, you have a persuasive speech.

Think of several possible subject areas for your speech and then think about how you could approach that as an informative or a persuasive speech. Does the fact that these topics can be addressed in either an informative or persuasive manner suggest something about the importance of purpose?

While focusing on the subject of electric cars, a speaker could develop a number of different focuses. Some of those focuses would be more informative in nature, while others would be more persuasive.

INTENT OF THE SPEAKER

We have talked throughout this chapter about informative and persuasive speaking as being two different types of messages you can present to your audience. The underlying message has been with each type of speaking your overall purpose and focus is different, so there isn't much more to say about this point. But, we do need to recognize that the speaker's intent is one of the most fundamental differences between informative and persuasive speaking. In an informative speech your goal is to educate, to add to the audience's base of knowledge. We could say, quite simply, that the goal is to inform, but we should not define a word with that word, but the goal of an informative speech is certainly self-evident in the way we label that speech. Likewise with a persuasive speech, the goal is quite self-evident—to persuade or convince. You want to do more than just provide information; you want the audience to think about that information in a particular way and perhaps to act in a particular way because of how they look at your material.

REACTION OF THE AUDIENCE

Just as you are trying to accomplish something different in informative and persuasive speeches, you expect the audience's reaction to be different. If your goal is to inform, you want the audience to learn; if your goal is to persuade, you want the audience to believe or act. In either case, you want to be successful and success is defined by your intention, so because your intention is different, the desired reaction needs to be different. However, it is not as simple as wanting a different reaction from the audience; we must also understand that a typical audience is more amenable to learning than to believing. To learn the audience simply needs to be open to new information and most audiences will be, because most people are open to intellectual growth, at some level. Therefore, the primary issue for you as a speaker is to get the audience interested in the particular information you will present. On the other hand, when you engage in persuasive speaking you want to change the audience's mind about something. You want them to look at an issue the way you think it should be looked at, not the way they have looked at it before, and people are more resistant to that kind of change. So, when you engage in persuasive speaking, you will have to work harder to get your desired result. In Chapter 12 we will discuss how you build effective arguments to help you accomplish that goal.

ROLE OF EVIDENCE

What should become clear from the previous discussions is that your goal is very different in informative and persuasive speaking. As we will see in Chapter 6, it is very important that you have supporting material in your speech and that the material is tailored to your intent. Logically, then, we can see that the way you use evidence in informative and persuasive speeches will be different. In an informative speech the role of supporting material is to provide the audience with facts about your topic. Whereas in a persuasive speech, the evidence will provide support for your position that the audience should think or act in a particular way (i.e., that they should buy an electric car). As we saw in Chapter 2 the speaker always has an ethical obligation to provide high quality information to the audience, and that doesn't change whether the speech is informative or persuasive. What does change is how you will use that evidence, and that may affect what you consider to be the best evidence for that speech. In an informative speech, the focus is on sharing information, so information that is factually accurate and clear and easy to understand is generally best. On the other hand, in a persuasive speech you will be making arguments to convince the audience to look at a situation the way you want them to. As you will see in Chapter 12, an argument consists of three parts, one of which has to do with explaining how your evidence relates to the argument you are making. In situations like that, the best evidence will be that which relates best to the argument you are making. In addition, because you are trying to change the audience's mind about something, you have to recognize that they will be more resistant to your argument. Therefore, it is important that you select the evidence that will be easier for the audience to accept. That may mean using evidence from sources that are more acceptable to the audience or looking for evidence that makes a point in a way that makes more sense to the audience. Overall, the thing you should notice here is that supporting material, while important to all speeches, plays a more crucial role in persuasive speeches and therefore, you need to give more thought to the evidence you use.

The supporting material you decide to use in a speech should be selected based on how it will help you achieve your purpose.

SUMMARY

In this chapter we have seen that your speech can be geared to different purposes. In the classroom, that purpose will be dictated by the assignment your professor gives you. Outside of the classroom, the specific distinction may be somewhat less important and the focus more on what you can achieve with your particular audience. Either way, it is important to know what your general purpose is because that will affect a number of decisions you will make about how you construct and present your speech, as you will see as we move further through the speech development process in the next several chapters.

IN REVIEW
Persuasive and informative speeches differ in...

- The topics (or thesis) you select

- Your intent

- The way you want the audience to react

- The way you use evidence

Questions:

Reflections:

Do you think it is easier to give an informative speech or a persuasive speech? Why?

CHAPTER 6

RESEARCH

No idea stands alone; through research, you give your ideas appropriate support.

You need to give your audience high quality information in your speech and there is not one source that is always the best source for that information. You should be aware of all the available resources and work to find the best sources for each speech.

In the 1990s, the way most people conducted research began to change. The "information superhighway," otherwise known as the Internet, was suddenly accessible to most people. Instead of looking for material in library aisles, the preferred mode of research became a computer screen. However, the computer isn't always the best means of research. At times, we are lucky; our Google search brings up exactly what we need from a credible source. Other times it seems impossible to sift through the hundreds of thousands of websites that may or may not be helpful for our purposes, and other forms of research may be more effective. In order to help you conduct research that is both rewarding and effective, this chapter discusses the importance of research, presents a basic plan for gathering research, information about using the different varieties of supporting materials, standards for evaluating the materials you find, and strategies for effective research that will be helpful within this course, as well as other college courses.

IMPORTANCE OF RESEARCH

Before we begin the discussion of research plans and such, the concept of this chapter ultimately raises the question, why is conducting research an important step in the speech-making process? Arguably the number one reason that research is important has to do with the concept of *ethos* (which was discussed in Chapter 2, and will be addressed again later on in the text as well). When we research, we are either learning about the topic, or expanding the knowledge base we already have about the topic. In either case, we are contributing to our ethos. From a different perspective, we are accumulating information that we will be using to deepen our understanding of our topic area and to support the ideas or arguments we are presenting. While speakers can use their own knowledge and opinion during their speech, this type of support/evidence is not always viewed as legitimate. When we conduct research through credible sources, however, we are adding more legitimacy to our topics. In essence, to reference another aspect of ethos, we are also contributing to our "moral character" by showing the audience we care about them and the

Why do we need to do research and gather information about our topic before presenting our speech?

topic enough to give quality information. Furthermore, we are showing concern for the audience, or "good will," by researching. We want our audiences to have the best information and ideas possible before they make an ultimate conclusion about our topic (or before they, hopefully, accept our persuasive claims). Research shows that when you show you care for the best interests of your audience they are more likely to respond favorably to your message.

All in all, when we research our topic, we are showing the audience that we are prepared to give our speech, and are knowledgeable enough to do so.

PRELIMINARY RESEARCH PLAN

The first step in research is creating a plan. When doing research, people often sit in front of a computer and type the first string of words that comes to mind. Sometimes this works, but often such an effort can become unfocused, unproductive, and lead to problems down the road. Therefore, it is helpful to begin by creating a plan to guide your efforts. Depending on the type of project you are conducting, research plans can be elaborate, but for our purposes, there are three simple steps. Before beginning your research, ask the questions:

1. What do you know about the topic?

2. What should you learn about the topic?

3. What is the best way to find the information?

The first step is to map your knowledge of the topic. Write down what you know. This highlights the knowledge you have, keeps areas of the topic organized, and helps you identify any gaps in necessary information.

Second, it is important to realize that no one knows *everything* about a topic. *Breaking Bad* may be your favorite television program and you may know a lot about it, but chances are you need more information. If your purpose is to persuade the audience that *Breaking Bad* is the best drama in television history, you may already know how many seasons it was on, who the characters are, and where to find the show now. But think about this information in terms of how it helps you achieve your purpose. What would an audience need to hear to accept your claim? The audience may not rely solely on your opinion, so you would need to locate reviews of the show from critics. The audience might favor other popular shows, so you would need to have information about what makes *Breaking Bad* different and better. In other words, you will spend time in this step filling gaps in your own knowledge and determining what information your audience requires in relation to your specific purpose.

Finally, once you have identified your needs, think about where the information is located. You may be able to find information on the Internet, but the Internet is not always easier or faster. When you have trouble narrowing a search online, it can be helpful to interview a person with expertise or specific experience related to your topic. An expert may be able to answer your question more clearly and specifically than Google. It may also be more helpful to search a newspaper or magazine database. Be aware of all the available resources. The Internet *is* a great place to do research, especially if you are using all the specialized options available. You can conduct web searches, but also news searches, image searches, and video searches. It can also be helpful to narrow your results by searching specific credible websites, as opposed to searching the entire web. But remember, the Internet is not the *only* place to research and not always the *best* place to do research. Do not rule out more traditional sources, such as:

- Encyclopedias
- Government documents
- Almanacs
- Quotation books
- Dictionaries
- Personal interviews

- Newspapers
- Librarians
- Magazines
- Television and radio
- Journals
- Article databases

When conducting research, do not rule out traditional, printed sources of information.

Each one of the above sources has advantages and disadvantages that you can consider in the research worksheet at the end of the chapter. There is not one source that is better than another in general. Make your decision based on the kind of information you need.

TYPES OF SUPPORTING MATERIAL

After you think about your answers from your preliminary research plan, you will need to take the next step and locate information from books, news transcripts, or credible websites. When you conduct your research, you will find different types of supporting material. Common sense tells you to choose only information that supports the specific purpose of your speech, but even then, you have choices to make. Each type of support has a certain strength attached to it. One type may be more effective than another to help make a specific point. Nevertheless, when considering the overall message, it is important to incorporate a variety of supporting materials to promote a sense of balance and appeal to needs of the audience.

STATISTICS

Statistics are a type of supporting material using numerical data. For example, "Nine out of ten dentists agree that Brand A is better than Brand B at preventing gum disease." Statistics can be used to show how large or small a phenomenon is, how popular an item or idea is, and in other ways that emphasize the scope of an issue.

In a speech about film actor Ben Stiller, statistics could be used in a number of ways. If you want to establish Stiller's popularity, you might report the amount of money his most recent films brought in at the box office or count the number of awards he has received. If members of an audience are number-oriented, statistics lend an air of credibility to your message.

NARRATIVES

Along with statistics to support your ideas, you can also use narratives (more commonly referred to as stories or anecdotes). While statistics give what are referred to as "the cold hard facts," narratives do a better job at "painting a picture" for an audience. Stories contain a human element, so in addition to clarifying ideas, they can add a level of emotion to a message.

These narratives can be from real or imagined experiences (hypothetical scenarios must always be disclosed as such to an audience). If you want to convince a friend not to support a local restaurant, statistics regarding the number of closures by the health department can be helpful, but a narrative detailing the poor service, high prices, and your visit to the hospital to be treated for food poisoning afterward, can really drive that point home. Narratives add a more human connection to the issue.

EXAMPLES

Examples are specific pieces of information that are representative of a larger claim or idea. They are used to clarify unfamiliar or difficult concepts. When giving the previously mentioned speech on Ben Stiller, you may claim he is especially talented in executing physical comedy. You may then support this claim by showing a short clip from the film *Night at the Museum* and pointing out his technique. This specific example of his acting is meant to represent his talent on a larger level.

Examples, like narratives, can be real or imagined. As with narratives, you must declare any hypothetical examples as being such. In addition, you can use very brief examples or extended and developed examples. It is possible for a narrative to serve as an example, depending upon how it is incorporated into the message.

TESTIMONY

The final type of supporting material is testimony. Testimony in a speech is similar to testimony given in a courtroom. A person who is considered qualified to speak on an issue gives their experience or viewpoint on a specific idea. However, we do not usually bring people in to testify during our speeches, so for our purposes, testimony is given in the form of direct quotation or paraphrasing. Testimonies can add an authoritative air to your claim or a personal element, depending on the type of quotation you find.

Identify the type of supporting material used in each example below and explain how you could most effectively use it in a speech.

I had always heard that Elgin Airlines had poor customer service, but I didn't believe it until I flew with them last summer. Let me tell you about my flight…

According to government data, in October of 2014, 89.7% of Hawaiian Airline flights at all U.S. airports were on time, giving it the best on-time performance in the industry.

Patrick Smith, a commercial pilot and blogger, says all airlines, even regional carriers, are very safe, telling *The New York Times*, "there's nothing that makes a large plane safer than a small plane; it's simply that you're more disconnected from the sensations of flight on a large plane."

The downing of Malaysia Airlines Flight 17 in the Ukraine demonstrates the need to better identify dangerous fly zones.

Whatever its purpose, remember to qualify the source of testimony as being credible to speak on your issue. Give your audience a reason to accept the word of your source. For example, "Toni Morrison, who won the Nobel Prize in Literature in 1993, claims that truly great writing..." is more effective than the claims of "my friend, Sam."

RESEARCH GUIDELINES AND TESTS

People tend to look for information in many places. As mentioned previously, many head right to a computer and the World Wide Web. Others tend to rely more on books, newspapers, online databases, or journals. Wherever you find your information, it needs to be critically evaluated. While you need to be most careful with sources from the World Wide Web (because many are not critically or editorially reviewed), faulty evidence can be found anywhere. So, before incorporating a source into your message, take the time to determine its legitimacy.

CRITICALLY EVALUATE THE SOURCE OF INFORMATION

We all know there is no censor for the Internet; for as many credible, objective sources you find, there are as many with misleading, false, or biased information. Likewise, newspapers run opinion columns, in addition to reporting objective news. Organizations with names that sound neutral may be corporate or party sponsored. When you use information in your speech, the audience must know that it comes from a valid and appropriate source, so make sure you can tell them that by looking critically at the source of your information.

If you are not certain of the background of the person, paper, or organization, check. On a website, visit the link entitled "About Us" (but recognize such sections are often written by the authors of the source and therefore may not be the best way to determine the quality of the source). You can also run an Internet search on the source of your information. You will not always be able to judge credibility by the appearance of your source; it is better to spend a little extra time to ensure the validity of your information. For printed sources, double-check the background of magazines, journals, or newspapers that you may not know very well. Are the contents written for an audience with specific interests or views, or not? Sometimes you can find this by looking at the editorial statement of the publication; other times you may actually need to research your research source.

Finally, when using the Internet, the endings .org, .edu, or .gov do not ensure legitimacy of information. Some universities, for example, post student papers, blogs, or personal web pages. Consider this before using the information.

©2015 The Christian Science Monitor (www.CSMonitor.com)

Screenshot of DHMO.org used with permission of website owners.

You need to get beyond appearances to really determine the quality of a website. While both these sites look legitimate, the Christian Science Monitor is a far better source. If you want to know the problem with DHMO.org, find out what DHMO is.

CHECK FOR AUTHORSHIP

Just as the source of the information needs to be credible, so too does the author. So, ask yourself: "Who wrote this information?" For many printed sources that is relatively easy to find. However, the authorship of a website may not be as apparent. Again, try the "About Us" link. You can also try to use the first part of the URL address and see if it indicates authorship. For example, if you have an article on the URL http://www.elgin.edu/speech101/pprw589, try eliminating the "pprw589," or even everything after the .edu, to see if you can find any other information about the source.

Once you have identified the author, check to see if that author is credible. Before you take any information at face value, you should check to see if the author knows what they are talking about, and determine how credible they are as a source.

In some cases, websites may not offer information for a specific author. For example, if you determine that info you found on the WebMD website for a speech about the disease Ebola was appropriate to use in your speech, you might not find a specific author associated with that entry. In cases like this, cite the website as the source of the information, as opposed to a specific author. However, you will need to be sure to determine if the website itself is considered credible, and you may even need to explain that credibility to your audience during the speech. Even if an author isn't cited, you should also try to find out who the site generally uses as authors (i.e., does a medical site use doctors) to see if such people would generally be considered credible by the audience.

Finally, if you cannot find the author of any source, or do not feel the source is considered credible based on your research about it, do not use the information within your speech. If the information is legitimate, you will be able to find it elsewhere.

DETERMINE BIASES

Along with determining if the source you would like to use has verifiable and credible authorship, it is also noteworthy to examine if that source is also biased. In a general sense, bias refers to the amount of prejudice or favoritism given to one side of an issue over another. For example, you may have found some strong statistics for a persuasive speech about marijuana legalization from a magazine called *High Times*. While many people may likely just take the information and use it, a further examination of the leaning of that source may be warranted. Specifically, *High Times* is a publication printed by a group that endorses marijuana legalization. Therefore, the information from that source is likely biased because the group favors one side of an issue over another. Also, as mentioned earlier in this chapter, if you are conducting Internet research do not assume that because a website ends in .edu or .org that it is automatically unbiased, as some schools or organizations have specific ideologies. Finally, remember even if the information appears "right" or consistent with what you believe, the particular source you are looking at may still be biased, as it favors a position similar to what you think is right or correct.

Generally, audiences will reject biased sources because they are not seen as objective or credible. Because of that, you should work to find better sources to make your point rather than use a biased source. As noted above in the discussion on authorship, if the information is legitimate, you will be able to find it elsewhere.

Why is it important to use credible sources? What characteristics does a credible source of information possess?

What characteristics does an appropriate source from the Internet have? An inappropriate source?

BEYOND THE FUNDAMENTALS

RELUCTANT TESTIMONY

While much of the testimony you find in your research is given willingly, occasionally you will encounter what is called **reluctant testimony**. This is testimony from a person who is speaking against his or her own interests. For example, if the president of a company testified that their brand of product was inferior to the competition, this is against the company's best interest. The theory associated with reluctant testimony states that an audience would attach more credibility to this type of support because they would view it as unbiased. This holds true for many audiences, but communication scholars Arnold and McCroskey argue the credibility of testimony is attached to audience attitudes as well as to speaker interest. This is important to keep in mind as you are researching. What you perceive as a credible source may be perceived as biased by the audience. For this reason, it is important to keep your audience analysis in mind as you are selecting materials to support your ideas.

Find five pieces of supporting material and evaluate the quality of the evidence. How would you cite these sources while giving your speech?

CONSIDER THE CURRENCY OF THE SOURCES

As a researcher, you want accurate and up-to-date information. Information that was true 10 years ago (or 5 years ago or 1 year ago or 1 month ago) may not be true today. Use the most current sources possible, ones that are new enough to still be valid when you present your speech. With newspapers, magazines, and other print resources, it is usually easy to locate the date. You may have to spend more time searching on a website, but it is important to determine when the site was last updated and how current the information was when it was added to the site. If you cannot verify the currency of the information, it may be better to look for another source.

There are some topics where the currency of an article may not be critical. For example, an article detailing baseball's famous "Black Sox Scandal" may not be as time sensitive as topics related to terrorism or immigration.

IN REVIEW
To determine the quality of your source you must...
- Critically evaluate the source
- Check authorship
- Determine bias
- Consider the currency of the source

Questions:

RESEARCH STRATEGIES

When you have formulated a plan for conducting research, there are strategies that can help the process flow more smoothly. Keep them in mind to make your search more productive, but also to simplify the organization and citation processes.

Reflections:

USE APPROPRIATE TIME MANAGEMENT

Block out an appropriate amount of time and begin researching early. When researchers wait too long to begin the process, they are more likely to feel frustrated with the results. So, beginning early can allow you to stay calm, cool, and collected. In addition to avoiding last minute problems, starting early gives you more choices in terms of which research is most appropriate for your presentation. It also gives you time to fully investigate a topic and make decisions as to the direction and thesis of your speech.

BRAINSTORM A LIST OF WORDS AND PHRASES RELEVANT TO YOUR TOPIC

Before you begin researching, identify key terms that are relevant to your topic and purpose. Think not only of the words you would use, but what language would the authors of your research use. Identify any variations on wording that might be likely and keep track of which search terms you have used on which search engines and databases. If you can only think of one way to phrase your key terms, use those. When you find your first reasonable source, quickly scan through for the language the authors use. You might find a more common or a more scholarly variation on the terms that you can use in your searching. If your source is a journal article or similar source (particularly from a library database) look for a list of key terms and utilize those for future searches.

MOVE FROM GENERAL IDEAS TO SPECIFIC IDEAS

Begin by searching for general ideas and information on your topic. Starting with a general overview can make it easier to see how ideas connect to each other and help determine the most appropriate focus for the speech and, perhaps, the audience. It also helps you avoid dealing with an overabundance of details that may never make it into your presentation. At the point you feel confident about the focus, search for more specific details.

KEEP A DETAILED RECORD OF WHERE YOU FOUND INFORMATION

Use note cards or another method of recording your findings. It is exasperating to read through several articles, decide upon an example or statistic in one of them, and not be able to find it later. Research records can also be useful when it is time to organize the ideas into main and supporting points. Finally, in an academic setting, a "Works Cited" or "Reference Page" is generally required. Keeping track as you move through the research makes it easier to create a thorough and accurate document. Keeping detailed records also helps you find the information you need to properly cite your sources in your speech.

Use a system to organize your research material to save yourself time in both the research and writing of your speech, and to avoid any possible problems.

APPLYING THE FUNDAMENTALS ▬▬▬

VERBALLY CITING SOURCES

In an academic paper, research that is not considered "common knowledge" must be accompanied by citations. The same holds true for speeches where you would use verbal citations of sources. It is important to verbally cite your sources while you give your speech for various reasons, one of which is the continued establishment of ethos. By citing sources, a speaker can establish that they have done research for the speech and found worthwhile statistics, testimony, etc., to use that supports their purpose. Another reason for verbally citing your sources is so the audience can do further research on your topic if your speech piques their interest.

Since writing and speaking are two different forms of communication, the style in which you cite will be slightly different, but the idea is the same. When incorporating a citation into the speech itself keep the following in mind:

- Give an abbreviated citation. Complete citations can be found in the works cited page. Do not include page numbers, web addresses, or other cumbersome information that may likely overwhelm the audience.

- Cite in a way that emphasizes your source is current and credible. For example, "On July 12, 2014, *The Chicago Tribune* reported that..." Your audience knows when the article was written (establishing currency) and is from a reputable source.

- Qualify unfamiliar sources for your audience. If you are using information from Public Citizen, your audience may be unfamiliar with this group. You would want to qualify, "In March of 2014, nonpartisan political watch group Public Citizen released a report..." or "Renowned brain surgeon Ben Carson claims...".

- Citations work best when the source is stated and qualified *before* the information is given. Therefore, you will need a "lead-in." These are short phrases or key words, such as "according to" or "as stated by," that let the audience know a citation is about to be used.

In a classroom setting, some instructors may ask their students to add more or less information to citations, so be sure to check with the instructor for other suggestions or a preferred style of citation.

REALIZE WHEN IT IS TIME TO STOP RESEARCHING

While some people don't give themselves enough time to engage in thorough research, others get caught up in the process and fail to leave enough time for constructing the speech. Give yourself a deadline and stick to it. If you find that when you are putting together your message you are lacking a piece of information, go back and find it then. Meanwhile, keep to your timeline. It is important to have all the information you need to develop your thesis, but often students will get "off track" and start researching interesting tangents that are not related to the speech. Having a fixed deadline can help you focus and stay on track.

Why should you cite sources during your speech?

IN REVIEW

Some strategies for effective research include...

- Use appropriate time management

- Brainstorm key words and phrases

- Move from general ideas to more specific ones

- Keep detailed records of where you found information

- Realize when it is time to stop

Questions:

Reflections:

SUMMARY

Researching is a crucial step in creating an effective message with adequate support. Create a simple plan to help focus your research efforts. Allow enough time, brainstorm key terms for your topic, move from general to specific ideas, keep records, and stay focused. Know when to move ahead in the process. Before incorporating the research, conduct a critical evaluation of its worthiness. Incorporate a variety of supporting materials, including statistics, narratives, examples, and testimony. Remember that no idea stands alone; through research you give ideas the appropriate support which makes for the most effective speech.

RESOURCES FOR BUILDING COMMUNICATION EFFECTIVENESS

RESEARCH SOURCE CHECKLIST—INTERNET SOURCES

Things to Consider	Website Name (not the URL)			
	Website 1	Website 2	Website 3	Website 4
Who is the author of the information?				
How do you know the author is credible?				
What type of website is it? (ex., college, private organization, private company, personal, newspaper, etc.)				
When was the site last updated?				
When did you last visit the site?				
Briefly summarize why you think this is an okay source to use in your speech.				

RESOURCES FOR BUILDING COMMUNICATION EFFECTIVENESS

RESEARCH SOURCE CHECKLIST—NON-INTERNET SOURCES

Things to Consider	Source Name			
	Source 1	Source 2	Source 3	Source 4
Who is the author of the information?				
How do you know the author is credible?				
What type of source is it? (ex., newspaper, magazine, journal, book, etc.)				
When was the information published?				
Briefly summarize why you think this is an okay source to use in your speech.				

CHAPTER 7

TOPIC AND THESIS

Your speech is most likely to be effective if you have a clear and focused goal to accomplish in the speech.

Sometimes the weather can be beautiful to look at and often it is fun to discuss, but there are also many other things to talk about, and effective speakers find one that will be interesting to their audience.

Oscar Wilde once noted that "conversation about the weather is the last refuge of the unimaginative," noting in his own unique way that people often have difficulty deciding what to talk about, and that is true of speakers as well. While the information in Chapter 5 will help you think about the purpose of your speech, that is only one issue you need to address. You also need to decide what you will talk about. There are literally thousands of different subjects you could tell the audience about and as many ideas you could try to convince an audience to believe. You need to focus on something specific to talk about, and the more specific that focus ultimately is, the more likely your speech will be successful. In this chapter, we look at developing that focus, starting with a general idea of what you will speak about and eventually developing a very clear statement of what exactly you will (and won't) do in the speech.

TOPIC

The first step in this process is to select your topic, or the general area you will speak about. Topics can be very general like "transportation" or "warfare," but because your ultimate goal is to be highly focused in your presentation you will want to start at a point that gives you a good chance of success. So, unless you are developing a speech that will be hours long, you probably want to start with more of a focus, perhaps "hybrid cars" instead of "transportation" or "the Iraqi Conflict" instead of "warfare." For most speeches you will give in class, even topics like hybrid cars and the Iraqi Conflict are still too broad to properly focus a speech, but they are an okay place to start.

How would you describe the subject of this photo? As a car? Yes, but could you be more specific? It is a blue car. It is a hybrid car. Picking a topic for a speech requires you to think about the same level of specificity.

SELECTING A TOPIC

Choosing a topic is a crucial step in preparing an effective speech. If you choose a mediocre topic, you limit your own potential to connect with the audience or to offer them something new. For some people, choosing a topic is the easiest part of preparing a speech. Others get stuck before they begin, worrying the audience won't share their interests or feeling overwhelmed by all the possible choices. While picking a topic is an important step, it is important not to get bogged down this early in the process, so let's look at ways to select a topic so you can then get on with the process of developing your speech.

The first step in selecting a topic is to generate a list of possible topic ideas. You need some place to start, so first generate a list of topic ideas that identifies broad, general areas of interest that the speech could address.

You may already have some idea of what you want to talk about in the speech, so that could be the start of your list. However, if you are not sure or you have no idea what you want to talk about, there are several ways to find a strong speech topic. For example, you can begin by brainstorming. Brainstorming is familiar to most students as a process in which you list as many ideas as quickly as possible with absolutely no censorship. When the list is complete, you explore each idea and find a possible topic in the list.

BRAINSTORMING

Art
Pain
Vincent Van Gogh
Ear
Nose
Body
Heart
Health
Exercise
Bicycle
Gym

MENTAL MAPPING

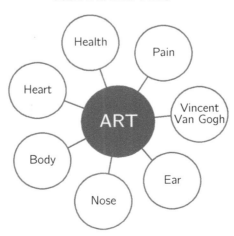

In addition to traditional brainstorming, you can brainstorm in the form of a mental map. To mental map, put one idea in the center circle and then brainstorm five or six ideas surrounding it. Repeat the process for each circle and see what you come up with. Mental map brainstorming has the benefit of branching off from topic ideas, rather than moving down a straight line. Essentially, the list you create from a traditional brainstorming session becomes the basis for many more lists. If you have five topics on your first list, you will create at least five more lists. You can see in the image below that a brainstorming session beginning from the word "art" leads to topic ideas ranging from the art of Frida Kahlo, to the cultural significance of tattoos, to sign language, all of which serve as excellent topics for a classroom speech.

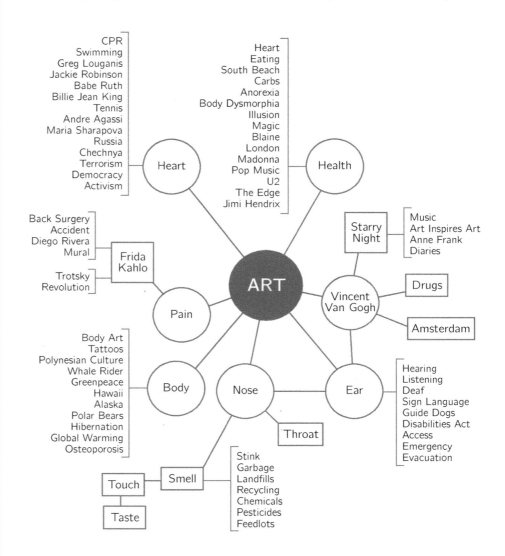

A mental map is nothing more than a visual representation of how you come up with topics. Sometimes you will think of a topic, like ART, and several ideas will come to mind (Van Gogh, Pain, etc.). Other times you will relate one topic with another, eventually drawing a chain of ideas (like Ear to Hearing to Listening, etc.). Do not worry if you can't see all the connections the authors made in putting together this sample. The key, ultimately, will be for you to map your own connections.

In addition to brainstorming for topic ideas, you can perform a personal inventory of your interests. There is a sample personal inventory at the end of this chapter. Looking at that, you will notice that you create columns with headings designed to elicit your own interests and knowledge. The sample suggests some questions like "what do I do during my free time?" or "what are my favorite TV shows?" among many others. You may want to explore other categories. Ultimately the questions are not as important as the answers. Like brainstorming, the goal of a personal inventory is to provide a starting point from which you can start to think about possible topics. So, if you are having trouble thinking of your own questions, use the Personal Inventory worksheet at the end of this chapter to provide you with those questions. Remember, the answers are more important than the questions, so focus on finding the answers: your hobbies, TV show preference, and the like. If you feel stumped, ask a friend or family member for their ideas. Sometimes other people have a clearer idea of our talents, interests, and abilities.

Finally, another way to find a topic is to expose yourself to information and choose something you find interesting. Pick up a newspaper or magazine or see what's on the Discovery Channel, 20/20, or the History Channel. Is there something you would like to learn more about? Something you find absolutely fascinating? Inspiring? Infuriating? Chances are it will make a good topic.

Looking through the newspaper is a very effective way to find speech topics.

IN REVIEW
You can come up with a topic by...

• Brainstorming

• Mental Mapping

• Personal Inventory

• Informational Review

Questions:

Reflections:

EVALUATING A TOPIC
Once you have a few good topic ideas, you must decide on one. You don't want to pick just any topic; you want to pick one that is likely to produce an effective speech. In order to evaluate your choices and determine the best topic for your particular speech, ask yourself four questions.

The first question is, "Am I interested in this topic?" If the answer is no, move on. If you are not interested, you will have a difficult time conveying interest to your audience and you must show enthusiasm for your topic to really connect with your audience. If you are bored with your speech, the audience will notice and they will be bored too. That is not a good way to get them interested in your material. Also, if you are

Construct a list of thirty possible topics. Which of those do you think would be the best for you to give a speech on in class? Why?

not interested in your topic, you will be more likely to procrastinate and not really spend the necessary time preparing your speech. Again, that tends to lead to an ineffective speech that isn't likely to connect with the audience. On the other hand, if you are interested in your topic, you will likely be more enthusiastic in preparing and delivering your message. Also, when you feel attached to your topic, you are less likely to experience anxiety while speaking.

The audience will draw their enthusiasm for your topic from you, so make sure you pick a topic that excites you so you can excite your audience.
Otherwise, your audience will be bored and the speech will not be effective.

You should also ask yourself, "Is this topic relevant?" While it is important to be interested in your own topic, your topic must also be important to your audience. You must have some information or ideas to offer your audience that are socially significant, personally significant, or interesting on some level. When you choose a topic with which the audience is overly familiar or that does not apply to their lives, it is difficult for them to pay attention to your message. In fact, you are missing the point of speaking to an audience in the first place. You are there to offer them something, some new information or a new perspective on a common theme. The purpose of speaking to an audience is to connect with them; you will not connect if you speak on a topic that is of no interest to them. You will essentially be wasting time, both yours and theirs.

Occasionally you will choose a topic with relevance, but the audience will not immediately see it. It is your job to show them. However, in order to do that, it must exist in the first place. So, in answering the relevance question, it is not necessary to choose a topic that influences the entire world. There are different levels and styles of relevance. Third-world growth and its impact on animal habitats is relevant on a very large scale, but to the people in your classroom, the price of textbooks may also be relevant. Additionally, they might find relevant such topics as what constitutes date rape, how to prepare for a job interview, impressing a date on a small budget, or how Jon Stewart's *The Daily Show* has affected politics. Remember to do your audience analysis as a first step in preparing any speech, because what is relevant depends on who is in your audience.

How relevant a topic is depends on your audience. You do not always have to pick a large global topic, like the impact of economic development on animal habitats. For your class, a speech about the cost of attending college may be more relevant and thus more effective.

The next question is, "Is the topic appropriate?" Your topic must be appropriate to both the audience and the situation. Some topics are relevant, but they can still be inappropriate for a specific audience. For example, mathematics has a profound impact on our daily lives. However, an informative speech on how to do three-dimensional graphing might require the audience to have an understanding of advanced mathematics. It might be too complex for an introductory speech class where many audience members have not completed college algebra. On the flip side, an informative speech on how to do laundry or how to avoid skin cancer might be relevant, but also inappropriate. Because most audience members will already know this information, these topics are too simple for a Speech 101 class unless you can find new information or a unique way of presenting it.

Appropriateness applies to the situation as well as the audience. Some relevant topics feel awkward in a classroom setting. For instance, having a debate on a spiritual topic can be interesting and important, but convincing your audience to convert to a specific religion or to abandon religion altogether might lead to discomfort for your audience when they are in a classroom at a public school. An interesting conversation in a hallway might become an awkward situation in a classroom where an audience might have some of their social expectations violated.

The final question is, "Is the topic focused?" Ultimately you will need to develop a thesis that can be completely developed in the time you are given to speak. You will have a chance to address that issue as you narrow your focus while moving from topic to thesis. However, it is worthwhile to begin thinking about that issue now, so the whole process will be easier. It is a common mistake to attempt to cover too much in a speech. This often leads to information overload and decreased understanding of the message. In a six-minute speech, it is not possible to cover the entire life of Albert Einstein, at least not in a developed way. It may make more sense to cover just one of his scientific theories (or even one implication of one of his theories), or one of his political views, or how his work affected his spirituality.

Why will some topics work in some situations, but not in others?

The point is to choose a narrow focus and develop it thoroughly. Additionally, some topics are too controversial or require too much thought or too much information for the allotted time. Returning to one of the earlier examples, not only may some audiences feel uncomfortable with a discussion of religion, it is not reasonable to expect an audience to adopt a new religious ideology in an eight-minute speech. Do not set yourself up for failure by having an overly broad topic.

As you will learn as you move through the process of developing a speech, the more focused you are, the more effective you are likely to be. So, don't try to say everything about Albert Einstein; focus instead on one very small facet of his life or work and deal with that completely.

IN REVIEW
A good topic is...

• Interesting to me

• Relevant to my audience

• Appropriate for the audience and situation

• Focused

Questions:

Reflections:

Your topic is a good starting point in putting together your speech, but it is not the final step in focusing your presentation. As you will see in Chapter 8, the more focused your speech is, the more likely it is to be effective because of the way the audience will process the information in your speech. Topics are not focused enough to provide that level of effectiveness, so you have to continue to narrow down your speech. What exactly do you want to say about hybrid cars? What facet of the Iraqi Conflict do you want to focus on? As you answer those questions, you begin to develop your thesis statement and it is that statement which will ultimately tell the audience exactly what to expect in the speech.

THESIS

The thesis identifies the goal of the speech. It is the statement that tells the audience exactly what you hope to accomplish. It also gives you a clear sense of what your purpose is and that helps you organize your speech into an effective message. The thesis statement is different from your topic. It is narrower and more focused. A topic may be something like "computers" or even "the role of computers in education," but a thesis statement would be even more focused. For example, your thesis within that topic area may be, "I wish to persuade my audience that computers have become too important in grade school classes."

A topic identifies a broad subject, like computers, but a thesis identifies the very specific and narrow focus of the speech. So, a thesis may suggest that computers have become too important in grade school classrooms.

Here we come to one of the most important points in developing a speech, so it bears repeating and further discussion: a thesis and a topic are not the same thing; a topic identifies a broad subject area that a speech addresses while a thesis statement identifies the very specific and narrow focus of the speech. The diagram below may help you see the difference. The large circle represents a large topic area, like computers in education. The smaller divisions represent narrower possible thesis statements that could be the focus of a speech within that topic area. Those divisions could focus on different facets of the topic, or even respond to different purposes. Thesis 1 may represent a speech that argues that elementary education overly relies on computers (which would be a persuasive speech), and thesis 2 could represent a speech discussing a new technology that is changing the way history is taught (which would be informative). Beyond those examples, notice that there is still a lot of area within the circle. That space would represent other possible thesis statements within the topic area. This diagram highlights two key points about developing your thesis statement. First, you do not have to (and should not) include everything about your topic area in your speech, and, second, the information you include in your speech should relate to your thesis, not solely to the topic.

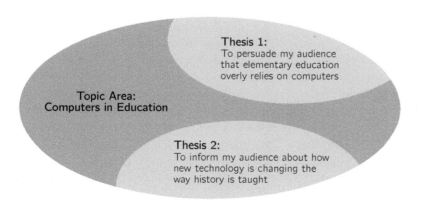

TOPIC AND THESIS

Which of the following are more or less topics and which would work better as thesis statements? What makes the thesis statements good thesis statements and how could you narrow the topics down to thesis statements?

Baseball

How to effectively kill a penalty in hockey

Solar energy

Impressionist painters

The differences between classic country and modern country music

The impact of global warming on polar bears

How to manipulate depth of field with a DSLR camera

What the diagram does not show as effectively is a third key point about your thesis statement: your thesis statement should always be the narrowest possible thesis that you can fully develop in the time allotted for the speech. Having a narrow focus makes it easier to relate the information to a clearly stated theme, and, as you will see in Chapter 8, the narrower your thesis is, the easier it will be for you to build relationships among your material which will make it easier for the audience to process and remember your information and the main point of your message. If you make your thesis for a five-minute informative speech, "I want to say some things about the Vietnam War," you will certainly be able to fill your time, but since you cannot say everything about that war in that time frame, your information will be incomplete, it will be hard for the audience to follow your information, and they will be more likely to miss your point (think of it as trying to follow a map when one section is missing). On the other hand, if you say you want to show the audience that Americans' reactions to military personnel when they returned from Iraq and Afghanistan were influenced by the aftermath of the Vietnam War, then your audience can see more easily how the information you are presenting serves your purpose. Ultimately, the more focused your thesis is, the clearer your organization, thesis, and message will be to the audience, and the more effective you are likely to be.

The Vietnam War was certainly a significant event in our history. Because there is so much to say about it, to have an effective speech you will need to find a narrow focus within that broader topic area, perhaps how Vietnam affected our perceptions of the Iraq and Afghanistan conflicts.

One challenge in determining the thesis is having a thesis which is narrow enough to be effective but not so narrow as to make developing the speech difficult or impossible. Your knowledge of your topic area, which will come from your research, will help you address that challenge. As you saw in the last chapter, you will need to gather information which helps you develop your thesis. Further, one of the benefits of the research process is that it helps you get to know your topic area better. So, before you do some research you may not know exactly how you want to narrow your topic, but you also would not want to have to research everything about, say, the Iraqi Conflict.

You can respond to this challenge by developing your thesis statement in phases. Start with your topic. You can always be sure that your topic will be too broad to address in the allotted time. Then think of a statement of purpose that highlights a particular focus within your topic area. Ask yourself if you could legitimately say everything about that narrower statement in the allotted time. Be honest and really think about all the facets within that statement. If, after doing that, a true and well-thought-out answer is "yes," you have your thesis statement. If not, repeat the process, looking at an even narrower focus within your last statement. Each of these intermediate steps can be considered what are sometimes called specific purposes. While any particular specific purpose will not be the focus of the speech, the process of identifying these specific purposes can help you in two ways. First, by thinking through this narrowing process you get a good idea of what you hope to accomplish and what information you will include and exclude from your speech. That helps you keep your speech more focused. Second, working through the specific purposes can help you identify key terms as you do your research.

To see how this process works, consider the prior example. The Vietnam War or the Iraqi Conflict are topics—too broad to be effective for a speech. Saying that your speech will show how the Vietnam War affected our response to the people affected by the wars in Iraq and Afghanistan is a good example of a specific purpose. It is relatively narrow, but your research will probably show you there are many effects on many people and so you may still have to decide exactly which of those effects, or which group of people, will be the focus of your speech.

Why is it important to narrow your topic to a specific purpose and then to a highly focused thesis statement?

© Leena Krohn

Working from your topic of the Vietnam War, you may narrow down to how the Vietnam War changed the way we thought about people involved in the Iraqi Conflict. If you find that is still too broad you could then focus on either military families, soldiers, or war protestors to develop a more manageable thesis.

SUMMARY

An obvious first step in putting together a speech is figuring out what you will talk about. In this chapter you have seen how you move through the process of topic selection and thesis development to find a very clear and narrow focus for your speech. You have been offered several effective techniques for selecting a topic. You have also seen the importance of moving past the topic to a more focused thesis statement. Hopefully you have been able to use these techniques to decide what you will speak about in your classroom assignments and you will also be able to use these techniques any time you are asked to present a speech.

APPLYING THE FUNDAMENTALS

USING RESEARCH TO DEVELOP YOUR THESIS

One of the false assumptions many people make about research is that the only reason to do research is to find information to use in their speech. This leads to a corollary false assumption that every piece of information they find must be (or even should be) used in their speech. This often leads to very unfocused speeches which are hard for the audience to follow and hence are not likely to be effective. This can be a particular problem when a person has a sense of topic, but not of thesis. In that case, early research should help develop the thesis before there is any thought of what information should be used in the speech. Instead, what many people do is start researching their broad topic area and when they have enough information to fill their time they put together a speech that just lists the information. As has been mentioned in this chapter, and will be more developed in Chapter 8, that is not likely to be an effective speech. What you need to do instead is use your early research simply to find the focus for your speech and then you can implement a research plan, as discussed in Chapter 6. The diagram at the end of this section demonstrates this concept using the topic of immigration as an example.

Let's say you are asked to give a seven-minute informative speech. You decide you want to say something about immigration, but as noted in this chapter, your speech needs to cover everything within your area of focus (which, ultimately, is the thesis) and you know you can't say everything about immigration in seven minutes, so you know you need a narrower focus. Your problem is that you don't know much about immigration, so you don't yet know what you want your focus to be. That's okay. What you can do in that case is do some research to learn about immigration and determine what some possible focuses might be. The diagram suggests you might find three possible focuses: border security, reasons for immigration, and President Obama's new immigration policy. Even basic research shows you that you can't cover all three ideas fully and properly in a seven-minute speech, so you know you still need more focus. You decide to focus on the reasons why people immigrate to the United States and do some more research and find out two major reasons why people immigrate are for educational or economic reasons. Again, your preliminary research tells you that you can't fully and properly address both reasons, so you decide to focus on the education reasons. Knowing that, you can now begin the actual research for the speech.

Two important things to notice in this example: First, the narrowing lines on the thesis development side of the following diagram represent the narrowing of your focus as you move from topic to thesis. Notice that by the time you are done, only the education reasons why people immigrate to the United States are inside those lines. That is the focus of your speech and only information about that should be in the speech. Everything else you found helped you find your focus, but now that you know your focus, that information is beyond the scope of your speech and should not be used as you develop your speech. Second, only when you reach the thesis at the bottom of the diagram are you ready to start the research plan discussed in Chapter 6. Your preliminary research has told you much about immigration and the reasons why people immigrate to the United States, and even more specifically, the educational motivations for people to come to the United States, so you are in good shape on the first step in the plan. Your research has also probably given you a good broad understanding of what you will need to cover in the speech, so you also have a good start on the second step in the plan: you know what you still need to find. So, while you are just starting with a research plan, you are rather far along in that plan and are really in good shape for the third step: determining the best place to find the information you now need to write the speech.

Finally, don't be discouraged about the material you found that you won't use. The process has helped you focus your approach and put you in a good position to develop that focus effectively, so the whole process was useful in helping you develop an effective speech.

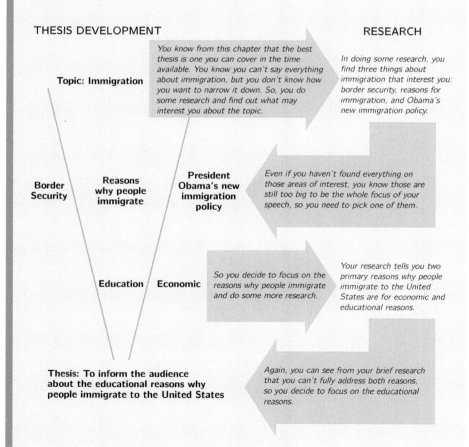

THESIS DEVELOPMENT

Topic: Immigration

You know from this chapter that the best thesis is one you can cover in the time available. You know you can't say everything about immigration, but you don't know how you want to narrow it down. So, you do some research and find out what may interest you about the topic.

RESEARCH

In doing some research, you find three things about immigration that interest you: border security, reasons for immigration, and Obama's new immigration policy.

Border Security

Reasons why people immigrate

President Obama's new immigration policy

Even if you haven't found everything on those areas of interest, you know those are still too big to be the whole focus of your speech, so you need to pick one of them.

Education **Economic**

So you decide to focus on the reasons why people immigrate and do some more research.

Your research tells you two primary reasons why people immigrate to the United States are for economic and educational reasons.

Thesis: To inform the audience about the educational reasons why people immigrate to the United States

Again, you can see from your brief research that you can't fully address both reasons, so you decide to focus on the educational reasons.

RESOURCES FOR BUILDING COMMUNICATION EFFECTIVENESS

PERSONAL INVENTORY

During my free time I like to…				
When I have a chance to read, I read…				
The best things I have ever done are…				
The hardest thing I have ever had to learn was…				
I seem to be really good at…				
My favorite TV shows are…				
I get angry when…				
The most important social issues today are…				
I would like to learn more about…				
If I could do anything, I would…				
The most unusual jobs I have had were…				
If I could travel anywhere, I would go to…				
The most important thing about me not yet on this page is…				

CHAPTER 7

RESOURCES FOR BUILDING COMMUNICATION EFFECTIVENESS

FOCUSING WORKSHEET

TOPIC AREA:

Possible Subdivision	Possible Focus	Possible Thesis
		Possible Thesis
	Possible Focus	Possible Thesis
		Possible Thesis
Possible Subdivision	Possible Focus	Possible Thesis
		Possible Thesis
	Possible Focus	Possible Thesis
		Possible Thesis
Possible Subdivision	Possible Focus	Possible Thesis
		Possible Thesis
	Possible Focus	Possible Thesis
		Possible Thesis

CHAPTER 7

CHAPTER 8

ORGANIZATION AND OUTLINING

The primary goal of organization is to ensure you have an effective speech.

Random facts (like a grocery list) are hard to remember, but when there is a way to organize the information (like a recipe) the information is easier to remember. Make sure your speech is a "recipe" and not a "grocery list."

Imagine your mother sends you to the grocery store for a couple of items. How many do you think you could remember without a list? Most students honestly answer three, two, one, or even zero. Psychologists say we should be able to remember about seven items, but most of us generally cannot remember that many items without help. Now let's say you are going to be making a taco salad for a party tonight. It is a salad you have made many times and you know the recipe very well. There are twelve ingredients in this salad. Even though there are many more than seven ingredients in the recipe, you probably can remember them all, if you just follow the recipe in your head as you move through the store. Let's take this analogy one more step. After you serve the taco salad tonight at the party, you are going to serve homemade chocolate cake for dessert. That cake requires another nine ingredients. Now we are up to twenty-one items that you need at the store. Chances are you can still get them all without a list, by moving first through the taco salad recipe then the cake recipe. Why can you now get twenty-one items without a list, when initially we said you would struggle to remember more than seven? Because you have created a thought pattern to support your mental list—an organization in your mind that helps you process the information.

What does a trip to the store have to do with speech preparation? In both cases you are using organization principles to help process information. Remember psychologists tell us that people can only process about seven items of random information. In a speech of any length you will most certainly ask the audience to process more than seven pieces of information, and your audience will need all of that information to understand your message and you need them to understand your message if you are to accomplish your thesis. Therefore, your speech will be ineffective if each audience member remembers just seven (or less) randomly selected facts. So, you have to help your audience process your information and see your thesis by providing the "recipe," or organization for the speech. This chapter guides you through that process.

PUBLIC SPEAKING IS PURPOSEFUL

In the last paragraph we noted that organization is important to accomplish your thesis. That statement is based on an obvious, but important, observation we first made in Chapter 1: you have some reason or purpose for presenting a speech. As you move through the process of putting together a speech you must remember that speech writing is driven by a desire to accomplish a particular goal, your thesis. Someone does not get up in the morning and decide, because they are bored, that they will just give a speech that day. More seriously, the goal of a speech cannot merely be to provide a list of facts. As we have already noted with the grocery shopping analogy, if someone is confronted with a list of random items they are likely to remember very few of them. That means that a speech which simply lists information is likely to be unsuccessful because the audience is likely to forget most of the information. Therefore, for a speech to be effective, it must be focused on accomplishing the specific task which is identified in the thesis statement, and you use the information you gathered in the research process to accomplish that goal. That means the information that you present is really not a series of random facts, but a collection of information which will help you accomplish your thesis. Stated another way, a speech should not be a period of time in which you just list information; it should be a unified effort to use information to accomplish some goal, your thesis. The key, then, in organizing a speech is to take the seemingly random information and develop the structure that will help the audience use the information to understand your thesis. Once you have thought through your organization, you can use an outline to represent that organization and help you make that structure clear to the audience.

It is important to note that, technically, organizing and outlining are two different steps. However, as we mentally engage in the process of organization, we tend to see it in outline form. Therefore, to some extent, the steps get blurred. In this chapter we will try to separate the mental process of organization from the practical step of outlining.

Why is strong organization so critically important for an effective speech?

STEPS IN ORGANIZING A SPEECH

It will be easiest for the audience to follow a speech if there is a clear structure to help them do that. That structure will basically consistent of three things: a clear thesis which indicates what the goal of the speech is, main points which clearly relate to and help develop the thesis, and supporting material which supports the points and relates them to the thesis. The process of organization helps ensure you have all of that and that it fits together in an easy-to-process package.

DEVELOP A CLEAR THESIS

We have already discussed this first step in great detail in Chapter 7. This step is very important because as you have already seen, the key to an effective speech is to organize your information to serve some purpose. Without that purpose, there is no basis for the organization. So, having a clear sense of your goal, your thesis, is essential if you are to have a well-organized and effective speech.

There are two important things to remember as you move from the thesis step in the process to actually organizing your speech. First, remember your research may have initially been driven by your specific purpose or even your topic. Now as you start to organize your material, you should be focusing solely on your narrower thesis. As we discussed in Chapter 7, that means determining the theme which ties all your information together.

The second thing you need to remember at this point is that organization needs to be driven by the thesis, not the topic. The opening grocery store metaphor showed the importance of developing strong relationships among pieces of information to help us process the information. Those strong relationships extend from the more focused thesis statement. Think of the topic area as the store and the thesis as the particular dish you are going to make. Just like you wouldn't go to the store and buy everything, but rather only the ingredients you need, so too, you would not include everything about a topic in a speech, but only those facts and analysis that you need to develop your thesis. If you needed to buy the ingredients for the taco salad and the dessert, but also five other random items, the entire organizing schema would be undermined.

Just as grocery shoppers should only buy what they need, speakers should only include in their speech what they need to accomplish their thesis.

IDENTIFY YOUR MAIN POINTS

The first step in developing an effective speech is to clearly establish your goal, or thesis, for the speech. Once you have determined your thesis, the next step is to identify the primary steps you will need to take to accomplish that thesis. For example, if your thesis is to convince your audience that the government should place greater limits on handgun ownership, you would probably need to show that there are problems associated with widespread gun ownership and that the particular limits you want to propose will mitigate those problems. Or, if you want to tell the audience about the game of baseball, you may decide that they must know the history of the game, the rules, and the basic strategies. Whatever your goal is, there will be key points that will have to be developed in order to help you accomplish your goal. These will become your main points in the speech. Remember, these are key points that have to be well developed in order for you to be effective, so there is a limit to the number of main points you can have in a speech. Some people say there have to be exactly three main points in a speech. While there is some logic to that, to state that as a hard and fast rule is probably overstating the case. Much will depend on how much time you have to present your speech. In many of your class assignments, the assigned length will be such that two main points will be enough. On the other hand, if you were asked to speak for a couple of hours, you could probably develop more than three main points. The important thing to remember is that these points have to be well developed in order for your speech to be successful, so even in a classroom speech you should expect to spend at least a couple of minutes developing a main point and in longer speeches you may spend even more time developing a point. So, you can look at the assigned length of your speech as a guide to how many main points you can have.

If you find that you have more main points than you can legitimately develop properly, there are a couple of things that you can do. First, and most importantly, make sure all your information relates to your thesis and not the topic area. If the information does not directly relate to the thesis statement, eliminate it. For example, if you were preparing the baseball speech discussed above, you could eliminate information about a particular current baseball league because that information does not fit with the particular focus you have created.

If, after eliminating unrelated information, you still have two much information, there are two ways to address that problem. First, consider narrowing your thesis to reduce the number of points that need to be addressed. Going back to the example of the speech about the game of baseball, you may find that given the amount of time you have you cannot properly develop all three of the points you were originally going to address. So, you decide instead to focus on the history of the game and make your main points the early development of the game and the modern game. Another option is to redevelop the points. In this case you will cover the same areas but you may not cover everything in the same depth. Again, returning to the baseball example, you could choose to make your main points the history of the game and how the game is played. Notice that the second point now combines the two points about rules and strategies into a single point, a strategy which basically means you will develop those individual ideas in less depth, perhaps using rules and strategies as examples to demonstrate how the modern game differs from earlier eras, as opposed to discussing every rule and strategy, as the prior thesis suggested you would.

CHARACTERISTICS OF EFFECTIVE MAIN POINTS

As noted previously, these key points will become the main points in your speech. In addition to the issues associated with your specific speech discussed previously, there are some general characteristics of main points you should consider as you develop your speech. Good main points will be discrete, balanced, simple, parallel, and complete. **Discrete** means that each main point deals with a clearly separate part of the speech. As you attempt to place your information into particular main points, it should be very clear which point a particular piece of information goes into. If it seems the information could go into multiple points, then your points are not discrete. For example, if you were doing a speech about places to go on vacation, you would not want one main point to be amusement parks and another main point to be places in Florida, because where would you put information about Disney World, which is an amusement park in Florida. You could either divide your material by state or by type, but you should not mix the two.

Because Disney World is in Florida, the main points in a speech about vacations should not be "tourist spots in Florida" and "amusement parks," because Disney World is both and so there is not a clear and distinct place for that information.

IN REVIEW
Effective main points are...

- Discrete
- Balanced
- Simple
- Parallel
- Complete

Questions:

Reflections:

Balance says that each point should be roughly the same size. So, again, looking at a speech about vacation spots, you probably would not want one point to be about amusement parks and another point to be about a specific civil war battlefield. Because one point is very broad and one is very specific, you would probably not be able to develop those points in roughly equal ways. **Simple** points are just that—simple. They are constructed in a way that is easy for the audience to process. So, you are better off dividing a speech about amusement parks into main points about Disney World and Cedar Point, for example, rather than making the division "parks with more than 20,000 acres" and "parks with less than 20,000 acres." Most audiences have no sense of how large a park is, or even what an acre is, so it will be harder for them to process that division and that is what you want to avoid. The concept of **parallelism** says that the points should be similar in nature, again so it is easy for the audience to process. For example, a student in a basic speech class recently divided a speech about the health effects of obesity into main points labeled "stress on the heart," "stress on the lungs," and "stress on the muscles." The use of this parallel structure makes it easy for the audience to process the information. Finally, **completeness** is as much a test of the thesis as it is a test of the main points. Your speech is complete when you have covered all the information associated with your thesis. So, you do not want to have a thesis like, "There are six major amusement parks in the county, but because I only have a limited amount of time, I am only going to talk about three of them." If you really can only discuss three amusement parks in the time allotted, then build your thesis around that, for example, something like, "There are three amusement parks that everyone should be sure to visit sometime in their lives." With the later thesis, you are able to cover the whole thesis area in the time allotted and that will seem most complete to the audience.

PLACE YOUR RESEARCHED MATERIAL INTO THE APPROPRIATE POINTS

After you have determined your thesis and main points, the next step is to place your information into each point. If each of your points is well developed, particularly if the points are clearly discrete, this step should be easy. As you choose the information you will include in the speech, think carefully about what point that information helps develop. Going back to the baseball example, the question is: is your information about history, rules, or strategies? Whichever of those ideas the information is about, that is the main point where you would include the information. If the answer is "none of the above," then you should not include that information in the speech. If the answer is, "well, it could be placed in either the first or second point," for example, then you need to reframe your main points so they are more discrete.

DETERMINE THE ORDER OF YOUR MAIN POINTS

The next step in the process is to determine the order in which you should address the main points. The answer to that question is really very simple: you should present the information in an order that will seem logical to the audience. For example, think of someone who is good at giving directions. They start at where the person currently is and move logically step by step to the end goal. They do not start in the middle. They do not skip around. The directions are easy to follow because they are in a logical sequence and your speech should be easy to follow for the same reason. So, look at your points and see if there is a logical sequence to the points and use that sequence. For example, if you were giving the gun control speech previously mentioned, you would need to convince the audience there is a problem before you could talk about how to fix the problem. In the baseball example, you would probably want to discuss the history before discussing the modern game because most people tend to approach time from past to present. In the speech where you were going to talk about three amusement parks, you could find some list of the top three amusement parks and then discuss them from one to three, or, because we are so into lists and countdowns, maybe from three to one. Regardless, you probably would not cover the second most significant then the most significant, then the third most significant, because no one counts 2, 1, 3.

Arranging your speech in a logical order helps the audience make sense of your information. In a speech about baseball, for example, you might discuss the game from past to present.

- Identify the thesis
- Identify the main points
- Place your supporting material in the appropriate points
- Determine the order of the main points

Questions:

Reflections:

COMMON ORGANIZING PATTERNS

There are common organizing patterns for both informative and persuasive speeches. Many informative speeches can be organized using a **spatial pattern**. This is based on the geographic relationship among the points. So, for example, if you were going to give the speech about the three amusement parks, rather than doing a countdown, as suggested in the last paragraph, you may choose, instead, to take a trip across the country from east to west or north to south and let that relationship drive the main points. The key to spatial organization is to follow the relationships in a straight line, because that is what is more likely to make sense to people because most people tend to be linear thinkers.

Another common organizing pattern for informative speeches would be the **chronological pattern**. In this organizing schema, points are taken in chronological order. This is a common pattern when discussing events. You can talk about each step in the event in the order the steps occur. Also, many speeches about historical topics lend themselves to the chronological pattern. It is important to note in the chronological pattern we are still taking about organizing points, not individual pieces of information. Many speakers seem to think that a chronological speech is just a listing of events. As we have already noted, lists of random facts are not likely to make effective speeches. So, even in a chronological speech it is important that you organize your information into more fully developed points, and it is those points which are then placed in chronological order.

BEYOND OUR PERSPECTIVE

DIFFERENT WAYS OF THINKING ABOUT TIME

When it comes to time, some cultures (such as the United States and other European countries) have a monochronic time orientation, meaning time is viewed in a way that emphasizes scheduling and measurable units of time. This is perhaps why making schedules is emphasized in a Study Skills course and why organizers such as calendar apps are so popular. Promptness is valued and meeting deadlines is crucial.

Other cultures (some Native American, Hispanic, and others) hold a polychronic time orientation, meaning time is viewed as "less tangible," and while the involvement of people and completion of tasks is important, the urgent constructs of measurement are not emphasized in the same way.

When it comes to organizing a message, time orientation is just one cultural value that might have an impact on how an audience might receive a speaker's message. When measurements of time are important, it might make sense to organize a speech on a historical topic by decades. For example, your preview of main points might sound something like, "Today, I'll highlight the major political shifts of each decade, looking at first, the 1950s, second, the 1960s, and finally, the '70s." When speaking to a group of people who view time differently, it might be more helpful to choose a topical organization pattern, rather than a chronological one. "Today, I'll highlight the major political shifts after World War II, by looking at first, the evolution of civil rights, second, the women's movement, and finally, the anti-war movement."

> There is not one orientation that is more valuable or more logical than another. These differences exist because they work for the groups of people who have them. All cultures are constantly in flux and we shift, sometimes, in response to each other, but it is important as a communicator to note that time may be a noun to one group of people and a verb to another. Some people focus on the present (for example, Spain, Greece, and Mexico) and others are more future-oriented (most U.S. cultural communities, especially the middle class). In addition to time, different cultures have radically different perspectives on human nature, the relationship between humans and nature, and more. While we will certainly take into account these differences while thinking about how best to explain an idea or construct an argument, they might also help us organize a more effective message for our audiences.

There are, however, many informative speeches where the information does not easily follow a geographical or chronological pattern. Often the organizational pattern for those speeches is grouped under the heading of **topical organization**, which simply means the points are organized in a way that makes sense for that particular topic. The "countdown" organization for the amusement park speech is an example of that approach. Other patterns may include compare and contrast, order of importance or significance, even alphabetical order. The key is to find some pattern that will be easy for the audience to follow.

Determining the appropriate organizing pattern for a persuasive speech is a bit different. In Chapter 5 we discussed the different types of persuasive speeches: the persuasion of fact, persuasion of value, and persuasion of policy. Remember the persuasions of fact and value are predominately focused on changing how people think, while the persuasion of policy is focused on changing how people act. The commonly used organizing patterns respond to those particular focuses. Because persuasions of fact and value focus on changing how people think, the focus is on giving the audience reasons to think differently. Each of those reasons could be a main point. In that case, the speech is organized topically, with each point developing one of the reasons why the audience should agree with you. Often those points could be placed in any order, but most would agree that your best arguments should begin and end the speech, because those are the points which tend to be the most memorable. The flexibility to place your main points in any order works if you have **independent arguments**, meaning that each main point is a complete argument that does not rely on evidence or reasoning from another point. In some cases, your reasons for supporting your thesis will be **dependent arguments**, meaning that one argument depends on information or reasoning contained in another point. If that is the case, you need to organize your points so that a dependent argument comes after the point or points which contain the information or reasoning you need to make the argument you want to make.

Because persuasions of policy are focused on actions, the organization of those speeches tends to focus on the action. The most common way to do that is with what is called **problem/solution organization**. This is usually a two-point speech where the speaker first convinces the audience there is a situation that needs to be addressed because it is in some way undesirable and then shows how the problem can be mitigated or eliminated. The speeches are almost always presented in this order, because that is the order which is most logical for the audience. If the audience does not believe there is a problem, they are not likely to be too concerned about any actions that could be taken, because there is no reason for the action. As with

IN REVIEW
Common organizing patterns for informative speeches are...

• Spatial

• Chronological

• Topical (also commonly used in persuasions of fact and value)

Questions:

Reflections:

any persuasive speech, it is important in problem/solution speeches to make sure you completely defend your position. In the problem step that means making sure that you make the argument that the situation really is undesirable—do not assume that the audience shares your outlook on the situation. Even death, which we tend to universally think of as a bad thing, is accepted in some situations, like wars. So, your audience may feel, within the particular context you are discussing, that the situation is acceptable—you must convince them otherwise.

In the solution step, the issues become even more complex. You must present a clear **plan**, a course of action to be taken; you must show that it is possible to implement the plan; and you must demonstrate the plan will eliminate or mitigate the problem. You must also show that the plan will not create other situations that are worse than the problem you are trying to address. Let's say for example you want to address the issue of poverty in America. Your plan could be to simply give everyone in the country enough money to get them above the poverty line. That would certainly solve the problem, as poverty is currently defined. However, such an action would likely create inflation which would drive up prices and hence alter the definition of a living wage. In the long run, the problem would not be solved. Even more simply, you could change the poverty line so that fewer people fell below the poverty level. While that would also change the number of people living in poverty, it would not actually address the issues which make poverty a problem. So, you can't just present a plan and assume it will work; you actually have to demonstrate that it will work. This issue is referred to as **practicality**, and it must be addressed along with the plan in the solution point of a problem/solution speech.

Do you have an idea for empowering the people who live here?
You could present that in a persuasive speech. As part of that speech,
you would have to make arguments to show your solution would work.

BEYOND THE FUNDAMENTALS ▬▬▬

MONROE'S MOTIVATED SEQUENCE

One particular approach to the persuasion of policy was developed by Alan Monroe and is referred to as Monroe's Motivated Sequence. Monroe's Motivated Sequence really reflects the standard problem/solution speech, along with the introduction and conclusion. Monroe identified five steps: **attention**, where the speaker gets the audience to want to listen to the speech; **need**, where the speaker indicates there is a need for action; **satisfaction**, where the speaker tells the audience how to address the need; **visualization**, where the speaker shows how the steps identified in the satisfaction step will address the need; and **action**, where the speaker makes a final appeal to get the audience to accept his or her ideas. As noted in the following table, those steps match well a typical problem/solution speech:

Function	Monroe	Problem/ Solution
Draw the audience in	Attention	Introduction
Establish there is a situation that needs to be addressed	Need	Problem
Present a way to address the issue*	Satisfaction	Plan
Show that this way of addressing the problem will work*	Visualization	Practicality
Make a final plea to get the audience to be a part of the solution	Action	Conclusion

* Note: Just as Plan and Practicality are frequently grouped into one point in a problem/solution speech, so too can the Satisfaction and Visualization steps be combined. Likewise, just as Monroe tends to separate the Satisfaction and Visualization steps, the Plan and Practicality steps could be separated in a problem/solution speech.

There are other organizing structures for persuasion of policy speeches like comparative advantage or goals/criteria but they still get at the issues of identifying a problem and finding a way to eliminate it.

The **comparative advantage speech**, as the name implies, involves comparing various alternatives to addressing the identified problem. Generally, speakers use this approach when there is more agreement about the existence of a problem, but less consensus on how to solve the problem. In this situation, the speaker does not need to spend as much time arguing the problem point and hence can focus more on possible solutions. So, speakers then identify possible solutions and then through a comparison process, showing the strengths and weaknesses associated with the various approaches, make a case for the solution they wish to support.

The **goals-criteria persuasion** is a slight variation on the comparative advantage speech. In this case, there is generally complete agreement that a problem exists and needs to be addressed. However, there is disagreement over what an effective solution would be and that disagreement stems from alternate perspectives about exactly how we should look at the problem and possible solutions. That disagreement usually focuses around the question, what is most important to us? For example, imagine there is an old, abandoned, dilapidated building in your neighborhood.

Everyone agrees it is an eyesore and a danger to the community and want it torn down. However, there is disagreement about what to do with the land. Some people want new retail development, others want it remodeled into urban condominiums, still others prefer the land remain undeveloped and turned into a park. The disagreement over the solution, then, comes from the different goals people have. To address that situation, you need to get people to agree on a particular goal. The goals-criteria speech allows you to do that. In your first point you argue for your particular goal, building arguments to express why your goal is correct. If you think there should be new retail development, you would express why retail stores are an important component in neighborhood redevelopment. Likewise, you could argue why your city needs urban housing or more open space. Once you have convinced your audience to accept your goal, the second part of the speech is showing how one particular solution meets that goal. While that is essentially a comparative advantage approach, the difference is a particular context has been created for that comparison and if you have done your job in the first point, the conclusion in the second point will be very clear. That, obviously, means establishing agreement on the goals is the critical element in an effective goals-criteria speech.

People may agree the dilapidated building should be torn down, but they may disagree on how to use the land after that. Should there be new retail, housing, or parkland? If you want to convince people you have the best idea, you may want to use a goals-criteria speech to make your point.

WRITING THE OUTLINE

After all the mental activities of organizing your speech, the next step in the process is to write the outline. The outline is basically the visual representation of the steps you just completed. Commonly such an outline will begin with the introduction and end with the conclusion, but you have not written those yet, nor should you have written them yet. The role of the introduction is to set up the speech, and until you finish working on the body, you do not know exactly what you need to set up. There are questions that you will ask yourself about your introduction before you finish your speech and you will have better answers to those questions if you outline the body first. Likewise, the conclusion serves to close the speech by reviewing the body and, again, that cannot be done until the body is completed.

OUTLINING THE BODY

Chapter 9 talks more about how to develop an effective introduction and conclusion. For now, we need to focus on developing the outline for the body of the speech. Traditionally, the main points would be identified by Roman numerals (I, II, III, IV, etc.). Subpoints are identified by capital letters (A, B, C, etc.), then numbers (1, 2, 3, etc.), then small letters (a, b, c, etc.). We have already discussed that main points serve to fully develop the specific purpose and thesis statement. Similarly, subpoints are simply divisions of a main point or higher level subpoint and they serve the same relationship as main points to the thesis—they help clarify and develop a particular point. Each level of the outline is also indented so it is easy to see how points relate to each other. The general form looks something like this:

I

    A

        1

            a

            b

        2

    B

II

    A

        1

            a

            b

        2

        3

    B

Notice that in the outline, each point, if divided, is divided into a least two points. That is because you cannot divide a point into one subpoint. Think of it this way: if you slice an apple, what is the smallest number of parts you can have? Two. In the same way, if you split a point you have to create at least two subpoints. If you find you only have one subpoint, that subpoint probably defends a greater level of focus for that point. So, if your outline looks like this:

I.   Rides at Disney World

   A.   Space Mountain

II.   Shows at Disney World

   A.   Hall of Presidents

you would probably first want to think about completeness. But, if this really is all you want to say, then the first main point should say something like "Space Mountain is the only ride worth waiting for at Disney World," and the second main point should say something like, "The Hall of Presidents is the best show at Disney World." Because those attractions are the only part of each point you want to address, you can establish that by more narrowly focusing your point.

We should make one last note about outlining: the symbols you use are less important than the relationships they reflect. Remember, subpoints should help clarify the point they are subordinate to (that is why they are called subpoints). Main points (and the subpoints under them) should help develop the thesis. By using consistent symbols and indenting you can check to see if those statements are true. If they are, you probably have a well-organized speech. If they are not, you should reevaluate your speech's organization and make changes to make the speech clearer to the audience.

INSERT CONNECTIVES

After you have developed your outline for each main point the next step in preparing the outline is to insert what we call connectives. These are words, phrases, and sentences that help the audience see the progression of the speech. There are three common forms of connectives: transitions, internal previews and internal summaries. **Transitions** highlight the fact that you are moving from one point to another, something like, "After you get off of Space Mountain, you should head immediately to the Hall of Presidents because it is such an awesome show." **Internal previews** let the audience know what they should expect next. "The Hall of Presidents is really neat because it celebrates the history of the United States without political agendas and the animation is outstanding," is an example of an internal preview. An **internal summary** is very similar. It reviews for the audience what you have just completed, so the audience gets one more chance to remember and process the information. You might say something like, "So Space Mountain is a great ride because it is tied to a theme and the track is almost invisible in the dark." Note that you can sometimes combine all three of these into one statement: "After you have enjoyed the theme and thrill of Space Mountain, you should head immediately to the Hall of Presidents because it is such an awesome show because of its apolitical theme and outstanding animation."

BENEFITS OF EFFECTIVE ORGANIZATION AND OUTLINING

You can now finish your outline by writing your introductions and conclusions (a process we discuss in detail in the next chapter). You may be happy to know you have reached the end of this process; you may in fact be thinking that this process seems overly involved. However, many beginning speakers tend to underestimate the importance of the organization and outlining processes. They know what they want to say and because the message is clear to them, they assume it will be clear to the audience. But, remember, your goal is to clearly communicate a message to an audience and you will not be in that audience, so the speech needs to be clear to someone other than you, someone who is not as familiar with the topic area. The steps described in this chapter will help you have a clear message and once you see that clearly you will be better able to effectively communicate that message to the audience. There are four specific ways that these steps help you organize and clarify your message.

The first two benefits are closely related to each other and have to do with helping you effectively accomplish your goal. First, giving careful thought to the organization of the speech will help you to clearly identify the goal of your speech—that is, you will have a clear sense of what your thesis is. Second, once you have a clear sense of your goal, you can see what exactly you need to do to accomplish that goal. That will give you a clear sense of what your main points should be and how you should construct those to fully develop your thesis.

Third, you can see what supporting material you will need to make those points and be sure you have the information and that you present it in the correct point. Remember in Chapter 6 we talked about knowing when to stop with our research. It is important to note that we cannot stop until we have all the information we need to accomplish our task, which is why avoiding procrastination is so important. Knowing when to stop means recognizing that it is okay to have three examples for a point instead of five. However, if that point is important, you do still need to have at least some examples and/or pieces of supporting material to develop the point. An effective outline, born from a well-developed sense of organization, will show you if there are places where you still need to find information to support your speech.

Finally, developing a strong organizational structure for your speech will help you to see the relationship between your information, your main points, and your thesis so you can clearly present your message to the audience. It is this last benefit that brings us back to our initial discussion of the primary goal of organization: to be sure you have an effective speech. When you can present a speech that is easy for the audience to follow, you are most likely to be successful for three reasons. First, as we have already discussed, grouping the information into small and easy-to-process categories makes it more likely that the audience will remember your information. Second, if you have a clear sense of your purpose and communicate that to your audience then they will know how you want them to use that information you have helped them to remember. Any particular piece of information could be used in many different speeches with different goals. To extend the grocery store analogy at the start of the chapter, lettuce is used in many different dishes; you need to tell the audience what dish you are making. For example, in the speech about baseball, are you using the information about the rules of baseball to further the audience's understanding of baseball or are you trying to compare and contrast baseball and cricket? If the audience knows the answer to that question, they are more likely to use the information you present to them in the way you want them to use it. Finally, stronger organization will help the audience attend to your specific message. If a speech is disorganized and hard to follow, the audience will have to work harder to access the information. The mental energy they have to expend making sense of the information is mental energy they do not have to actually process your message and you do not want their attention divided in that way.

Because speakers have had the advantage of researching their speech and organizing their material, the message will generally always be clear to the speaker. But that isn't what is necessary for an effective speech. Make sure your speech is clear to the audience; if they don't understand your message, the speech won't be effective.

IN REVIEW

Effective organization and outlining...

- Help clarify the goal of the speech
- Help determine what you need to accomplish that goal
- Help evaluate the completeness of your research
- Help you understand your message so you can communicate it to your audience

Questions:

Reflections:

BEYOND THE FUNDAMENTALS

THE DIFFERENCE BETWEEN PREPARATION OUTLINES AND SPEAKING NOTES

As noted in this chapter, the basic benefit of outlining is that you end up with a clear sense of your message, which allows you to communicate effectively with your audience. Interestingly enough, these steps can also help you when you deliver that message. In Chapter 10, you will read about the different styles of delivery. One of those styles is extemporaneous delivery, and, as you will see, it is generally the preferred mode of presentation for speeches. It often surprises beginning speakers to find out that what makes extemporaneous speaking so effective is that it does not rely on a word-for-word manuscript. Manuscripts actually tend to limit a speaker's effectiveness because when a person reads a manuscript they tend to neglect the components of good delivery. To avoid that trap, extemporaneous delivery does not require speakers to learn a word-for-word script, but rather to be familiar enough with the speech material so they can discuss it in a natural and conversational style. Thus, the benefit of the organization and outlining process is that speakers have an opportunity to become intimately familiar with the material and how they will present it.

There is also a danger, however, that comes with all this work. Often speakers will decide the outline they have written at this stage of the process, what we call the preparation outline, is so good that it would also make effective notes, but that is not the case. Remember the benefit of extemporaneous speaking is that it tends to lead to the most natural and conversational style of delivery, as opposed to manuscript delivery, which tends to be the more stilted. The fundamental distinction between the two styles that allows for that difference is the use of a manuscript versus the use of brief speaking notes which remind the speaker of the key points he or she wishes to make. In addition, these two styles of delivery identify the two ends of a continuum, so we can say that the more notes a speaker has (the closer he or she gets to a manuscript) the greater the negative impact on the delivery of the speech will be. That is why you should not use your preparation outline as your speaking notes—it is too detailed.

Once you complete the outline of your speech, including the introduction and conclusion, the next step will be to work on your presentation. In Chapter 10, you will see that there are many elements of effective delivery and you want to be able to concentrate on those, not your notes, when delivering a speech, and that means your speaking notes need to be much briefer than your preparation outline.

How do you get from the preparation outline to speaking notes? One of the key elements will be practicing the speech so you become familiar enough with the material so that you don't need many notes. Chapter 10 will give you some tips for practicing your speech, and with adequate practice, you can reduce your dependency on any notes. Here, however, we focus on the mechanics of transforming your preparation outline into speaking notes, and here are some tips for doing that.

First, focus your speaking notes on the material that requires the greatest precision. Remember, extemporaneous speaking does not require that you follow an exact script. However, there are still certain items that require greater precision like citations, statistics, and direct quotations. These are the items that you are most likely to need in a speaking outline, regardless of how much you practice (however, the more you practice, the more you will become familiar with these parts of your speech). Therefore, these are the items that should make up the majority of your notes. The rest you really should know by the time you present the speech.

Second, be very mentally engaged in the preparation process and trust your knowledge of your thesis that has come from that preparation. Think about how you have learned other things in your life. Usually it is by repeated exposure to the material, and while you are preparing a speech, you should have lots of exposure to your material. That is why many people say you start practicing your speech when you start to prepare your speech. While we address the topics of preparation and delivery separately, they really are closely interrelated and the work you do preparing your speech really can help you prepare to deliver the speech, if you are willing to make the effort in this step in the process. And, if you make that effort now, you will find that, with a little practice, you really won't need many notes. Ultimately, you just have to trust that your efforts will pay off, and they will. You will be more effective because you have less notes and hence a greater ability to connect with the audience.

With these two principles in mind, you can begin to pare down your preparation outline to a much briefer document. Eliminate all or most of the detail, using only words and phrases to remind yourself of major concepts. Keep extra detail only where it is most necessary, when you are dealing with those few items that require precision. And, do focus on what is necessary, not what you think may be helpful. If you prepare well, and trust yourself, you will find that with some practice prior to the speech, you really can get by with very limited speaking notes.

SUMMARY

In this chapter we have seen that organization is a very critical step in the process of putting together a speech. A well-organized speech allows speakers to easily accomplish their goal. A disorganized speech is far less likely to be successful. Since our goal should be to accomplish our purpose, we can see that having an organized message is a key step in our efforts to effectively communicate our message, and this chapter has given you lots of information to help you develop a well-organized, and effective, speech.

APPLYING THE FUNDAMENTALS

EFFECTIVE SPEECHES

As you finish your outline, you will want to look back and make sure you have developed an effective speech. In this chapter, we have covered the basics for building an effective speech, but there is always more that you can do. Here are some questions you can use when you review your speech outline. Some have been addressed in this chapter, and others identify those little extras that separate a good speech from a great speech.

When you review your informative speech, think about these questions:

- Do I have a clearly stated goal?

- Can I achieve my goal in the allotted time?

- Is my structure clear? Is it logical? Would another pattern/order be more effective?

- Do my details support my purpose? Am I giving extraneous details?

- Can I simplify my ideas?

- Am I speaking in generalities? Can I give more specific support or explanations?

- Is my information correct? Is my message slanted? If my message is one-sided, do I make that clear to my audience?

- Am I giving a speech (or information) my audience will not have heard before?

- How can I move my speech beyond the "standard" presentation?

- Can I add an unusual or extraordinary element/story/perspective?

- Have I spent time thinking about my audience, their experience, and their motivations?

- Will my audience be familiar with my language/terminology?

- How can I connect new information to what the audience already knows?

- Where can I make specific references to my audience's situation or experience?

- Have I incorporated a human element to my message?

- Can I incorporate a local element to my message?

When you review your persuasive speech, you should think about all of those, and you should also consider these questions as well (many of these issues will be discussed in more detail in Chapter 12).

- Will the audience clearly know my position? Is that position argumentative?

- Are my points argumentative and are they well supported?

- Is my message logical? Have I avoided the use of logical fallacies?

- Have I answered all counterarguments or questions the audience is likely to have?

- Have I properly incorporated pathos by using vivid description and examples?

- Have I established ethos by including argumentative strategies that boost the audience's perception of my competency?

- Have I taken advantage of places where I can establish common ground with my audience?

- Is my use of argumentative appeals effective and ethical?

CHAPTER 9

INTRODUCTIONS AND CONCLUSIONS

The introduction and conclusion should solidify the impact of your message and help you connect with the audience.

A direct question, such as, "How many of you have been to Mexico City?" is one way to start a speech as it first gets the audience thinking about your topic.

We are trained to give firm handshakes as a method of impression building. When we meet and part with someone, we focus on creating a sincere, positive, and lasting impression. In movies and television, beginnings are crafted to draw you in immediately, to keep you from changing the channel, and endings are made to leave you with an important idea, or at least a sense of closure. The same is true with speeches. Once you have completed the body of the speech and have a strong sense of thesis developed throughout, it's time to think about how you will open and close your speech. This chapter will focus on ways to make a strong impression on your audience by creating effective introductions and conclusions.

THE INTRODUCTION

"You never get a second chance to make a first impression." This old saying holds true when it comes to meeting people, job interviews, and speeches. The first impression given by your speech should be that your topic is focused, interesting, important, and that you, as a speaker, are ready to give it. There are five elements of an effective introduction that can help you build this positive impression and connect audiences to your topic and purpose.

Why do you think it is important that your attention-getter be relevant to your topic?

GAIN THE ATTENTION OF YOUR AUDIENCE

Put simply, if you cannot gain the attention of your audience immediately, they will be less likely to pay attention to the rest of the speech. So spend some time thinking of a unique way to draw the audience in. This section includes several common methods of gaining attention. There is not one "best" method; what will be most effective depends on your topic, purpose, and audience. Whatever you choose, make sure it is interesting and directly related to your topic and thesis, or you may leave the audience with an unclear sense of what your speech is about.

ASK THE AUDIENCE A QUESTION

The first method of gaining attention is to ask the audience a question. There are two types of questions you can ask: direct and rhetorical. A direct question is a question that asks for a response from the audience. For example, a question asking, "How many of you have been to Mexico City?" is an example of a direct question. Most likely, the speaker is looking for a show of hands from the audience. A rhetorical question, on the other hand, is a question that is not meant to be answered. Instead, the speaker wants the audience to think about the issue or topic of the question. For example, "What is wrong with a world that allows people to go hungry when there is more than enough food to feed everyone?" This question is worded in a way that does not impel the audience to shout out an answer.

Before beginning a speech by asking a question, consider some possible scenarios. How would you respond if you asked a direct question to your audience and no one answered? Or answered in a way you had not anticipated? Likewise, how would you respond if you asked a rhetorical question and someone shouted an answer? Be prepared. When you engage an audience, any response is possible.

USE A QUOTATION

Quotations are often used because they encapsulate a powerful idea or give an insight into the person who made the saying famous. They can be effective ways of quickly gaining attention from the audience. For example, a quotation from Mickey Mantle might work well for a speech about baseball. A quotation from Wolfgang Puck might be appropriate if giving a speech on a culinary topic. Remember to keep the quotation relevant to the topic. If you use a Mickey Mantle quotation expressing a political viewpoint, it will not fit a speech on the history of baseball, even though Mantle is an important part of that history. It is the quotation that needs to link to the topic, not necessarily the person.

A quotation from a person associated with your topic provides a powerful opening for your speech. For example, in a speech about cooking you might begin with a quotation from a famous chef.

USE A POWERFUL STATISTIC

Some statistics are so strong and so surprising that an audience can't help but have their curiosity aroused. You might tell an audience, "According to the U.S. Census Bureau in 2013 more than 45 million people lived in poverty in the United States. That is more people than live in the state of California, our most populous state." Most people are surprised by a number this large and will take a moment to hear what you are going to do with this information.

USE A NARRATIVE

Another way to create interest is to tell your audience a story. Narratives give a speech a more personal feel. In addition, if you begin with a powerful or curious story, your topic becomes more interesting. One warning: if the story is too long, the speech loses focus and the audience may lose interest. Keep it brief, make sure the point is apparent, and focus on details that set up the focus of your speech.

TELL A JOKE OR USE HUMOR

Telling jokes or funny anecdotes are great ways to quickly involve an audience. But remember, as with all attention-gaining devices, the humor should be relevant to your topic. Also, make sure it is appropriate for the topic and the audience; you don't want to offend your audience in the first thirty seconds of a seven-minute speech. Humor can be tricky to use, so be prepared for *any* kind of response. Some people may find your joke hilarious, others may chuckle, and still others may not laugh at all.

STATE THE TOPIC OF YOUR SPEECH

This may sound simple and obvious, but too often speakers forget to tell you what they are speaking on. It is frustrating for an audience to be unsure of what a speech is about until it is completely over. You will have a more focused and attentive audience if they are not trying to figure out what your topic is.

What do you think is the most effective way to gain the audience's attention?

DISCUSS THE IMPORTANCE OF THE TOPIC TO YOUR AUDIENCE

Once the audience knows your topic, they will want to know why they should be listening. While the significance of your topic may be obvious to you, your audience may not have the same background or passion for your topic. Let them know what they stand to gain from your speech. Will they save money? Have a more fulfilling life? Better understand their own community? Audiences can be open to different levels of significance, from improving the lives of people suffering around the world to a new and entertaining way of looking at an old idea. The point is that there should be some importance to your audience and it should be clear in the introduction.

ESTABLISH PERSONAL CREDIBILITY ON THE TOPIC

As Aristotle emphasized, speaker credibility is of great importance to an audience. Listeners may be interested in your topic, but in order to effectively connect your message with them, they need to trust you as someone qualified to deliver that message. In formal speaking situations, credibility is often established by a person who introduces the speaker and lists their relevant accomplishments. In other situations, a speaker can establish credibility through their preparation and style of delivery; they create the impression of a professional or an expert. For beginning speakers, that can be difficult, so it becomes important to make some type of credibility statement. Whether you have personal experience with the topic or have conducted sufficient research, let your audience know. If you are teaching the audience how to perform CPR, let them know that you have been certified for the last three years, or that you saved someone's life last summer while working at the pool. There are many different ways of emphasizing your credibility. Be aware that it is possible to overstate your credibility and appear arrogant or overconfident to the audience, so when you choose this strategy, be brief and sincere.

BEYOND THE FUNDAMENTALS ━━━

SPEAKERS AND CREDIBILITY

The concept of speaker credibility, on one hand, is very simple to grasp: establishing what makes you, as the speaker, believable and/or trustworthy on your selected topic. Interestingly, the idea of credibility can actually be broken down a bit farther, and its influences can be seen on multiple levels. Specifically, there are three types of credibility that can influence the audience/speaker relationship: initial credibility, derived credibility, and terminal credibility.

Initial Credibility Before speakers begin their message, audiences create general positive or negative impressions of the speaker, often based on appearance, and then use this impression to determine to what extent they will likely listen to the message. In many cases, initial credibility is part of a social construct (students assume teachers are credible, patients assume doctors are credible, and so on), but this is not the case with public speaking. Therefore, speakers need to treat the speaking situation with respect, which can include things you may, at first glance, consider tedious: dressing appropriately, having all your items ready before class starts (even if you may not be asked to speak), etc. When an audience feels a speaker is taking the situation seriously, the initial credibility is often higher, and there is a better chance the audience will listen to the message.

Derived Credibility This is the credibility that you earn (or in some cases, lose) during the speaking situation. As your speech progresses, you are going to meet all the required elements for your specific project (citing sources, transitions, audience adaptations, etc.). You are also hopefully going to speak with passion, energy, eye contact, and come across as a knowledgeable individual for the topic. When you do these things, you are building a sense of trustworthiness and believability between yourself and the audience. This credibility stays with you longer than initial credibility because you are showing the audience your skill set. In other words, you are not just "dressed to impress," but you also have good sense and are speaking with good will. Of course, by not doing any of these things described above, you do run the risk of losing credibility, which negatively influences the extent to which your audience may listen to you.

Terminal Credibility This form of credibility is the lasting impression your audience has of you as a speaker. For example, you may find yourself excited to hear a speech from one of your classmates because they had performed well on previous assignments, or you decide to enroll in a certain professor's class because you enjoy their teaching style and how they apply their knowledge of material. It is important to note, also, that a lot of work needs to go into developing the first two types of credibility in order to create positive terminal credibility.

In Chapter 2 we noted that people tend to associate greater credibility with some professions (doctors) as opposed to others (used car salesmen). Based on our discussion here of credibility, why do you think that is the case?

Should a speaker have to state the topic and thesis as well as preview the main points in the introduction? Shouldn't the audience just have to figure it out?

119

PREVIEW THE THESIS AND MAIN POINTS OF YOUR SPEECH

Just as the internal preview discussed in Chapter 8 lets an audience know the information they are about to hear within a main point of the speech, the introductory preview forecasts the thesis and main points of the entire speech. If there are three points in the body of the speech, the audience should hear what those three points will be in the introduction. Remember, a speech will often contain more blatant statements of organization than a paper. This is because a reader can re-read a sentence or a paragraph, but the listener cannot rewind a speaker. Making the structure clear helps listeners better understand and remember a message.

Although an introduction needs to fulfill the five requirements in regards to attention, topic, significance, credibility, and preview, they do not need to happen in the order presented. The gaining of attention should obviously be first. In addition, you should end the introduction with your thesis and preview because that signals the end of the introduction and prepares the audience for what is to come next—the body where you will develop the ideas you set up in the introduction. The other elements can be addressed in many ways: in different sequences or even combined into a single statement that serves multiple functions. For example, if you gain attention with a narrative that highlights your own expertise, you are likewise establishing credibility and may want to highlight that issue first. Some speakers may combine the statement of topic with the more specific thesis and the preview of main points. As long as you give thought to the most effective way to complete all five functions, you are making strides toward an engaging opening and a memorable speech.

Do you believe a speaker can overcome a poor introduction? Why or why not?

APPLYING THE FUNDAMENTALS

INTRODUCTIONS IN FAMOUS SPEECHES

Many students in speech classes struggle with developing the types of introductions their professors ask them to create. The five components listed in this chapter and how they are presented seem very blatant, and students don't always see such an overt approach in more famous speeches.

But most of those components are there, although they may be more subtle. Consider, for example, the famous "I Have a Dream" speech by Dr. Martin Luther King, Jr. In this speech, Dr. King addresses one of the largest civil rights demonstrations of the 1960s and his goal is to energize and justify the ongoing civil rights movement. While most of the components are rather subtle, at some level he addresses most of the common issues in an introduction.

He starts with an attention-getting device. Standing on the steps of the Lincoln Memorial, he begins with a narrative that makes a clear allusion to one of Lincoln's most famous speeches, the Gettysburg Address. Then, in one well-written paragraph, he discloses his topic, emphasizes the importance of that topic, and reveals his thesis when he says,

> But one hundred years later, the Negro still is not free....One hundred years later, the Negro is still languishing in the corners of American society and finds himself an exile in his own land. So we have come here today to dramatize a shameful condition.

Most importantly, note that the last statement establishes a thesis. It tells exactly what he wants to do in the speech; he wants to "dramatize a shameful condition." Admittedly, there is no preview, but that is not unusual in many famous speeches, because many of these speeches are what we call special occasion speeches, and, as you will see in Chapter 14, these speeches respond to very specific rhetorical contexts. Because of that many are rather short; they are essentially one-point speeches and don't need to be previewed. Longer speeches like business presentations and classroom lectures will tend to have previews, but few of those become famous. In addition, while there is no preview, the entire body is still closely tied to the thesis and the points King makes about the conditions "one hundred years later," so the audience does have a very clear sense of what he is trying to do and how he wants to accomplish that. Dr. King uses the metaphor of a bad check; he speaks of inequality and he mentions trials and tribulations that people have faced in the battle for equal rights. Every one of these could be considered a "shameful condition," and, therefore, draws directly from the theme presented in the thesis.

The one component that is lacking is an explicit statement of personal credibility. However, by then Dr. King was well known in the civil rights movement and would not have needed to establish his credibility. As we saw in Chapter 4, your audience analysis should examine your relationship with the audience, so that you respond appropriately to the needs of an effective speech, and, clearly, Dr. King did that.

The key point here is that most famous speakers have spent a lot of time honing their craft. Some of their early introductions probably were more blatant and overt, but over time, they learned how to serve the functions of an introduction in more subtle and artistic ways, and eventually you may learn that as well. But, you need to learn the basic skills before you can enhance them. You learn to ride a bike before you learn to do tricks, and that is the stage you are at in a basic speech course. So, make sure in this class you learn the basic skills and then over time you can develop more advanced techniques that could make you the next great speaker.

IN REVIEW
Effective introductions...
- Gain the attention of the audience
- State the topic of the speech
- Establish credibility of the speaker
- Give the audience a reason to listen
- Preview thesis and main points

Questions:

Reflections:

THE CONCLUSION

The ending of a great film provides not only a sense of finality, but also a great feeling or strong image. An effective speech ends in a similar way. Your closing should, once again, create an impression that is positive and lasting. In order for your conclusion to be effective, it should fulfill three functions. It should review the main points of the speech, restate the importance of the message, and provide a logical and positive closing statement.

REVIEW THE MAIN POINTS OF THE BODY

Similar to the preview of points in the introduction, you need to review the main points in the conclusion. When you have finished delivering the body of the speech, signify to your audience that you are about to close. Reviews not only reinforce the structure and thesis, they provide a clue to the audience that the speech is about to end. This is important so the speech does not feel "unfinished."

What do you think is the most important element of a conclusion? Why?

121

IN REVIEW
Effective conclusions...

- Review the main points of the speech
- Reinforce the importance of the message
- Provide a logical sense of closure

Questions:

Reflections:

REINFORCE THE IMPORTANCE OF YOUR MESSAGE

By the end of your speech, the importance of your topic should be pretty evident. Your conclusion provides one last opportunity to bring it together, tie it to the audience, and perhaps build a climax of emotion. In the conclusion, the significance of your thesis and message should be stated in the most powerful way possible.

HAVE A POWERFUL AND LOGICAL CLOSING STATEMENT

Speeches that conclude with, "Well, that's all I have," "I'm done," or perhaps worst of all, "Sorry that was so bad," can be disappointing endings for an audience. They are sometimes the anticlimactic closing to an otherwise good speech. You do want to let your audience know that the speech is finished, but it should be done more effectively. Just as your opening statement makes a first impression, your last line can alter the way an audience thinks about you. Take time to think of a closing statement that is as strong as your opening. Again, you have options. You can end with a quotation, question, example, etc. Some speakers choose to relate back to the opening idea to give a sense of having come full circle. As with the gaining of attention, there is not one right or best way. It should evolve from your message. Whatever you choose, make sure it leaves a positive and lasting impression; give your audience something to think about.

SUMMARY

The introduction and conclusion of a speech are important because they communicate the first and last impressions to an audience. Strive to create a strong introduction that gains attention, states the topic, previews the main points, and highlights the importance of the topic and the credibility of the speaker. A closing should leave the audience feeling positive by reviewing the main points, reinforcing the importance of the message and providing a logical sense of closure. When all is said and done, an abrupt or inarticulate beginning or ending can weaken the impact of a very strong message. A weak opening loses listeners; a poor closing confuses them. Use the introduction and conclusion to solidify the impact of your message and to connect fully with your audience.

RESOURCES FOR BUILDING COMMUNICATION EFFECTIVENESS

CHECKLIST FOR A FORMAL OUTLINE

CONCEPT	COMPLETED
All elements accounted for: 1. Introduction 2. Body 3. Conclusion 4. Clear/logical transitions between main points	
The introduction to my speech is written word for word to include: 1. Attention-getter 2. Statement of topic 3. Statement of credibility 4. Statement of importance 5. Thesis and preview of main points	

The body of my speech is broken into outline format, so that:
    I, II, III, etc. tag my main points
    A, B, C, etc. tag my second-level points
    1, 2, 3, etc. tag my third-level points	

Each notation (Roman numerals, capital letters, numbers, etc.) has sufficient context for an outside reviewer to understand my goal and to help me present the speech. (This would include complete sentences for the most significant points but could use words and phrases for some of the substructure—remember to be consistent with the requirements of your professor.)	
I have clearly written in my _____ source citations to meet assignment requirements.	
My citations are written as I plan to say them.	
I have written into my speech qualifications for sources I think my audience may be unfamiliar with.	
The conclusion to my speech is written word for word to include: 1. Review of main points 2. Reminder of thesis and importance 3. A powerful (and logical) closing	
I have a Works Cited page, Source Checklist from the text, or Annotated Bibliography, as required by my professor.	
Upon final review of my formal outline, my main points are discrete.	
Upon final review of my formal outline, my main points are parallel.	
Upon final review of my formal outline, my main points are simple for the audience to process/understand.	
Upon final review of my formal outline, my main points are balanced.	
Upon final review of my formal outline, my main points help complete my thesis/purpose.	
Upon final review of my formal outline, my main points match what is previewed in the introduction.	
I have asked my professor any necessary questions to make sure I have completed the assignment correctly.	

CHAPTER 10

MODES OF PRESENTATION AND DELIVERY

Effective delivery enhances the message without drawing attention to itself.

© Corbis

John F. Kennedy was a master of presentation and delivery. The way he said something was as memorable as the words he used to communicate the message.

The common saying, "It's not what you say, but how you say it" emphasizes the importance of delivery, or the nonverbal aspect of communication. We have spent much of this text discussing the verbal element of communication (verbal meaning the words or the message), but it is important to understand and practice the nonverbal aspect, the actual speaking, as well. While we may not go so far as to say that the delivery of the message is more important than the message, as stressed in the saying above, it is important. An ethical listener and a critical listener will look past a weak delivery and focus on the importance of the message, but because we want an articulate message that is easy to hear and because so many listeners find it easier to focus on the message when the delivery is clear and confident, we do seek to improve our delivery. This chapter will focus on both vocal and physical elements of delivery, as well as some different modes of delivering a message.

The elements of delivery can be divided into two categories: the vocal delivery, how you use your voice, and the physical delivery, how you use your body. The following sections will highlight a few of the many elements of delivery.

Effective speech delivery includes vocal elements, physical elements, and a speaking style that is appropriate for the setting and the topic.

VOCAL DELIVERY

Vocal delivery involves the use of your voice to communicate a message and includes such elements as volume, rate, energy, and the use of pauses.

VOLUME

Effective vocal delivery has an appropriate level of volume. No matter how well you seem to do with every other aspect, if an audience cannot hear you there is no point in speaking. If they need to strain to listen, they are putting so much energy into the process it becomes tedious and easy to give up. Adapt your volume to the size of the room and adjust for interference, such as a loud class next door. While being too loud can also cause interference for the listener (why is that person yelling?), it is important that your audience is able to hear you.

RATE

Rate is the pace at which you deliver your speech—how fast or slowly are you speaking? Nervousness can cause speakers to speed up their message in an attempt to "get the speech over with," but speaking too quickly can make you seem nervous. On the other hand, speaking too slowly can make you seem bored. What is a proper rate of speech for a classroom setting? It varies depending upon the complexity of your topic and the expectations of your audience. The key to determining an effective rate is to make sure you are not speaking so fast that you cannot articulate or that your audience cannot focus and not speaking so slow that you seem to lack energy. Keep in mind that if you find yourself using too many vocal fillers (umm, uh) or tripping over words, it is more helpful to slow down than to speed up.

As an audience member, how does a speaker's vocal delivery affect the way you receive the message?

ENERGY

When it comes to vocal delivery of speeches, the focus is on keeping your audience interested in you and your topic. A voice that exhibits energy adds that necessary interest. Being energetic does not mean you need to speak quickly or sound happy when speaking on a somber subject; instead, it deals with vocal variety. Messages that are monotone seem to lack enthusiasm or sincerity. A delivery that feels natural will demonstrate variance in pitch and tone. Additionally, there will be variance in volume, rate, and the use of pauses. Energy is created collectively by all the other elements of vocal delivery.

PAUSES

While overly long pauses can make you seem unfocused or unprepared, you do not have to fill every moment with some vocal utterance. In fact, many effective speakers use appropriate pauses as a tool to enhance the emotion in speeches (and as a way to catch their breath). Look at your message to determine where you can use pauses for impact or to build suspense. As with many things in life, moderation is the key. Too many pauses or extremely long pauses will make your delivery feel choppy and awkward to your audience.

PHYSICAL DELIVERY

Nonverbal communication encompasses everything other than the words. The vocal quality of delivery refers to how you use your voice, and all other aspects of nonverbal communication fall into the category of physical delivery.

EYE CONTACT

Maintaining eye contact is of great importance, but it is the most challenging element of delivery for many speakers. It can enhance the feeling of being the center of attention or feeling judged, as discussed in Chapter 3. Some people recommend looking at the back wall or staring at foreheads rather than eyes, but audiences can often sense when you are not making eye contact. It is a better idea to use **visual anchors**, or audience members you feel comfortable looking at while speaking. Make sure to have anchors in all parts of the room. A speaker will sometimes look only to one person or one half of the room, leaving a large portion of the audience feeling ignored. During your speech, actively look to all parts of the room and make eye contact with at least several different audience members.

APPEARANCE

While there is no dress code for public speaking, it will benefit you to consider your appearance before giving a speech. Based on how you look, your audience forms an impression of you before you open your mouth to speak. Show the audience you are taking them seriously. In regards to dress, adapt your attire for the audience and situation. For example, while a backwards cap, ripped t-shirt, and pajamas may feel very comfortable, it would be inappropriate in almost every situation. A good rule of thumb is to match at the highest level what your audience is likely to be wearing. In a work presentation, wear your most professional work clothes. In a classroom situation, wear your nicest school clothes. There may be certain situations that call for you to dress more formally than your audience; use your audience analysis skills to determine the appropriate clothing.

Why do you think it is so important to make eye contact with the audience?

IN REVIEW
Vocal delivery involves items such as...

• Volume

• Rate

• Energy

• Pauses

Questions:

Reflections:

GESTURES

Using gestures can help you look comfortable as a speaker and emphasize certain points of your message. Keep in mind that using appropriate hand gestures is not necessarily the same as "talking with your hands." Like so many of the other elements of delivery, you can overgesture and undergesture. No gestures at all can make you seem stiff. Too many gestures, too big of gestures, or repetitive gestures can make you seem nervous or unfocused. The trick is, once again, finding the appropriate balance. Often, reducing the level of nervousness and practicing your speech will move you to the amount of gesturing that works effectively for you.

As an audience member, how does a speaker's appearance affect the way you respond to the message?

Gestures can help you emphasize certain elements of your message when giving a speech and make you look more poised.

MOVEMENT

In addition to gesturing, you have the option to incorporate physical movement into your delivery. Some speakers prefer to stay behind the podium, but this doesn't work for everyone. Some speakers feel stifled behind a lectern. Others become so comfortable that they lean onto it, creating a sloppy appearance. If either of these is the case, incorporate purposeful movement into your delivery. Some speakers pace back and forth in a way that is not purposeful. Movement should seem natural and controlled. Move to one spot of your stage and speak for a while, then move to another spot and speak there. Moving occasionally helps you appear confident and connect with different parts of the audience.

POSTURE

Posture also plays a part in the physical delivery of a speech. Poor posture can send a message of laziness or boredom to the audience. Some research suggests that height lends an air of credibility to a speaker. Additionally, there is the benefit of effective breathing. Straight posture makes it easier for air to get to your lungs, which improves your vocal quality and increases your volume. So stand up straight. It can help you to seem more confident and powerful to your audience.

IN REVIEW
Physical delivery involves items such as...

• Eye contact

• Appearance

• Gestures

• Movement

• Posture

Questions:

Reflections:

As a speaker, how can you determine which mode of delivery will be the most effective?

With all the elements of vocal and physical delivery, you may have noticed there is no exactly right or wrong amount. There is no one standard for what works; delivery should meet certain expectations, but also be unique, reflecting a speaker's personality. Ultimately, an effective delivery is one that enhances the message without drawing attention to itself. To improve requires awareness and practice. Filming or recording yourself while giving your speech can be helpful in determining whether or not you are loud enough, make appropriate eye contact, incorporate purposeful movement, have repetitive gestures, and more. Practicing will absolutely help you find a style that is comfortable, engaging, and that helps you connect with your audience. Ultimately, that is the point of public speaking.

APPLYING THE FUNDAMENTALS

THE IMPORTANCE OF PRACTICE

The importance of practicing your speech was discussed in Chapter 3 as a method of reducing nervousness. This chapter mentions some of the other benefits associated with rehearsing your speech. In fact, practicing the delivery of your message is an essential element of the public speaking process.

Think about the sport of baseball for a moment. Before the game starts, you see players on the field taking ground balls, playing catch, and swinging bats. The reason players warm up is not to calm their nerves, but to perform their best during the game. They get on the field and go through the motions so their bodies are prepared to execute them more effectively during those crucial plays. Practicing a speech helps in much the same way; it serves as a warm-up to a successful communication experience.

You have taken the time to choose, research, and develop support around a specific topic. Now take the time to make sure it works. Practicing your speech can help determine if there are elements that need to be corrected, added to, or something that just doesn't "sound right." Also, the more you practice, the more confident and comfortable you become with presenting the material. This often enables a speaker to develop a more personal and unique style.

Even amazing athletes aren't amazing with every swing of the bat. They practice. Similarly, great communicators don't instinctively give a great speech; they work on it. Studying this text is helpful in terms of gaining knowledge, but the only way to improve as a speaker is to practice.

STYLES OF DELIVERY

There are four modes of delivery that will be covered in the remainder of this chapter. Each style has advantages and disadvantages, dependent on the specific situation, so it is important to conduct a situational analysis before deciding upon the type of delivery you will use in a presentation.

MANUSCRIPT SPEAKING

Many students will write word-for-word papers, outlines, or note cards of their speeches. This is referred to as manuscript speaking: a completely pre-written, prepared message which is read to the audience (think of someone reading a prepared statement to the press, or a speaker reading from a teleprompter). The benefit of using a manuscript is that you will not have to worry about forgetting words, or missing a section of the presentation. However, the challenge becomes that it is more difficult to sound natural, to interact and connect with your audience. People who are reading usually sound like they are reading, not "speaking." There are certain limited situations where manuscript speaking is desirable, for example if there are significant political or legal implications attached to your exact wording. For our purposes in the classroom, this is not the case. The disadvantages of manuscript speaking outweigh the benefits in most situations.

How does straight reading of a manuscript impact the effectiveness of a speech?

Speaking from a manuscript can help you remember the wording and organization of your speech, but it usually sounds like reading rather than speaking. Consider the formal stilted delivery of a person speaking from a teleprompter.

MEMORIZED SPEAKING

Memorized speaking is similar to manuscript speaking in that the content is written word for word, but instead of reading, the message is memorized. The advantage to memorization is being able to speak without notes and, again, having precise wording. It also allows for more eye contact than manuscript reading. The dangers are greater than with the use of a manuscript. In the event of a memory lapse, there are no notes to get you back on track. Additionally, the more memorized a speech is, the greater the chance that it sounds unnatural or "rehearsed." Speaking from memory is appropriate in very limited situations where the precise wording is important and the message is brief.

When might it be necessary to use memorized delivery?

IMPROMPTU SPEAKING

In an impromptu speech you are given a topic with very little time to prepare your message. Just as with any other speech, impromptu requires organization. If someone can quickly organize a message, the benefit of impromptu speaking is the natural and conversational style of delivery. But not everyone can create an effective impromptu message. In fact, Mark Twain once stated, "It takes me two weeks to write a good impromptu speech." The challenge of impromptu speaking is thinking of appropriate ideas and maintaining an organized structure. This style of speaking

Why is it important that impromptu presentations still be organized?

IN REVIEW
The four styles of delivery are...

• Manuscript speaking

• Memorized speaking

• Impromptu speaking

• Extemporaneous speaking

Questions:

Reflections:

Is it possible to have an effective speech without good delivery? Can good delivery overcome a poorly constructed message?

requires you to speak on a topic area in which you are already knowledgeable. You are very rarely asked to speak impromptu unless you are considered to have the necessary information. Perhaps at work you will be asked to present an update on a project you are leading, or a politician may be asked to speak impromptu on his or her own political platform. Otherwise, impromptu speeches are usually only conducted as method of practicing organization and delivery.

EXTEMPORANEOUS SPEAKING

Extemporaneous speaking combines the research, preparation, and practice of manuscript and memorized speaking with the conversational tone of impromptu speaking. After conducting research and outlining the speech, the speaker practices and delivers the speech from an outline of limited notes (see the example of speaking notes or a speaking outline in the appendix). While this style lacks the precise wording of a manuscript, the amount of preparation and practice usually produces a strong, coherent message delivered in a natural style because the speaker is not straining to remember the exact next word. Extemporaneous speaking is the style that is the most useful in the largest number of situations. For that reason, it is the style that is practiced in most classrooms.

SUMMARY

This chapter discussed various important elements of both vocal delivery (the use of voice) and physical delivery (the use of body and environment), as well as the different modes of delivery. After considering the situation, work for a delivery mode and style that is most likely to be effective in that situation. All types of delivery have advantages and disadvantages, but you will most likely find extemporaneous speaking to be the most appropriate in the largest number of situations.

Delivering a speech is stressful for some, but practice and self-awareness can help you make choices that improve the strength and natural tone of your delivery. As mentioned in Chapter 3, many speakers experience communication apprehension during the delivery of a message. If you find yourself nervous while speaking, keep in mind some of the strategies for coping with anxiety from that chapter.

CHAPTER 11

LISTENING

*Effective communication not only involves sending messages,
but also making the necessary effort to properly receive messages as well.*

When someone is speaking, they generally have important information to share. Therefore, we must pay close attention and listen effectively so we know what that information is.

Why are we, as a society, such poor listeners? Why do we overestimate our listening skills?

Listening plays an important role in effective communication. When someone speaks to us it is usually because they have important information to share, and we must pay close attention so we know what that information is. That process of receiving and processing messages is listening and we must work to hone those skills so we are sure to receive the information we need. But developing those skills takes work. When asked to rate their communication abilities, people in the United States consistently report they think they are skilled listeners. They say they can capture important information in a lecture and lend an ear to a friend in need, while reading the paper, checking for text messages, surfing the Internet, watching a television show, or doing homework. But, they are wrong. Listening takes dedication to the primary task and a willingness to avoid distractions, so it should not surprise us that testing reveals most of us are actually poor listeners. We are easily distracted. Even when paying attention, we listen for details and miss the big picture. Or we listen only for holes in other people's arguments. We even spend time thinking of responses before someone is finished speaking, rather than focusing on the actual message being sent.

While listening is not difficult, we often fail to listen effectively because we don't know how. We are trained extensively in the communication areas of reading and writing, somewhat in speaking, but very little in listening. We view it as a passive, natural skill and, thus, have oversimplified the process. This chapter focuses on improving listening abilities by understanding more fully what is involved and giving specific strategies for increased effectiveness. As public speakers, we obviously want our audiences filled with good listeners, but improving our own listening goes hand in hand with improving our speaking. As we improve in listening, our capacity to improve as speakers grows.

LISTENING DEFINED

When most people say, "I'm listening," they actually mean, "I hear you." The phrases are used interchangeably, but the meaning is vastly different. While hearing is a passive physical activity, listening is active. **Listening** is the process of recognizing, understanding, and accurately interpreting the messages communicated by others. Hearing is only the first of five stages that define listening.

STAGE ONE: HEARING

Outside of physical impairment, either temporary or permanent, hearing is automatic. The ear picks up sounds created by traffic, television, the furnace, our own voices, other voices, and almost everything around us. We do not decide what or how well we hear (although many of us subject ourselves to a reduced ability to hear by playing loud music or working in extremely loud environments, such as construction with jackhammers); we do, however, play a more active role in determining how well we succeed in the next four stages of listening.

STAGE TWO: ATTENDING

If we paid close attention to everything we heard, we would be overwhelmed before reaching the middle of the day. We wouldn't be able to sleep through the night due to the whirring or ticking of our electric clocks. Luckily, we take an active role in listening when we decide how much attention we will pay to the sounds our ears are picking up. We mentally block out the ticking clock. We mentally block out other conversations as we walk through a busy hallway with a friend. We mentally block out our parent's request to take out the garbage. We decide to pay more attention in a classroom when we hear cues from a teacher, such as the repetition of important ideas or the words, "this will be on the test." We immediately become alert. Not because we have no choice, but because we decide it will benefit us to pay close attention. In all our listening, we have the choice to pay attention or not pay attention. Someone being "boring" or "offensive" may make it more difficult for us, but the choice to attend is still ours. Effective and respectful listeners make the choice to attend.

Research indicates that the introduction of television into most U.S. homes has had an impact on how people process information. Listeners have become accustomed to sound bites and their attention spans have decreased. Also, audiences have come to expect a higher level of entertainment from their speakers. With the Internet, cell phones, and other technology devices, listening habits and preferences will very likely continue to shift.

In which stage of the listening process do you feel you can make the most improvement? (The listening reflection at the end of the chapter may help you answer this question.)

STAGE THREE: UNDERSTANDING

Once we decide to pay attention, we must somehow make sense of the message being sent to us. Before we can fully grasp it, we need to understand it on different levels. We must certainly understand the language and vocabulary being used by the other person. We must also understand the context and concepts being discussed. These elements of understanding rely partially on our own background and previous knowledge. If someone is speaking in French and we don't speak French, we will not understand. But the construction of the message may also affect our understanding; we need to be able to organize the information in a way that is clear to us.

Understanding does not rely alone on the choices of the person speaking. A large part is dependent on our willingness to understand what another person is saying. If we do not attempt to understand a point of view because it contradicts our own, we are accountable for our listening failure. We must approach this stage of listening with an open mind and an effort to make sense of other people's messages. Just as we discuss speakers giving respectful consideration to their audiences in Chapter 4, an audience must give the same consideration. It is not only the key to more effective listening; it is an ethical obligation as noted in Chapter 2. Remember, communication is other-centered. Even as listeners, we strive to connect.

STAGE FOUR: RESPONDING

Remembering from Chapter 1 that communication is a transaction, responding becomes a natural part of the listening process. In conversation, it is obvious that having verbal and nonverbal responses is crucial, but the same is true in a public speaking format. According to Adler and Rodman, in *Understanding Human Communication*, giving observable feedback, i.e., responding, not only shows support and good will toward the speaker, it helps you, as a listener, to clarify your own understanding of the speaker's message.

STAGE FIVE: REMEMBERING

Finally, listening is considered effective when there is memory of the communication that has taken place. Unfortunately, by the time a message has been completed, studies show that listeners will only remember about half of it. Within hours, even more of the message will have been lost to the listeners. Indeed, effective listening is more of a challenge than most people realize. While it should not be our goal to remember every word of a message, we would definitely benefit from increasing the amount of effort we put into listening.

Many people question the importance of memory in the listening process. What are your thoughts on this criterion?

BEYOND THE FUNDAMENTALS ▬▬▬

LEVELS OF LISTENING

In the famous book *Seven Habits of Highly Effective People*, author Stephen Covey forwards the idea that effective people, "Seek first to understand, and then to be understood." Covey is essentially telling his audience how important it is to not only listen to others, but to understand their message. While this quotation, and other elements of this chapter, will serve to highlight the importance of listening, have you ever given thought to *why* you listen?

Communication scholars Wolvin and Coakley utilized some of their research to break down listening into various levels. It is interesting to also note that we can rapidly "flip" between the levels in one interaction. As you review the levels below, take the time to consider when you utilize that level of listening, and even make some determinations as to ways you can improve your listening skills as a whole.

Level	Definition	Example
Discriminative Listening	Using auditory (and visual) cues to discriminate between items	A mother is able to discriminate between the sound of her child saying "Mom" and another child saying the same
Comprehensive Listening	Listening with the intention of gaining knowledge	A student in a psychology classroom listens to her teacher discuss a specific theory
Empathic Listening	Listening to others as a form of emotional support	Your best friend is telling you about troubles he is experiencing with his fiancé
Critical Listening	Listening with the intent of evaluating/judging a message	The judging panel on the show *Shark Tank* carefully listen and evaluate the "pitch" from the contestant to determine if they want to partner up
Appreciative Listening	Listening as a form of enjoyment	Listening to the latest single from Coldplay while hanging out in your room

IN REVIEW
The five steps in the listening process are...
- Hearing
- Attending
- Understanding
- Responding
- Remembering

Questions:

Reflections:

As requested in the "Levels of Listening" box, list some of the times you engage the different levels of listening and think of some ways you can improve your skills for each level of listening.

IMPACTS OF LISTENING

ON COMMUNICATION

Listening, as an active process, impacts many facets of our lives. Because we spend so much of our communication time listening (over 50%), it impacts every aspect of our lives, including how informed we are, how effective we are at work or school, and how successful we are in relationships. Diane DiResta, training coach, speaker, and consultant to Fortune 500 companies, tells us in her 2005 book that listening reduces stress, improves relationships, increases sales, saves money, and empowers people to make better decisions. These are just some of the general benefits derived from effective listening. In a public speaking situation, both speaker and listener gain additional benefits.

Of the five benefits listed by DiResta, which is most important to you? How can you improve your listening to help you achieve that benefit?

Consider how your listening response can impact the person speaking.

ON PUBLIC SPEAKING

Who bears more responsibility for effective communication: the speaker or the listener?

As mentioned earlier in the chapter, it helps a public speaker to have an audience filled with active listeners. It becomes easier to speak when an audience is attending and responding in a positive way. While "the sender" is in control of his or herself, it is easier for a speaker to be confident with an audience who appears interested and supportive. A confident speaker is capable of speaking more clearly and enthusiastically. Not only is delivery affected, but content is affected as well. When a speaker is confident, it is easier to stay organized and develop a message in an enjoyable way. When you are presented with a "boring" speaker, ask yourself what your role might be. Remember, communication is a transactional process, and while you can't take responsibility for a boring speaker, you can help create an environment that promotes success. At times, you may be adding to your own boredom or the ineffectiveness of the speaker with your own actions.

BARRIERS TO EFFECTIVE LISTENING

With so many incentives to listen effectively, why are we still poor listeners? Why don't we make more of an effort to improve our listening? There are several reasons and we must work to overcome each one of them.

LACK OF KNOWLEDGE

The first reason, as mentioned earlier in the chapter, is we simply don't know how. Most people don't understand the listening process and lack training. Reading this chapter is your first step to improving. Learn about listening. Approach it with the attitude you would any other form of communication (or any skill you want to learn), as a challenging ability where you always have the potential to improve.

PRE-JUDGMENT

A second challenge associated with listening is our tendency to pre-judge a message. We reject messages without listening to them if we suspect they contradict our worldview. We tune out a message from a person we perceive as different, weird, radical, or wrong. We respond emotionally to certain words or topics. Or we spend time thinking of arguments before a speaker has completed the message, sometimes even before the speaker has completed a sentence. The second and third stages of listening, attending and understanding, require us to hear speakers out, to let them get through their message and take into consideration the context or any other variables before making a decision.

> **BEYOND OUR PERSPECTIVE** ━━━
>
> ### LISTENING TO OTHER COMMUNICATION STYLES
>
> Culture can be a factor in how people deliver speeches. Some countries, like Mexico and Japan, are considered to be *high-context cultures* because they deliver messages in a less direct way. They depend on context to help them interpret messages. For example, to directly refuse a request by saying "no" is uncommon. Very often refusals will be vague, but a listener from the same culture will be skilled in understanding that something like "it appears difficult" means "absolutely not." High-context cultures sometimes rely on stories or more roundabout ways of developing a point and sometimes do not make direct requests.
>
> While the United States is considered to be a low-context culture valuing directness, many high-context co-cultures exist within the United States. For example, we have different ethnic groups with different communication styles; we have styles that can be determined based on age, gender, ethnicity, and sometimes on factors like occupation.
>
> Although problems may arise when communication occurs between different styles, one style is not considered more effective than another. Effective speakers and listeners will be open to cultural styles different from their own.

Which of these barriers is the hardest for you to overcome? What can you do to overcome that barrier?

Why do you think it is so hard to listen to people who use communication styles that differ from our own?

FAILURE TO AVOID DISTRACTIONS

We may find ourselves arguing and questioning a speaker mentally, in part because we feel strongly about their topic, but also because of a third challenge tied to listening. We are easily distracted. Our brains are capable of processing information much more quickly than people are capable of speaking. The average person speaks at about 100–150 words per minute, but we can process information at the rate of 400–600 words per minute. This creates an "excess capacity" in listening where it's easy not only to argue with the speaker, but tempting to go over our grocery list. Unfortunately, while excess capacity is a real issue, the ability to listen while going over the grocery list is not real for most people. Remember, most people overestimate their listening skills and if you are really missing important parts of a message, you are likely to be unaware of it.

Finally, we can be distracted by our own lives, the stress of an upcoming test, the lack of sleep the previous night, hunger, thirst, or emotional upheaval in our personal lives. Any of these could easily occupy our minds and push out the message being sent by a speaker.

FEAR

Winston Churchill once said, "Courage is what it takes to stand up and speak. Courage is also what it takes to sit down and listen." Here he acknowledges one of the greatest barriers to effective listening: we are afraid of what we might hear. So, Churchill tells us it takes courage to listen effectively. There is an element of risk in true listening; you may be forced to acknowledge a problem or admit you have been wrong. Overcoming fear requires that we be willing to take that risk. Interacting with others means being willing to listen to what they have to say and give the message a fair and open-minded evaluation. Sometimes that will mean receiving a message we don't like or having to change our mind. That is just part of life in a world where we must deal with other people and therefore we must embrace that risk.

BEYOND OUR PERSPECTIVE ▬▬▬

"LISTENING" TO SIGN LANGUAGE

With approximately 22 million hearing impaired people, American Sign Language (ASL) is a commonly "spoken" language in the United States. For people who cannot hear, seeing becomes the first stage in listening and the process becomes 100% active. Listening to someone who speaks sign language requires looking directly at the speaker and paying close attention. With hearing, you may get some of the message without paying close attention, but ASL requires a listener to be focused and actually look at the speaker. When watching a speaker, in addition to getting the words, a listener gets more *context*, for example, facial expressions and body language that emphasize the personality of the speaker or the energy and passion attached to a message. The speaker also has an easier time reading the listener's responses.

IN REVIEW
The common barriers to effective listening include:

- Lack of knowledge
- Pre-judgment
- Failure to avoid distractions
- Fear

Questions:

Reflections:

Some teachers of American Sign Language classes give their hearing students earplugs to enhance their ability to *listen* to the signer. Using sight adds a richer dimension to the listening process. Deaf culture offers an example of fully engaged communication. Whether we hear or not, we always have the opportunity to be involved this fully in the listening process.

What does the discussion of sign language suggest to you about how we "listen" to stimuli we perceive through other senses (like sight, or even smell or touch)?

IMPROVING LISTENING

AS AN AUDIENCE MEMBER

Understanding the impacts, as well as some of the causes, of poor listening gives us a basis from which to improve. As audience members, we grow from listening and we help create a supportive climate for a speaker. There are several strategies we can use to improve, the first of which is to better understand listening as an active process and make a commitment to more fully participate in that process. Take it seriously by sitting up and keeping eye contact, by giving observable feedback, and by attempting to understand the message. Secondly, decide to listen with an open mind to all messages. This is not a decision to agree with the speaker; it is a decision to listen to what has been said before judging. It is a decision to be open to the possibility that the speaker may surprise us and offer new, interesting, and useful information. Once we have taken in all the information and made sure we understand what has been said, we can decide to accept or reject the speaker's message, but not before.

What is the one thing you think you could do which would most improve your listening skills?

Another important consideration in open-minded listening is that not all speakers have the same style of constructing or delivering a message. As you are learning in class, there is not one best way to present information. We may have a preferred style as both speakers and listeners, but speakers using styles different from what we might choose are not necessarily "bad" speakers. Some people are direct; others like to use stories and build to the main idea. Some speakers are very energetic; some have a laidback style. Some people speak with accents different from our own, or in different dialects. It can be tempting to pre-judge a speaker and discount their message based on these or other factors, but it is both unethical and an exercise in poor listening.

Third, use the "excess capacity" your brain has to focus on the speaker and message, rather than to think about an unrelated topic. If possible, take notes. Otherwise, listen for the speaker's main ideas, observe the speaker's verbal and nonverbal cues, think about how the message might relate to your life, and review the organization of the speech.

Finally, stay focused. Avoid internal distractions by being rested, taking care of yourself, and detaching from any issues that cannot be solved at the present moment. Acknowledge that the speaker is there in an attempt to connect to you, the audience. Respect the speaker's effort to have a communication moment with you by being in that moment.

AS A SPEAKER

As speakers, we count on our audiences to pay attention to us. When we understand the process of listening and the challenges associated with it, we can make speaking choices that help our audiences listen. People pay attention to what they believe is important and to information that is somehow linked directly to themselves. If you remember these principles in preparing and delivering your message, you'll be more likely to keep an audience listening. The chapter on audience analysis gives more details, but remember that connecting to your audience through your message and delivery will increase the amount of effective listening that occurs during your message.

SUMMARY

Most people see listening as a passive activity, but listening is the active process of recognizing, understanding, and accurately interpreting the messages communicated by others. It includes five stages: hearing, attending, understanding, responding, and remembering. When a person doesn't engage all the stages, the listening process is incomplete and ineffective. When listening is practiced effectively people have the potential to experience reduced stress, improved relationships, increased earnings, saved money, and empowered minds. When it comes to public speaking, effective listening improves the confidence of the speaker, leading to a more energized delivery and more coherent message. The listener can create a more supportive climate for the speaker, potentially gaining more information and understanding.

There are many incentives for listening effectively, but most people are challenged when it comes to effective listening, in part because they do not take it seriously. They lack training and do not fully understand the process. Even when making a serious effort, we have a tendency to pre-judge messages or become distracted by the fast pace of our brains and our lives. We can however take certain actions and make a commitment to become a better listener.

Has this chapter changed your perspective on the importance of creating a well-organized and easy-to-follow speech?

Executives from major corporations have stated that listening is an extremely important skill they look for when hiring. Why do you think listening is so important to an employer?

RESOURCES FOR BUILDING COMMUNICATION EFFECTIVENESS

LISTENING REFLECTION

1. I engage in multiple activities while listening to another person.

   ☐ Always   ☐ Often   ☐ Sometimes   ☐ Rarely   ☐ Never

   The reason for this is:

   The benefit of multi-tasking is:

   The problems with multi-tasking are:

2. I often go through the motions of listening (eye contact, head nodding, etc.) to convince the speaker I am paying attention even though I'm not.

   ☐ Always   ☐ Often   ☐ Sometimes   ☐ Rarely   ☐ Never

   The reason for this is:

   How can you help yourself to really listen, instead of just pretending to listen?

3. When it comes to public speaking, I believe it is the speaker's responsibility to keep me engaged. If I am bored or annoyed by what the speaker is saying, it is the speaker's own fault.

   ☐ Strongly Agree   ☐ Agree   ☐ Neutral   ☐ Disagree   ☐ Strongly Disagree

   Explain your rationale:

Considering your answer, are your expectations of speakers realistic? For example, do you expect them to read your mind and agree with all your beliefs? Do you find less value in their message when they do not have a perfect or "entertaining" presentation style?

What do you think are some of the possible reasons for why you have developed this attitude toward the responsibility of a speaker?

How do you think your attitude impacts your listening?

4. There are certain topics or viewpoints that are difficult for me to hear without becoming angry or defensive.

    ☐ Strongly Agree   ☐ Agree   ☐ Neutral   ☐ Disagree   ☐ Strongly Disagree

    What are those topics?

    Why do you think you react that way to those topics?

    What are some of the impacts of refusing to listen openly to those topics or viewpoints?

5. I become distracted from a message by the person who is giving it; for example, by their appearance or my previous experience with that person.

    ☐ Always   ☐ Often   ☐ Sometimes   ☐ Rarely   ☐ Never

    In what situations does this generally occur? Why?

    What have been (or might be) the impacts of this pre-judgment of the message?

6. What might be some ways that I can improve on my listening ability or habits?

CHAPTER 12

CRITICAL THINKING

Effective arguments are based on sound reasoning that resonates with the audience.

*People tend to have strong opinions about many topics
and therefore do not change their minds easily, so an effective
persuasive message will have to use effective arguments to make a case.*

You and two of your friends are trying to decide where to go for dinner. One friend wants Greek food, the other wants Mexican. It is going to be up to you to decide, but all your friends say is "Greek" and "Mexican"—neither tells you why they want that kind of food. That is the difference between an opinionated statement and an argument. An argument is an opinion backed by evidence and reasoning. For example, you may know that the friend who wants Greek food is allergic to common ingredients in Mexican food, so you decide the Greek restaurant is the better choice. You now have some information (your friend's allergy) and a basis for using that information (a belief that people should avoid things that make them sick). From there you can build an argument: you and your friends should go to the Greek restaurant because there both of your friends will be able to find something to eat that will not make them sick. (In the "Applying the Fundamentals" box on page on page 149 you can see this argument in a common graphic form.)

When you engage in persuasive speaking, you will need to build arguments such as this and in order to be successful they must be effective arguments. As we saw in Chapter 5, persuasive speeches address controversial topics where people have different opinions about what is correct and the goal of the speaker is to get the audience to agree with his or her position on the topic. In order to do this, the speaker must have strong arguments that convince the audience of the validity of the position expressed in the speech. In order to help you build strong persuasive speeches, this chapter explores the argument-building process and explores what makes a good quality argument.

THREE TYPES OF PROOFS

According to Aristotle, when you make an argument there are three basic modes of proof, or ways to defend your position: ethos, pathos, and logos. **Ethos** is your personal credibility. In Chapter 2 we discussed the characteristics of an ethical speaker. Exhibiting those characteristics as you speak allows the audience to see you as trustworthy. If the audience sees you as trustworthy, they are more likely to accept your arguments. Or, stated the other way, if the audience does not believe a speaker is trustworthy, they are likely to be suspicious of the arguments presented. They will wonder what the speaker is not telling them and how that information could negatively affect the validity of the argument being presented. **Pathos** refers to emotional proof. When we utilize pathos we are attempting to respond to the fundamental emotional needs of the audience and structure arguments that convince them that our position will help them meet those emotional and psychological needs. **Logos** refers to logical proof. When we engage in logos, we are attempting to develop our argument based on the rules of logic.

This is the third chapter which has discussed the concept of speaker credibility. Why do you think this is such an important concept in public speaking?

While all three types of proof are critical in a good quality argument, in Western culture the most persuasive arguments tend to be logical arguments that resonate with the audience. In many cases how well the speaker connects with the audience will be a function of pathos, but that will depend on the rhetorical construction of the speech. In some ways, pathos, like ethos, becomes an issue that emerges from the quality of the construction of the speech (although it is possible to construct a quality emotional argument in much the same way one would construct a logical argument). Because issues of pathos and ethos can be addressed as a speech is constructed and many of those concepts have been discussed previously in this text, we will, for the most part, focus on the development of logical arguments in this chapter.

Which of Aristotle's three modes of proof do you consider to be the most important? The most effective? Why?

As we focus on those specific types of arguments, we note, again, that persuasive speeches are an attempt by a speaker to convince an audience that they should look at a situation differently, that they should think or act in a particular way that is counter to how they have previously thought or acted. People do not change their mind easily, so speakers need to build a convincing case for their positions. In order to do that a speaker must build arguments, detailed positional statements, which not only express an opinion but provide reasons why someone should accept that opinion as right and appropriate.

TOULMIN'S MODEL OF ARGUMENT

Why do we still regard Aristotle's three rhetorical proofs as important elements of persuasion more than 2,000 years after he first proposed them?

The basic argument consists of three steps. First, an argument is based on an opinionated statement that cannot be readily verified. For example, someone could say: "College students should be required to take a music class each semester." Obviously, someone else could say: "Colleges should not require any music classes." It is important to note that these statements cannot be verified. You cannot look in an encyclopedia and find out if a music class should be required, as you could, for example, look up the population of the United States. If a statement can be verified like that, it cannot be an argument. For example, it is not an argument to say that as of November 2014 the movie *Avatar* had the largest theater box office of all time because we can look that up. You could build an argument around the opinion that *Avatar* is the best movie of all time. You cannot look that up, but you can build a case to support that position, perhaps using theater box office as a criterion for greatness.

Merely having an opinion does not create an argument. That argument must be supported by some facts. Notice that in the previous paragraph we said you could not make an argument that *Avatar* had the largest theater box office ever. However, we could use that fact to support our contention that *Avatar* is the best movie ever. Think of it this way: you have stated your opinion to a friend and that friend has said, "Prove it, show me something that would convince me that you are right," so you go to the library and find some information that you think supports your position. For example, in a debate about the role of music classes in elementary education, the person who expresses the opinion that local school districts must maintain music classes even in these tight budgetary times is likely to encounter some skeptical people who will need some convincing. That person needs to do some research to find information that supports that position. In doing that research the person advancing this position may discover some recent work done by Canadian researchers which suggests music training improves memory and cognitive skills in younger children. The person making the argument can now back up the opinion with this information.

But the person building the argument is not done. More than likely the reaction of the skeptics will be: so what, why does that information support your opinion? So, in order to complete the argument, the arguer must also explain why the information really does support the opinion. For example, the arguer could point out that cognitive and memory skills are often cited as core skills that are necessary for all people to be able to learn and therefore schools are often expected to work on developing these skills from an early age. Likewise, if someone used the box office performance of *Avatar* to back the opinion that it was the best movie ever, the information would only support the opinion if theater-based ticket sales were a legitimate measure of greatness, and the speaker would have to convince the audience of that.

Before we move on, we should note that in many cases this connection between the opinion and the information is, in fact, another opinion. That is not unusual. Complex arguments, like the ones you will be making in your speeches, generally require multiple interrelated arguments in order to convince the audience. However, for the sake of simplicity we will focus on just a single argument for now (but you can see how arguments chain together in the last example in the "Applying the Fundamentals" box on page on page 150).

This step of developing the connection is often the hardest step for us when building an argument. Ironically, that happens not because the step is so difficult, but because in some ways the step is too easy. The research process is basically intuitive, meaning that when we look for information to support our opinion, we seek out information which we believe does, in fact, support our claim. That, of course, is obvious and that is the problem. We do not go to the library and think, "I need to support this opinion, so what is some trivial fact which has nothing to do with this topic?" Rather, what we think is: "I want a strong argument, so I want the best information to support my position." So, when we find something, and we say "this is it," that statement is based on some intuitive belief that the information supports our opinion. The problem is, while research is largely intuitive, arguments are not. Within an argument there is never any piece of evidence that inherently supports the opinion. If a piece of information inherently supports a position, that position is a fact, not an argument. As we noted before, you cannot build an argument around a position that is verifiable, so, by definition, if the information merely verifies the position, we do not have an argument. By extension, then, any evidence we use in an argument supports the opinion only by some manner of interpretation. That interpretation seems obvious to us when we do our research, but in order for us to have a strong argument we need to be able to explain that connection to the audience and in order to do that we need to get past the "this is obviously good stuff" reaction we have in our research and be able to explain why it is good stuff and to do that we need to think carefully about our thought process that led us to select that piece of supporting material. And, because it is so obvious to us, thinking that through can actually be quite difficult. That is why this is where you should focus a lot of your mental energy when developing a persuasive speech.

This description of an argument is based on a model of argument developed by Stephen Toulmin, and hence is referred to as Toulmin's Model of Argument. The opinion we advance is called the **claim**. The evidence we use to support the claim has been referred to as data, grounds, evidence, or supporting material. There are subtle differences in those terms, which are not very important here. For simplicity, in this text we will use the term **data**. Finally, the connection between the claim and the data, the reason why the data supports the claim, is known as the **warrant**. These three steps make up the first triad in Toulmin's model, and that triad defines the basic argument.

IN REVIEW
The basic elements of Toulmin's model (the first triad) are...
- Claim
- Data
- Warrant

Questions:

Reflections:

APPLYING THE FUNDAMENTALS

VISUALIZING ARGUMENTS

In Chapter 8 we discussed how outlines allow you to visually see your organization process and then noted that visual images provide a way for you to check the quality of your organization. We can treat arguments in much the same way by using a visual model for the argument (although the visual model of the argument does not translate directly to the outline). Toulmin's model is often depicted as shown below. Such a model allows you to see how the parts of your argument fit together and also provides visual evidence of the importance of the warrant: it is the foundation of the argument and ties the data and the claim together.

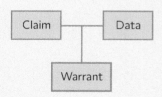

Here are some of the arguments discussed in this chapter, diagrammed using Toulmin's model, so you can visually see how a whole argument fits together. Note that the last example on the next page shows how sometimes you have to chain multiple arguments together to completely develop your position.

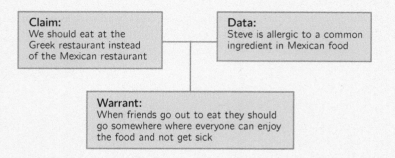

Why is it important to explain your warrants during a persuasive speech?

Identify the Data, Warrant, and Claim in the following arguments (work only to identify the components of the argument; don't worry about the quality of the argument).

The federal government should increase funding to the space program because the United States is lagging in scientific achievements.

Claim:

Data:

Warrant:

The state has cut funds for road repairs and hence it is more important that we adopt a mandatory motorcycle helmet law.

Claim:

Data:

Warrant:

Alternative medical treatments do more harm than good. People often delay necessary treatment expecting these untested approaches to provide a cure.

Claim:

Data:

Warrant:

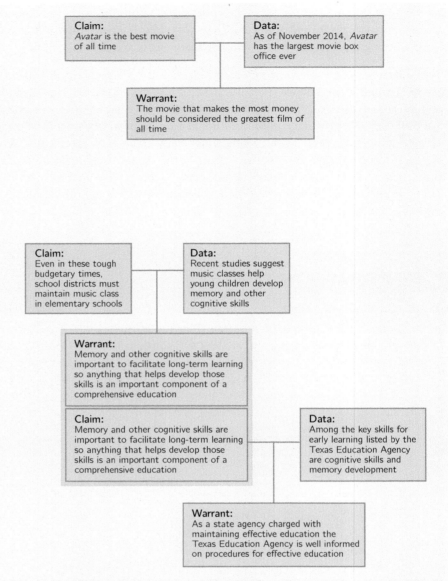

These arguments represent various levels of quality and after you have read this chapter you should have a better idea of how to evaluate that quality. You should also find it is easier to evaluate the quality of your arguments when you can see them like this and that is why it would be useful to model the arguments you think you will be using in your speech before actually adding them to your speech.

BEYOND THE FUNDAMENTALS

THE SECOND TRIAD

According to Toulmin, the data, warrant, and claim make up only part of the argument. In the full model, there are three more components to an argument. While these are more advanced concepts, which may not be entirely appropriate for a basic course, being aware of these components of the model can help you evaluate the quality of your argument. In fact, often you can use the concepts from Toulmin's second triad to better present a basic argument.

The elements in the second triad are the qualifier, the rebuttal, and the backing. The **qualifier** acknowledges that most argumentation is probabilistic, meaning that you will not be able to show that your claim is 100% true, but you can establish a high likelihood that your argument is true. The qualifier indicates the level of certainty you have in your argument. Often qualifiers will be expressed in the claim. For example, instead of saying "Smoking causes cancer," you may say "People who smoke are much more likely to get cancer than people who do not smoke." "Much more likely" is a qualifying term. In this case you are not saying that every smoker *will* get cancer, but you are indicating a much greater chance than if the person did not smoke. That is the qualifier.

Rebuttals attempt to anticipate and respond to the most likely objections to the argument. For example, you may think that when you say "Cigarette smoking causes cancer," someone will suggest that it is not the smoking but rather some environmental or personality issue that causes the cancer. You can address that by making your claim "All other things being equal, cigarette smoking increases a person's risk of getting cancer." Phrased in that way, you are acknowledging (and addressing) a key counterargument.

Finally, **backing** refers to cases where the warrant needs to be supported with additional data and arguments. In this chapter we have talked about chains of arguments where the warrant in one argument becomes the claim in the next argument, as shown in the last example on page 150. This is another way of looking at the issue of backing.

TYPES OF REASONING

In order to ensure that you have good quality arguments, you need to evaluate each component of the argument. However, since anyone is basically entitled to any opinion, there is not much evaluation that can be done to the claim. You can, however, evaluate the quality of the data by making sure you have quality supporting material, as discussed in Chapter 6. The new skill in this chapter is evaluating the quality of the warrants.

Warrants can be evaluated on two different levels. First, there is what is called field-specific analysis. This is essentially where you determine if the argument would be accepted as valid by experts in the field. Recall in Chapter 6 we discussed that research not only helps you gather information for your speech, but it also helps you learn more about your topic area. Here is one benefit of developing that knowledge. As you become more familiar with the topic area, or field, you begin to understand how people who work in that field generally think about arguments in that field. Knowing that, you can determine if the people who know your topic best would consider your argument valid. That is essentially the focus of field-specific analysis.

The second level is more generic. In this case, we look at the nature of the connection between the claim and the data. Many different arguments which support different claims with different data rely on similar warrants. For example, as you drive to school you notice a person sending a text message while driving and think that person will cause an accident. You pass another car and see someone smoking and figure that person will get cancer. Finally, you get to school and pass some students studying in the hall and assume they will get good grades on an upcoming test. The claims (a distracted driver will cause an accident, a smoker will get cancer, and conscientious students will get good grades) are all different, as is the data (observing someone texting, someone smoking, and students studying), but the connection, the warrant, is the same (one thing will cause another). These would all be based on causal warrants or causal reasoning, and all causal reasoning must meet particular standards of logic to be considered good quality reasoning. It is this level of analysis—identifying the connection between the data and the claim and applying common principles of logic to determine the quality of the warrant—that will be our focus in this chapter. Causal reasoning is one such connection. So is sign reasoning, reasoning by example, reasoning by analogy, and reasoning by authority. There are many others, but these are the ones you are most likely to use in your speeches (or encounter in your research), so we will examine the tests of those types of reasoning here.

REASONING BY CAUSE

Causal reasoning involves inferring that a certain factor produces a particular effect. Think of the old adage that one thing leads to another—that is the basis of causal reasoning. You have a causal warrant when your argument is based on a position that says an observed behavior (your data) will lead to your claim. So, in the example in the last paragraph, the warrants are: driving while distracted causes accidents, smoking causes cancer, and studying causes students to get good grades.

When evaluating the quality of causal reasoning there are two questions you should ask yourself: Is the alleged cause truly relevant to the effect, and are there other factors that could influence the relationship? The first question asks if the two events are really related. For example, every person who had a glass of water in 1865 is dead, but the water did not cause them to die (it was simply old age). So, we do not see any significant relationship between the cause and the effect.

The second question gets at an issue known as **correlation**. Here the two events may be related in some way, but it is not a direct causal relationship. Rather, both events are the result of some third event. For example, it is probably true that when ice cream sales increase in a park, so does crime, but it is unlikely that the ice cream causes the crime. More than likely, hot weather brings more people to the park to enjoy ice cream, and to be victims of crime. And, in fact, there are some statistics which suggest that petty crimes are more common in hot weather. So, the causal relationship is not between the ice cream and the crime. It is between weather and ice cream consumption and weather and park attendance and weather and crime. In order to argue for a causal relationship, you must demonstrate that other likely intervening factors have been eliminated. This is the basis of a controlled scientific experiment. Researchers try to be sure that the only thing that varies in the experiment is the one factor they want to study. That way they know any changes in other factors are more than likely the result of changes in the factor they are studying, because everything else remained the same.

REASONING BY SIGN

Sign reasoning is similar to causal reasoning in that it is based on a close relationship between the data and the claim. However, in this case the argument is not that one thing caused another to happen. Rather, with sign reasoning you are arguing that the presence of one variable (your data) indicates the presence of another. For example, when you see leaves falling off the trees you claim that it is fall. You believe that, not because leaves falling off a tree cause it to be fall, but, rather, because leaves falling off the tree indicate that the season of autumn has come. Think of it this way: if it were a hot summer day, you would not go out in the front yard and shake leaves off a tree believing that would cool the temperature down. To think that way would be to suggest a causal relationship, and we understand that is not true. However, leaves falling off the tree may be an indication of what season it is and that is the basis of sign reasoning. Or, consider this example: in the last paragraph we discuss that there is no causal relationship between the sale of ice cream and the amount of crime in a park. Yet, the police chief in that city may still want to know how much ice cream the local vendor is ordering, because the size of the ice cream order may indicate how many people the vendor thinks will come to the park, and that may be a reasonable determinant of how much crime the police chief should expect.

When engaging in sign reasoning you can determine the quality of that reasoning by asking yourself two questions: is there a logical link between the indicator variable and the claim, and does the presence of the first variable always and only lead to the presence of the second variable? The first question simply asks if there is a logical connection between the indicator and the claim. Simply put, does it seem reasonable to say that leaves falling off the trees are a sign of fall? Likewise, if you walked into your class one day and saw your fellow classmates intently studying their books and notes, it would not be unreasonable to think that there was going to be a test or quiz that day. On the other hand, let's say you and your friend are looking for a place to eat. You come to a nice looking restaurant with this sign out front:

Your friend refuses to eat there because "restaurants called 'Mom's' always have bad food." This is literally sign reasoning. Your friend is saying that the sign is an indicator of the quality of the food. Such a claim is probably unreasonable. The quality of the food probably has a lot more to do with where mom learned to cook (assuming "Mom" is even really doing the cooking).

The second question raises a more complicated issue. The sign must always and only lead to the claim. So, for example, can leaves falling off trees only be a sign of fall, or stated differently, do leaves only fall off the trees in fall? The answer, of course, is no. Leaves may also fall off trees when it is windy or when a tree is dying. The problem is, there are very few signs that indicate one and only one thing, and most of those are basically issues of scientific law (which would be virtually factual and not, as we have noted, the subject of persuasion). For example, when you drop a pen, it falls to the floor—a sign that gravity is present. And, as far as we know, gravity is the one physical force that pulls objects down to the earth. But, because we are so sure about the fact that there is not a second force that causes objects to fall, we really do not need to persuade anyone about the existence and role of gravity. This situation would seem to create a trap for the arguer. If you can argue for the type of relationship this question implies is necessary, there is no reason for the argument; if you cannot argue for that kind of relationship then your reasoning is weak. So, how do we get around that situation? Usually, the arguer can address this issue by using multiple signs. In this case, the argument is that any one of the signs could indicate multiple things, and probably different things, but all of the signs only have one thing in common. And, since all of the signs are present, it is legitimate to say that, taken together, the presence of all of the signs legitimately indicate the presence of the claim.

We should note one last important fact about sign reasoning. Remember we said that in your persuasive speeches you often end up with chains of arguments where one argument supports the claims inherent in the warrants of a previous argument. Sign reasoning is a good example of the necessity of building those chains. To claim that students studying hard is an indication of an impending test or that restaurant signs have nothing to do with the quality of the food probably will requires additional arguments. So, once you make this argument, you would present another argument in which you supported your claim that what you are claiming is a legitimate sign should be accepted by the audience as a legitimate sign.

In sign reasoning, the sign must always—and only—lead to the claim. Leaves, for example, may fall off a tree because of the season, the wind, or a disease. So to say that falling leaves always indicate the season of fall is faulty reasoning.

REASONING BY EXAMPLE

The next kind of reasoning we can look at is reasoning by example. In this case, a person argues that one or more specific cases allows us to make inferences about a whole group. So, if you go to a store and a clerk is rude to you, and you believe that all of the clerks in the store will be rude to you, you are relying on reasoning by example. The basic issues associated with reasoning by example have to do with the quality of the cases (or examples) that you use. For one thing, the examples should be representative or typical of the whole. We would not want to draw conclusions about the quality of the help we get in the store on the basis of one clerk who is about to be fired for treating customers poorly. That clerk would not seem to represent fairly all the employees of that store.

We would also want to know that we have enough examples. Chances are that at any store there will be one bad clerk, but is that person the exception, rather than the norm? By using multiple examples, we can start to detect a pattern. When we try to get help from three clerks and all are rude to us that could be the indication of a pattern that allows us to draw some conclusions about that store's approach to customer service (or lack thereof). How many examples are enough? Often that can be difficult to determine. Surveys are one type of reasoning by example and when doing a survey there are formulas to help researchers determine the number of examples they need. But, often we are using reasoning by example in more informal situations, where those formulas will not be much help, and argumentation scholars are not much help in these situations either. All will acknowledge that a sufficient number of examples are necessary for a good argument, but few will truly quantify what that means. However, in public speaking, we can get some good guidance for these types of arguments. Remember, in public speaking your goal is to convince the audience you are right and they are wrong, and most people will resist admitting that they are wrong. So, the question becomes: how many examples would it take to convince an open-minded audience that those examples represent the entirety of the class you are discussing? Because, in the end, the two issues really merge: the goal of having multiple examples is to ensure a representative sample, and we can address this concern in two ways. First, we can use a collection of examples which, in total, seems to cover all aspects of the class. In other words, rather than relying on one single clerk, you would base your conclusion on multiple employees and experiences, and those examples and experiences should be diverse (different age of clerks, different level of employees, different times of day, different degrees of busyness in the store, and so on). The second way to think about the number of examples necessary is to think about the degree of persuasion necessary to bring the audience around to your point of view. Generally, the more significant your argument, the more convincing that will be necessary, and the better your examples will need to be. For example, imagine you are walking through a shopping mall with a friend and you pass a store where you have had a couple of bad experiences and you tell your friend you are not going to shop there anymore. Your friend is not likely to see that as a big deal and may not question the fact that your sample is relatively small and perhaps not representative. However, if you tell your friend that you have had these bad experiences and now you are starting a campaign to put that store out of business because of its poor customer service, your friend might now be more concerned about the quality of your examples. So, if you can point out that you have been in the store many times, you have dealt with salespeople and supervisors, you have been there on weekdays and weekends, day time and night time, and you have been there when the store was crowded and when it was empty and despite all of these different experiences the employees have always been rude to you, you have a better chance of convincing your friend that something needs to be done about the store and its approach to customer service.

REASONING BY ANALOGY

Another type of reasoning that is similar to reasoning by example is reasoning by analogy. Reasoning by analogy is based on a comparison. The argument here is that since something is true in one situation, it will also be true in another similar situation. So, like reasoning by example, this type of reasoning begins with a specific case, but in reasoning by analogy, the conclusion is about another specific case. When you say, "if you can play tennis, you can play racquetball," you are making an analogy. You are saying that something that is true in one case is true in another (you have a set of physical skills that allow you to play tennis, and those same skills will allow you to play racquetball). Note that your claim is only about one other sport; you are not saying that people who can play tennis can play any sport. That type of generalization would be reasoning by example.

Reasoning by analogy may be the easiest to evaluate. Quite simply, if you want to make an analogy, you need to look at the two things you want to compare, see how they are similar and how they are different, and then be prepared to argue that the similarities are more important than the differences. For example, let's say you want to argue that, because campaigns for most local political offices last only a few months, we should be able to shorten the national campaign season. How are these two events similar? They both involve candidates seeking election for public office. The campaign and election rules are fundamentally similar, although that also highlights one of the most significant differences between these campaigns: national campaigns tend to be much larger in scope in terms of people to reach, resources necessary, and the issues to discuss. So, what is more important: the similarities in function and basic rules or the difference in scope? As we have said before, in a persuasive speech you often need a chain of arguments to support your thesis and here would be another case of that. In order to support your analogy, you would have to make another argument defending the claim that the similarities in terms of function and basic rules would be critical and scope a much more minor issue.

When you argue that what is true in one case will be true in another case—such as an ability to play tennis means an ability to play racquetball—you are making an analogy.

REASONING BY AUTHORITY

The final type of argument that we will look at here is reasoning by authority. In this case, rather than taking factual supporting material as our data and developing our own claim and warrant, we rely on a complete argument made by someone else. So let's say that your college recently had a significant tuition increase and you want to argue that the increase was a result of cuts in state aid to schools. You could make a causal argument that one event (a cut in state aid) caused the other (an increase in tuition). Or you could argue by analogy, noting that other colleges have experienced large tuition increases when state aid was cut. Or you could argue by authority and claim the tuition increase was the result of a cut in state aid by quoting the College President's address to the board on the issue. In the last case, you are relying on the quality of the College President as the source of your data to support your argument. In order to make that a good argument, you would want to be able to do two things.

First, you would need to convince your audience that the President was a credible source. Remember in Chapter 6 we looked at what makes good quality evidence. Here you would want to be very open with your audience and share whatever information you have to demonstrate that you have a good source. This should be relatively easy to do because, as we also noted in that chapter, you always need to provide a source citation when you present information and that citation should allow the audience to determine the quality of the information. The difference here is you may choose to provide even more information about the source, as the qualifications now become central to the argument.

The second thing you could do to improve the quality of reasoning by authority is identify and defend the type of reasoning your source used. It is possible that the College President used in her address to the board the causal or analogy warrants that you could have used to support this point. So, you can identify the type of reasoning and demonstrate that the warrants in that reasoning are sound. For example, tell your audience that the President made a basic cause and effect argument (state aid went down so tuition had to go up) and show how she established the legitimacy of that relationship (i.e., how did she show that she had controlled for correlative factors).

It is that last step in demonstrating the quality of reasoning by authority that makes it so critical that you be familiar with all types of reasoning. Many speakers will rely on reasoning by authority because in many ways it is the easiest form of reasoning: an expert says something is true and we rely on that in our speech. However, in evaluating the quality of that expert's opinion we need to be able to determine the quality of his or her conclusion and to do that we must be able to identify and evaluate the reasoning that expert used. So, even if we are using reasoning by authority in our speech, we will need to know about other types of reasoning to evaluate the quality of our sources.

FALLACIES

So far we have looked at good strong data and warrants working together to make good arguments. However, sometimes there is a problem with the argument that undermines the quality of the argument, and then it is referred to as a fallacy. Sometimes the data or warrants are flawed in some way, which undermines the quality of the arguments. In some cases, the connection between the data and the claim is simply flawed. Other fallacies are the result of poor efforts to use some of the types of reasoning discussed previously, resulting in poor quality warrants. In still other cases a speaker attempts to make strong pathos appeals, but the appeals are similarly flawed. In other cases, persuaders do not pick their words carefully and end up misrepresenting the argument. This section will examine three broad classifications of fallacies. As you learn about these types, think critically about the examples and what could be done to the argument to make the statements correct, as opposed to false.

IN REVIEW
The five types of reasoning discussed in this chapter are reasoning by...

* Cause
* Sign
* Example
* Analogy
* Authority

...and for each there are tests to be sure they are being used properly.

Questions:

Reflections:

FALLACIES OF DATA

As you have learned previously in this chapter, there is a natural order to arguments. Persuaders develop claims to support their purpose, and then offer data that they think will back up that claim. While this sounds like a fairly simple task, some fallacies committed by persuaders result from using data that does not necessarily, upon deeper examination, support the claim that was provided. Specifically, there are two main types of fallacies related to data.

BEGGING THE QUESTION

One common fallacy of data is the fallacy of begging the question. You may be familiar with the phrase, "you should never define a word with the word you are trying to define." The reason you do not is simple: the person you are speaking to still has no idea what the word means, so the definition will still not make sense. It is very similar in the example of an argument. In this case the arguer does not provide data to support the claim, either by not providing any data or by restating the claim as data. Whenever a speaker uses phrases like "it is obvious," look for the fallacy of begging the question. Never is an argument obvious. As we have seen throughout this chapter an argument needs to be developed and the claim supported with data and warrants. So, we should never say an argument is obvious because it is not.

NON SEQUITUR

Logically, when a piece of information is offered to support a claim, it should naturally be related. However, *non sequitur* occurs when the data presented has nothing to do with the claim, or does not support the claim being made. To be even more specific, when translated from Latin *non sequitur* means "no sequence" or "does not follow." An example of this fallacy can be seen in the following argument. The arguer claims that teenage pregnancy in America is increasing and uses data from a 2012 Yahoo Shine article that shows the teenage pregnancy rate in the U.S. is more than two and a half times that of Canada. The problem here is that in order to show an increase in teenage pregnancy, the arguer must compare current and past teenage pregnancy data in the United States, not American and Canadian teenage pregnancy data. So, the data, while related to the claim (because it is about teen pregnancy), does not support the actual specific claim being made (in fact, that Shine article actually shows that the teen pregnancy rate in the United States is declining).

FALLACIES OF WARRANTS

Hopefully the data that you utilize to support your claim makes logical sense, but that is only part of the story. The other element that needs to be considered is the use of a strong warrant to help show your audience how a claim and a piece of data are connected. What follows are examples of fallacies committed through poor warrants.

POST HOC FALLACY

The first of this type of fallacy is what we call the *post hoc* fallacy, which occurs when we make a weak causal connection. *Post hoc* is short for *post hoc ergo propter hoc*, which is Latin for "after this, therefore because of this." In other words, this fallacy occurs when you assume that because one event follows another, the first event caused the second. For example, you may have been walking into the math building at school and a black cat crossed in front of you, and then you proceeded to fail your exam that day. Likely you didn't fail that test for that reason, but you might assume those two events are related. If you do, however, you would probably be committing the *post hoc* fallacy because just because your failure came after you saw the black cat doesn't necessarily mean the black cat caused you to fail the test. Similarly, remember in our discussion of causal reasoning we talked about the fact that crime probably increases in a park when ice cream sales increase. However, just because the increase in crime comes after the sale in ice cream does not mean that the sale of ice cream causes the crime. To suggest otherwise is to commit the *post hoc* fallacy.

© Doubt.It Comic

HASTY GENERALIZATION

Just as poor causal reasoning can lead to a fallacy, so too can poor reasoning by example. In this case the fallacy is referred to as hasty generalization. Remember we said to have effective reasoning by example we need a sufficient number of representative examples. We cannot realistically tell if the Chicago Cubs will have a great (or poor) season after only ten games, especially because a baseball season lasts over five months. If we either do not have enough samples or properly representative examples to justify our conclusion, then we commit the fallacy of hasty generalization.

FALSE ANALOGY

Poor reasoning by analogy leads to a false analogy. Remember an analogy is justified if the similarities between the two cases are such that a comparison makes sense. However, when we cannot legitimately compare the two cases because of substantial differences, we commit a false analogy. You may be familiar with the saying, "comparing apples to oranges." That statement implies that there are key critical differences between two items that an arguer is trying to compare. For example, a student may argue that because one of the large universities in their state offers graduate degrees, the local community college should offer graduate degrees. The problem is, in some states the degrees a community college can offer are limited by law. So, there is a significant legal difference between a community college and a comprehensive university. That difference undermines the legitimacy of the comparison and thus we have a false analogy.

Identify the fallacy (or potential fallacy) in the following statements. What information would you need to determine for sure if this is a fallacy or not, and if you determined it was, how would you fix it?

I'm going to get a loan from Money Mutual because Montel Williams says they are the best place to get a loan.

There is no reason to make changes to social support programs like welfare and Social Security; they have worked fine since the Great Depression.

We shouldn't allow bow hunting in our community. Ted Nugent bow hunts and he is a rock star and we all know how irresponsible rock stars are.

The United States must use military force to maintain stability in the Middle East. If they choose to do nothing, the region will plunge into chaos.

Identify the fallacy (or potential fallacy) in the following statements. What information would you need to determine for sure if this is a fallacy or not, and if you determined it was, how would you fix it? (continued)

It is obvious our community college is the best in the state.

It's time to legalize the use of marijuana—a 2013 Gallup poll shows that almost 60% of Americans support such action.

During these difficult times it is more important than ever that governments operate like businesses.

Passive euthanasia reduces our respect for life which will lead to legalized active euthanasia and eventually the acceptance of murder in certain circumstances.

My math teacher can't relate to college-age students. There are no good teachers at this school.

DOUBTFUL AUTHORITY

Finally, poor reasoning by authority results in the fallacy of doubtful authority. Here, the argument is based on the quality of the source of the data, but the quality of the source is poor. This could be either because the source is unqualified or biased. Many television commercials are an example of the first issue. An actor, who plays a doctor on television, offers medical advice. The problem is, the person is an actor, not a doctor or any other trained professional in the medical community, and hence the person is not qualified to give medical advice and is hence a doubtful authority. The second situation occurs when the source of the information is biased. For example, if you wanted to argue that there were no known health risks associated with smoking and your source of that data was a cigarette company executive, the source would be weak because such statements serve the interests of the executive. In this case, we would have a doubtful authority due to issues of bias.

FALLACIES OF APPEAL

While the fallacies mentioned previously are directly correlated to either poor data or weak warrants, there are also other types of fallacies that are not associated with any particular form of reasoning. Some of the following fallacies are related to poor attempts at pathos appeals while others are a result of ineffective word choices.

AD HOMINEM

The first example of a fallacy not directly associated with any particular form of reasoning is the *ad hominem* fallacy. This fallacy occurs when a person attempts to support an argument by attacking a person associated with the issue. Ultimately, the speaker is trying to create contempt or dislike between the audience and the opposition. One genre where these fallacies are prevalent are political campaign advertisements (more specifically "attack ads"). Candidate "A" will say negative things about Candidate "B's" personal life, finances, etc., in an attempt to make the public dislike "B" and not vote for him. When this happens, an *ad hominem* is committed.

FALSE DILEMMA

Another common fallacy is the false dilemma. Arguers commit the fallacy of false dilemma when they suggest that a situation presents a choice between two alternatives, when in fact there are many alternatives. Often a speaker will use this strategy to argue for a particular action by arguing that another action is undesirable. The presented logic is since it is a bad idea to do one thing, we must do the other. That strategy is only legitimate, however, if the speaker can prove that there are in fact only two alternatives.

AD POPULUM

Speakers will sometimes attempt to influence audience choices by using public opinion as a base. When a speaker appeals to public opinion as a form of support, the *ad populum*, or bandwagon fallacy, is committed. This is considered a fallacy because the argument confuses logical support for a position with popular opinion. A presidential candidate, for example, may decide to speak out against capital punishment because their data shows 70% of voters are opposed, and speaking against it would likely help garner more votes.

APPEAL TO TRADITION

You may be familiar with the phrase, "If it ain't broke, don't fix it." This statement brings up another fallacy: the appeal to tradition. This fallacy assumes that breaking away from the status quo would be damaging, and replaces a logical reason to resist change. For example, family traditions during the holidays, such as playing Pictionary after Thanksgiving dinner, or driving around to see holiday decorations on Christmas Eve, have likely been around for generations, and people seem comfortable and complacent with them. When a new idea is offered, it is often met with some opposition. Recently, professional baseball instituted video challenges to certain calls made by umpires (the most substantial change to the rules of the game in quite some time). Baseball purists argued that this system was not needed because umpires (and hence, human error) had been a part of the game since the game's creation. Since these baseball purists relied on the history of the game as a defense against change, the appeal to tradition was committed.

SLIPPERY SLOPE

The slippery slope fallacy is also called the "snowball effect" or "domino effect" fallacy, asserting that one event will lead to some sort of catastrophic outcome. When a slippery slope is used, it attempts to play off the fears of the audience. An arguer may claim that the rising price of college textbooks will result in students dropping out of school, which will make it difficult for them to get a job, which will lead to more unemployment payments, which will place a greater strain on the government budget. As a college audience, you may hear this and feel shocked/startled or otherwise moved by that statement, and do not want that to happen to your fellow students. While it is natural to assume that some may not be able to afford textbooks, the likelihood of students dropping out of school seems a bit of a logical stretch and each step the arguer takes past that point becomes even more of a stretch.

With all of the fallacy types mentioned in this chapter (data, warrant, and appeal), it is imperative to consider the impact that using any of them may have on your overall persuasive message. As ethical persuaders with moral character, we are tasked with not only developing a logical argument, but also making sure the connections and appeals we make within the argument are valid and realistic. The good news is that even if you notice that you are using a fallacy, with some critical thinking and reframing you will likely be able to make the statement more accurate, and thus, more persuasive.

SUMMARY

In this chapter we have looked at how to build effective arguments, some common types of reasoning, and a number of common fallacies. There are other forms of reasoning and other fallacies that we have not explored. Ultimately, the key is to be sure that your arguments follow the rules of logic and seem valid to the audience. If you can develop those kinds of arguments, you have a good chance of convincing your audience that your arguments are valid and they should accept the position stated in your thesis.

RESOURCES FOR BUILDING COMMUNICATION EFFECTIVENESS

ARGUMENT DEVELOPMENT WORKSHEET

POSITION:		
Claim	Data	Warrant
		Warrant
	Data	Warrant
		Warrant
Claim	Data	Warrant
		Warrant
	Data	Warrant
		Warrant
Claim	Data	Warrant
		Warrant
	Data	Warrant
		Warrant

CHAPTER 12

CHAPTER 13

USING PRESENTATION AIDS

What we see impacts what we hear.

Visual imagery adds impact to many messages. Consider the emotional difference between hearing that 168 people, including 19 children, died in the Oklahoma City Bombing and seeing 149 empty full-sized chairs and 19 smaller ones lined up in the field where the Murrah Federal Building once stood.

Describe a situation where something made more sense to you, or became more real, when you could see an image of it, rather than just hearing it described.

When one of the authors visited the Oklahoma City National Memorial and Museum, the experience began by sitting in a room listening to the only known recording of the bombing: a tape recording of a government meeting that was being held across the street on the day of the bombing. Museum-goers heard the mundane functioning of government interrupted by the explosion and then the chaos that ensued. A few special effects heightened the experience, which was quite powerful. But then the visitors left the room and entered the actual display space of the Museum. Here people could see artifacts from the bombing: clothes and personal effects and even an unclaimed teddy bear. There was a display of the media coverage and the pictures that populated the front pages of newspapers. One room in the building which houses the museum (and which was damaged in the explosion) had been preserved in its post-bombing state so people could see the destruction caused by the bomb. There was the remarkable display of origami cranes which became the symbol of hope after the tragedy and even a wall lined with political cartoons that were published after the bombing. Then, outside the museum the author visited the Outdoor Symbolic Memorial and one of the most visually compelling parts of that Memorial: The Field of Empty Chairs. There 168 empty chairs offer a visual depiction of the human toll of the bombing. Nineteen of the chairs are smaller in size to represent the children who were killed in the bombing. The nine rows of silent chairs, and especially the 19 smaller chairs, provide another significant and emotional visual image of the events of April 19, 1995. For the author, the audio tape may have been powerful, but the visual displays were almost emotionally overwhelming.

The emotional impact of this visit speaks to the power of visual images, something we sometimes tacitly acknowledge without fully accepting or understanding. Other examples abound. When Ronald Reagan became president in 1981, he broke tradition and moved the location of his inauguration to the opposite side of the Capitol building where cameras would be able to pan the national monuments during his speech. He knew it would create a more dramatic visual effect.

Politicians speak while standing beside or in front of a large U.S. flag. In 1960, when Richard Nixon and John F. Kennedy were running against each other for the presidency, more people who heard the debate through their radios believed Nixon won. On the other hand, more of those who watched the nation's first nationally televised presidential debate believed Kennedy won, partly because they were able to witness Nixon sweating profusely and "looking nervous" while Kennedy appeared calm and confident.

Put simply, what we see impacts what we hear. It's an idea with which you are most likely familiar. It can be difficult to get through school without hearing about the different learning styles. Some of us learn by seeing, some by hearing, and some by doing. Regardless of your learning style, we are all impacted by what we see—or by what we don't see. And with the introduction of television into almost every home in the United States (the average home containing more televisions than people), the way we process information has changed. The visual element has become more important, even to those who are not visual learners.

However, the visual has always been important. Author Tarjei Vesass wrote in *The Boat in the Evening*, "Almost nothing need be said when you have eyes," noting how much can be communicated visually. It is easy to forget that when preparing a speech because in that moment you are focusing on the words that need to be said, on the process of talking and the sense of hearing (and the process of listening, as previously discussed), but we shouldn't forget about the visual element of communication. So, in this chapter we turn to the way visual imagery can add to a speech through the use of presentation aids (and we will also look at the use of audio aids, as well).

Audiences don't always need presentation aids, but the potential benefits from incorporating them into a presentation are so many, it is wise to consider using them. Not every speech needs a presentation aid, but think carefully before you decide to exclude them. In this chapter, we will look at the potential benefits of presentation aids, both visual and audio, as well as how to effectively incorporate them into your message.

Based on the topic of your speech, do you think a presentation aid would improve the effectiveness of your speech? Why or why not?

BENEFITS OF PRESENTATION AIDS

The first benefit of having a presentation aid is the potential to increase audience interest in your message. Even the most bored audience will look up to see what a speaker is uncovering. When music or a clip from a film is played, audiences seem to give added attention, at least initially. You have to work to keep them interested, but having a presentation aid can help catch their interest to begin with.

Another benefit from presentation aids is increased audience understanding of your message. A graph or a diagram might help to clarify a complex problem. While you may word your message in the simplest language with the appropriate amount of detail and explanation, for some people, it may not "click" until they can see it. Some people have an emotional block when it comes to numbers; for them, seeing statistics on a graph or pie chart may make the information more accessible. People can also become lost when a process contains many steps or requires behaviors with which they are unfamiliar.

Beyond emotional blocks, people just may not have the experience to "picture" what it is you're talking about. If someone has never been exposed to visual images of a particular place, person, or phenomenon, they may not be able to imagine what you are describing. We've all heard this dilemma in the age-old question, "How do you describe color to someone who has never seen?" Likewise, how do you describe the devastation caused to the New Orleans and the rest of the Gulf Coast without visuals? "Homes were subject to extensive damage" and "streets were impassable due to the amount of rubbage" are correct descriptions, but may be difficult to visualize without corresponding images.

A picture can help "describe" the indescribable. When Katrina hit the Gulf Coast, images such as these helped people all over the United States understand the devastation it wreaked.

Not only do visuals like these help to establish the extent of the problem, they can also strike an emotional chord in audiences. Presentation aids can help not only make a problem more "real" to an audience, they can help make it more important. The images of Hurricane Katrina's damage, like the displays in the Oklahoma City National Memorial and Museum, both clarify the situation and convey an emotion. Visual images can serve both of these functions to increase the audience's understanding.

©Corbis   ©Corbis

Famous photographs, such as these, are remembered, in large part, because of the emotional response they evoke in the viewer.

It follows that if an audience better understands your message, they will remember more of it for a longer period of time. The third potential benefit of visual aids, then, is increased audience retention (or memory) of your message. Sometimes a picture stays more vividly in the memory and helps to solidify the message. For example, a picture of someone smoking through their throat can help an audience remember smoking leads to cancer of the esophagus.

A well-chosen visual aid can help the audience visualize and remember your message. For example, this photo could reinforce the message that secondhand smoke harms children.

Another potential outcome is an increased level of comfort in the speaking situation. As you know, most speakers experience at least some nervousness while in front of their audience. Having something to show or play can give the audience a place to put their eyes other than directly on you, at least for part of the time. Knowing this, or having an object to work with, can help relieve anxiety for some speakers, allowing them to come across as more confident and natural.

Working hand in hand with your comfort level is the potential benefit of receiving a boost in speaker credibility from the audience. When you have presentation aids that are appropriate and professional in appearance, they can lend to the audience's perception that you are appropriate and professional as a speaker. They also show the audience that you've taken time to think through your topic and prepare a thoughtful message. Audiences tend to respond more positively to a speaker whom they perceive as credible.

All of these benefits work together to create a possible sixth advantage: increased effectiveness of your message appeal. When you are more comfortable and the audience is more interested, understands better, experiences an emotional connection, and perceives you as a more credible speaker, you are more likely to be successful in reaching your goal with them.

Many messages can benefit from effective presentation aids, but some topics absolutely require them. An informative speech on a particular work of art would not be effective without a visual of that art. A speech on how to take more effective photographs would not work without example photographs. A speech on the musical genius of Benny Goodman would not be complete without a sampling of his music.

Which of these benefits do you think a presentation aid would most add to your speech? If you choose not to use a presentation aid, which benefit do you think you would be most likely to lose? (It is possible the answers to these questions are "none," in which case you would need to think carefully about whether you should even use a visual aid.)

IN REVIEW
The benefits of effective presentation aids are...

- Increased audience interest
- Increased audience understanding
- Increased audience memory
- Increased comfort for speaker
- Increased speaker credibility
- Increased message effectiveness

Questions:

Reflections:

But attached to these potential benefits must be a warning. Incorporating presentation aids into your message does not guarantee these benefits. The outcome depends on how and what you incorporate into your message. These benefits are derived from *effective* visual aids, which are well thought out, nicely made, and incorporated appropriately. When your aids are irrelevant, confusing, unprofessional, inaccurate, or used inappropriately, they are no longer presentation "aids." They are not only *not* aiding your message, they are likely to be detracting from the effectiveness. You are usually better off having no presentation aid at all than to have one of poor quality. Poor presentation aids, or aids improperly handled, can actually reduce audience understanding and speaker credibility. Aids with inappropriate images or information can actually offend audiences, who then mentally shut out your message or focus their thoughts on why you would make such choices. Even attempts to boost your own confidence by putting your entire speech outline (or even your entire speech) on a PowerPoint presentation can be detrimental to the connection between the speaker and audience. In any of these cases, interest in the actual message is lost. Knowing that you did not put the appropriate effort into your aids can actually give you one more thing to be nervous about during your speech. As you can see, there are many reasons to incorporate presentation aids, but they must not be last minute additions placed without thought, effort, or practice. The rest of the chapter will focus on what you can add to your speech, along with some tips to make sure you get the potential benefits, and not the disadvantages, associated with presentation aids.

BEYOND OUR PERSPECTIVE

THINKING ABOUT THE AUDIENCE WHEN SELECTING PRESENTATION AIDS
While you may consider a presentation aid interesting and appropriate, your audience may not. As with all parts of the speech process, you must analyze your audience before you create or deliver your presentation aids.

If you are delivering a speech on the late stand-up comic George Carlin, you might consider playing a short clip from one of his routines. Comedy usually plays well with audiences made up of college students and profanity may be acceptable in a speech for many of them. However, this is not a given. Consider some of the cultures that might be represented in your audience. While Carlin was a comic who pushed the boundaries of what was acceptable in the 1970s, his arguments on society still resonate in the 2010s, and, even though he has passed, he still serves as a major influence and role model for many of today's younger comedians. However, some audiences will not respond well to an abundance of profanity in your audio aids.

Think about the age of your audience, the conservatism of the region, and any of the other variables that may influence their response. Your audience would influence your choice of routine, how much to play, or whether to play a clip at all. Similarly, certain graphic images (death, violence, illness, sex) may or may not be successful depending on your audience.

THINKING ABOUT THE BROADER CONTEXT WHEN SELECTING PRESENTATION AIDS

As mentioned earlier in this chapter, the Oklahoma City National Monument and Museum is a powerful reminder of the emotional impact of visual images. Ironically, many of the displays in the museum are of visual images, photographs taken in the hours and days after the bombing: a visual display showing the power of a visual display. One of those photos has become world famous and even won one man a Pulitzer Prize: a picture of a firefighter carrying a one-year-old girl from the wreckage of the building. That picture was one of the photos we were offered to open this chapter with and we consciously chose not to use it. While the photo is a great example of the power of visual imagery, it is also a worthwhile reminder of the need for us to respect that power. At the time of the photo, according to displays in the museum, neither the firefighter nor the family of the girl were comfortable being a part of the iconography of the event. In 2001, the mother of that little girl told *Southern Living Magazine* she still couldn't bear to look at that picture. There was a second, almost identical photo which became embroiled in controversy and legal battles. There were some hard feelings at the time about why these people became the image of the recovery effort. All of this speaks to the incredibly strong emotions which can surround a visual image. While more recent reflection, like a 2013 appearance by the mother and the firefighter on Katie Couric's show, suggest they are coming to terms with the tragedy, even then the firefighter had to acknowledge it is still hard for him to talk about the event.

We did not want to tread on any of those feelings, and that is something you need to consider when selecting a visual image as well. As noted in several places in this chapter, visual imagery can, and often does, have a significant emotional impact. Remember in Chapter 2 you learned that ethical speakers respect the power of communication. That responsibility includes not only vocal and verbal communication but non-verbal communication, like visual imagery, as well. Therefore, as in any emotionally charged situation, you need to think carefully about the impact of the messages you communicate. In this case, that means don't only think about how your audience will react to the image, but think also about the context which surrounds the image. Think about the feelings of the people represented in the image and those of the people who were equally impacted by the context of the image. Think about how people in general, not just those in your audience, think about the events, people, or objects depicted in the image. Be respectful of all of those feelings and factor those considerations into your decision about whether or not to use an image. While a picture may be worth a thousand words, your ethos and your relationship with your audience, not to mention the feelings of all who are impacted by your message, are worth far more than that.

Describe a time when a speaker used a presentation aid which bothered or offended you. Could the speaker have anticipated your reaction and how could the speaker have avoided that reaction?

TYPES OF PRESENTATION AIDS

When you are creating a speech, there are a variety of aids you can choose to work into your message.

VISUAL REPRESENTATIONS

The first type is an object. When it is possible, you can bring in the actual object that is the topic of your speech. If you are giving a demonstration speech reviewing the principles of CPR, you may bring in "Rescue Annie," the doll that is commonly used for practicing the steps. If you are teaching your audience about the influence of guitar in classical music, you may bring in a classical guitar and play a short piece of music as an example.

For some topics, bringing in an object is either impossible or inappropriate. For a speech explaining the contributions of the C_{60} molecule to the field of alternative fuel development, you may want the audience to understand the structure of this molecule. But even if you could manage to get ahold of C_{60}, it is invisible to the naked eye. This is an obvious example, but the principle holds true with objects that are visible, yet not large enough to be clearly seen by the audience. If you are giving a speech on crochet, we can see your hands using yarn and a hook, but we cannot see your technique. We can see a hat or scarf in the process of being created, but we have no idea how you are doing it or what it should look like. On the opposite end of the spectrum, you might give a speech on a rather large Rodin sculpture from the Art Institute of Chicago and want your audience to have a sense of what it is like in three dimensions. It is impossible for you to bring a museum sculpture to class. In all of these cases, though, it is possible for you to bring in models of these objects, models being scaled up or scaled down versions of the actual object. You can bring in an oversized model of the C_{60} molecule illustrating its unique structure. You can bring in an oversized crochet hook and a piece of rope to demonstrate the process of crochet. You can bring in a smaller version of a Rodin sculpture to give us a sense of the texture and emotion attached to the artwork. Models can give audiences an up-close look at a complicated process or a realistic representation of your speech topic.

When you can't bring in an object or model, you can often bring in a picture of that item. Photographs or illustrations are excellent mediums for representing an object, or anything else, in an impactful and vibrant way. While you can't bring to class a bustling marketplace from Hong Kong or someone crossing the finish line of a marathon, you can bring in photographs of these occurrences.

Another common visual representation, particularly for statistics and other forms of data, are charts, graphs, and other similar items. Illustrations, graphs, diagrams, and charts offer visual reinforcement of your message and often make complex statistics and data more accessible. Any of these can be put onto different mediums: posterboard, overhead transparencies, computer presentation software (such as PowerPoint), or paper handouts.

When using any sort of presentation aid, there are some definite strengths and weaknesses that need to be considered. In the context of visual representation aids, one of the major strengths is that it gives the speaker access to items they may not have access to in person (consider the C_{60} molecule or the Rodin sculpture mentioned earlier). If you consider these items to be of importance to help make your point, a visual representation aid might be helpful. Another strength was also mentioned previously: enhancing clarity. When you use a graph, chart, or even PowerPoint or Prezi, you are adding in a visual layer of info for the audience.

If you were doing a speech about golf, would you be better off using an object or a chart as a presentation aid? Why?

While there are some major positives, there are definitely some weaknesses to consider. Visual representation aids are often very engaging for the audience, but in a negative sense. When these sorts of aids are used ineffectively, they can take the attention off the speaker. When giving a speech, you want the audience to be engaged in the message because of what you are telling them, not solely because of the visual. For example, a speaker that uses a PowerPoint full of text and images may feel more comfortable, but the attention may wander off of them from the audience. So, think critically if a visual representation aid will help keep attention on you and your goal. Also, if you want to use one of these types of aids, use them in moderation, as they can easily be overused. Deciding to add photos, objects, slides, etc., may sound like a good idea, but the more you add, the less the main point of your speech will stick with your audience.

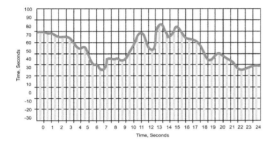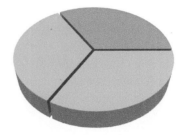

Graphs, diagrams, and charts can all be used to add visual impact to your message.

ELECTRONIC AIDS

If your speaking situation gives you access to a television, stereo, or projector connected to a computer, you have the ability to not only have still images, but video, music, or other forms of audio into your message. Are you giving an informative speech on the contributions made to modern music by The Edge of the rock band U2? You would be hard pressed to have an effective speech that didn't include examples of his music, as well as the music you are claiming he has influenced.

Chances are you have likely seen the use of electronic aids in classrooms, workplaces, etc. To many, these are often a "go-to" to add a bit of excitement into the presentation. However, just as with visual representation aids, there are some strengths and weaknesses that need to be considered. One of the biggest strengths of using electronic aids is that they tend to immediately engage an audience. Think of how eager you are to watch a video on YouTube when a speaker loads the website. Part of the eagerness comes from the fact that you get to see the information from the speaker "in action." This also coincides with another major strength: everyone in the audience has a chance to clearly see (or hear) the visual. You may consider putting pictures from your vacation to Hawaii into a slideshow, for example, so that all can see the image at once and nothing has to be passed around. Also, because you are utilizing this type of aid to clarify ideas, you may be more able to rely on persuasive appeals to ethos (discussed in Chapter 2), pathos, and logos (both discussed in Chapter 12).

Before you start scanning your mind for what videos you want to show within your speech, you will also need to weigh the weaknesses of using electronic presentation aids. One of the major weaknesses comes from technology problems. You may have access to a computer and projector and also have Internet access, but there may

If you were doing a speech about student loan default rates, would you be better off using a chart or an electronic aid as a presentation aid? Why?

If you were doing a speech about Gwen Stefani's musical accomplishments, would you be better off using a person or an electronic aid as a presentation aid? Why?

be problems with the quality of the video. Or, a projector may not be functioning properly, or you may have saved your files in a different format, and they do not open. Many speakers will often ask for a reprieve or a reschedule when these things happen, but do not think that this will always be an option. As a speaker, consider what you might do if your electronic presentation aid doesn't work. Will you be ready if your professor or an event sponsor tells you to continue? You should remember that if you have problems with your electronic aid, that doesn't mean you get to reschedule your speech.

Another weakness is that your electronic aid could possibly overpower the message you are sending. Too many moving visuals, or too long of a clip from YouTube can take the attention off of you.

PEOPLE AS PRESENTATION AIDS

Finally, you can use people as presentation aids. For example, you can bring in another person who will demonstrate the appropriate position or movement in a self-defense move or a dance step while you are pointing out to the audience the more subtle aspects of proper form. You may also use yourself as a visual aid. You may demonstrate a yoga pose to the class while giving a speech on the mental and physical benefits of practicing yoga.

When a speaker uses a person as an aid, one strength is that the attention level of the audience is often immediately heightened. Also, as a speaker, you can utilize a person to emphasize multiple parts of the speech. As mentioned above, you may decide to use a person as an aid while demonstrating self-defense moves. You will likely not want to show your aid performing just one element, but possibly more.

As with any aid, be aware of some weaknesses. First and foremost, when you recruit another person to use as a visual, you need to then rely on their credibility, professionalism, etc. When you are developing a PowerPoint, for example, you can easily determine how much time you want to use to write it, practice with it, and so forth. When you ask your sister, friend, or even classmate to help you, there is always the possibility that they may not come through for you. Also, while you may have taken the speech and preparation seriously, your best friend may think of the situation with more humor since she will be seeing you outside your comfort zone. Another possible weakness is that the use of a person as an aid can negatively impact the fluency of your speech. To use the previous example of illustrating dance moves, you might be forced to ask the person to perform the step again, or if the step is done incorrectly, you may need to take extra time restating the point. Plus, if you enlist the help of a friend, for example, you may not be able to stay focused on your speech. In essence, when you enlist the help of others, think critically about your choice.

IN REVIEW

The types of presentation aids are...

- Visual representations like:
  - Objects
  - Models
  - Pictures (photographs)
  - Charts, graphs, and similar illustrations
- Media (videos, music clips, etc.)
- People

and each type has different strengths and weaknesses which you should consider when selecting what type of aid you will use.

Questions:

Reflections:

THINKING ABOUT USING PRESENTATION AIDS: DEVELOPING THE PLAN

By now you should be aware of the many types of presentation aids that you can use within your speech, and also the many benefits for both the audience and the speaker. If you are like many other students, you may have read those benefits and thought, "I can't wait to include some kind of aid in my speech!" Before you start scouring the Internet for videos or get ready to create a handmade poster, you will want to stop and reflect on your eagerness. Was your eagerness to find that movie clip or picture grounded in critical thought of the topic and audience, or was it more of an impulse?

To help you consider that question a bit more, it may be helpful to look back on some of your previous encounters with presentation aids as an audience member. Have you ever been an audience member and felt that the use of a speaker's aid was awkwardly utilized? Distracting? Unprofessional in content or appearance? Not needed at all? If any of these questions resonate with you, that means you have made a critical decision on the effectiveness of aid usage, and you should use this same critical thought in regards to your speeches. Specifically, there are three questions you will always want to ask yourself to help you make those critical decisions:

1. Do I *need* to use a presentation aid for my speech?

2. If "yes," which type of aid will be the best fit to help me achieve the goal of my speech?

3. What does the speech setting allow me to do?

DO I NEED TO USE A PRESENTATION AID?

In some cases, this question may be the easiest to answer. For example, if your Communication Studies professor requires students to use presentation aids, then the answer is a simple "yes." However, many speaking situations will require the speaker to make the ultimate decision as to whether an aid is necessary. As a general rule of thumb, you likely will not need to use an aid if the topic of your speech, and the concepts within that speech, are reasonably simple enough for the audience to process. For example, a speech about the sport of tennis might be successful if visuals were not used because many of the items you may want to discuss are relatively simple to comprehend. However, this is not absolute, and some topics may be just complex enough where you may determine your audience needs to see or hear something to truly "get it." Consider the difference between talking about the history of tennis and telling your audience how to restring a tennis racquet or the proper form when serving. While the historical view of the sport may not need extra clarification, the other approaches might. In many cases, when a presentation aid is used by a speaker but is not actually needed for the context of a topic, it can negatively impact audience understanding and engagement.

WHICH TYPE OF AID WILL HELP ME ACHIEVE MY GOAL?

If you answered "yes" to the first question, your job is not nearly completed. As stated earlier, just because you know an aid needs to be used doesn't mean that any type of aid will work. What you must do next is think critically about which type of aid will help you achieve your goal. Earlier in this chapter, you learned about many of the different types of presentation aids (objects, videos, people, PowerPoint, etc.) and some of those types may help you achieve your goal more than others. If you want to teach your class proper form when serving a tennis ball, you may find that certain types of aids are better suited to helping you achieve that goal. You may want to bring in a tennis racquet and show the class in person, or have your friend that is on the college's tennis team be your model while you explain your ideas. You may also decide that a YouTube video of Serena Williams or Roger Federer can help you achieve your goal. But why didn't you decide to show a graph, pie chart, or play an instructional CD? The answer is very simple: you realized that some aids will work better than others for certain topics. Likewise, if you wanted to speak to the local school board about the underfunding of music programs compared to athletics, would you be able to better achieve your goal by showing a pie chart or

Think of a time you saw a speech using presentation aids. Were they effective? Why or why not?

If you are planning on using a presentation aid in your speech, what type of presentation aid would make the most sense for your topic, based on the strengths and weaknesses of each?

bringing in your trumpet from when you were in marching band? Or if you wanted to persuade your class that Fred Astaire was a better dancer than Gene Kelly, would it be more effective to show the class still images of them in mid-routine, or an actual video clip of their best moments? All in all, speakers need to understand that not all presentation aids are created equal, and should critically think about the goal of their speech and which type will help best achieve that goal.

WHAT DOES THE SPEECH SETTING ALLOW ME TO DO?

In Chapter 4 of your text, you learned about the importance of conducting a situational analysis of the speaking situation. As you may recall, this concept refers to understanding the entire communication environment, including items such as your relationship to your audience and the purpose for the gathering. However, this same idea comes in play here with presentation aids within the speech setting. Chapter 4 mentions that there are also logistic items that should be considered. For example, if you want to show a YouTube video of Serena Williams serving a tennis ball, you will need to make sure that the speech setting has the items to allow you to show that clip (a computer, a reliable network connection, projection screen, etc.). Or, from a different perspective, let's assume you determine that a live demonstration would be the best fit for a speech on serving a tennis ball. If so, you will want to consider if all members of your audience can easily see you from their seats. It is also important to note here that speakers should always be ready with a backup plan that is also suitable for the speech setting anytime a presentation aid is being considered. Planning a PowerPoint slideshow may be great in theory, but what if the classroom or meeting space doesn't have a projector? What if the video of Gene Kelly and Fred Astaire is no longer available, or the network connection is down?

In the final analysis, speakers aren't necessarily performing their duties ethically if a presentation aid is chosen haphazardly, or if speakers want to make handmade posters just because they like coloring posterboards, or decide to use a PowerPoint just to have a set of visual notes so they can read to the audience. In order for an aid to be as effective as possible, the speaker needs to think critically about the speaking situation, the goals for the speech, and the setting.

> Critically evaluate your decision to use visual aids in your speech by considering the three critical decisions:
>
> Do you really need a visual aid?
>
> What type of visual aid will you use?
>
> Will your plan work in the setting for your speech?

APPLYING THE FUNDAMENTALS

VISUAL AIDS AND THE 2008 REPUBLICAN CONVENTION

Throughout this chapter you have read information regarding how to use visuals in a manner that is effective. Doing so allows the visual to add something to your message and minimize any possible distractions. While these ideas should make logical sense, not all speakers tend to remember these sound pieces of advice.

One place where these ideas were disregarded was the Republican Party National Convention in 2008. At this conference, many high ranking (and popular) political figures such as presidential nominee John McCain and VP nominee Sarah Palin took to the stage. While the keynote speeches were being delivered from the podium on center stage, a large LCD screen behind the speaker constantly scrolled changing images of Americana (vast farm fields, major cities, main streets, etc.). While the visual was meant to rein-force American imagery, the viewing public, especially within the convention hall, had a different take: it was distracting because of the frequent changing of images. Not only did the images change frequently, but, as an article from the *Wall Street Journal* pointed out, "Republican nominee John McCain's acceptance speech here got off to a rocky start as the screen behind him interrupted his speech three times within the first 10 minutes."

Not only were there instances of distractions and technical glitches, there was also the question of the relevancy of the visuals. The images of Americana were seen as a point of confusion as they had little connection to the text of the speech. In essence they were meant to symbolize something generic (an American ideal), not something specific (like McCain's platform).

So, what is the takeaway from all of this? The point is to emphasize that when visuals are not carefully considered or carefully utilized the speaker runs the risk of losing audience attention. Remember that visuals are meant to *add* something to the speech, not cause distractions or confusion.

IN REVIEW
When developing a plan to use presentation aids, you should consider three issues…

• Need

• Type

• Situational constraints

Questions:

Reflections:

PREPARING AND USING PRESENTATION AIDS: IMPLEMENTING THE PLAN

Once you have decided that presentation aids will make your speech more effective and decided exactly what type of presentation aids will help you achieve that goal, you need to implement your plan.

CREATING YOUR PRESENTATION AIDS

The first step in that stage of the process is to prepare your presentation aids for use in your speech. Whatever, or whomever, you choose to use as a presentation aid, there are certain guidelines that should be followed. First and foremost, presenta-tion aids must make an actual contribution to the transmission of your message. You should not have a presentation aid in your speech just for the sake of having it. Remember, aids that are not well prepared or mishandled detract from the ef-fectiveness of your speech. Presentation aids are not decorations. Even if you have found something that is visually exciting, it must be directly related to your mes-sage. When used, aids must be used with purpose. Decide exactly where in the speech you will refer to your aid and for how long.

Try to keep one major idea for each aid. Putting too much onto one poster, PowerPoint slide, or any other type of aid that you use can end up confusing the audience. It can contribute to information overload and have your audience either jumping around in their heads or tuning out altogether. Additionally, restrict your-self to 6–8 lines of text per visual aid.

Use consistent formatting. If you have multiple visuals, they don't have to look exactly the same, but they should have some measure of uniformity. If you have

If you are going to use a presentation aid, it must help the audience understand your message and not become a distraction. Based on that, what do you think are some of the most important things you will need to remember when creating your presentation aids?

completely different fonts, sizes, colors, schemes, and layout with your multiple aids, it can be jarring to your audience. It can also look as if you have pulled information from many different places without owning it yourself. Even though you engage in research, the message you put together is your own message. You speak with one voice; your aids should reflect that.

Make sure your aids are large enough to be seen by all parts of the room (or loud enough to be heard by all parts of the room). It can be aggravating for an audience member to strain to see or hear a message. That might be the reason they choose to stop listening. It can also detract from credibility by impacting your appearance of preparedness and competence as a speaker. When using an overhead transparency or computer slide, you still need to enlarge the size of your text. Do not use anything smaller than size 18.

When possible, inserting color brings life and adds interest to visual aids. Be careful with color—it is possible to go overboard, having something too bright or lettering in a color that is hard to read. For example, if yellow is not against an appropriate background color, it can be difficult to see. Test it out first.

Create aids with a professional appearance. With the advances in technology, it is possible for anyone to create a neat and professional visual aid. In some cases, hand lettering or drawing is appropriate. In most cases, hand lettering or drawing results in visual aids that detract from credibility. It is tempting with presentation software to make use of all the bells and whistles, but it is easy to go overboard and appear unprofessional. Limit your use of these extras, especially when it is a sound that could interfere or overpower your speaking.

USING PRESENTATION AIDS IN YOUR SPEECH

Once you have created your presentation aids, you will need some guidelines for using them effectively during your speech. Begin by deciding on where they will be placed. In some situations, there will be limited choice. You must point any projector to where the screen in a room is mounted. In some rooms, the projectors may not move at all. But in most cases you can examine the room and choose positions for your objects, your posters, your projectors, and yourself. Set up your aids before you begin where all audience members will easily see them. As the speaker, feel free to move about your space, but don't stray too far from anything you will need to use or show your audience. Make sure you end up standing next to your aids at least a few seconds before you need them to avoid awkward silences as you move across the room or try to set them up.

As mentioned earlier, presentation aids must be used with purpose. Although it is common, it is unwise to set items on display for the entire time you speak. It becomes too easy for the audience to focus on something other than where you are in your message. Decide when and where your audience will see and hear your presentation aids. If you are using a poster, keep it covered until you are ready to refer to it in your speech. When you are finished, re-cover it. The same holds true for objects, slides, overheads, music, and any other type of aid.

Another key factor when using presentation aids is to avoid situations where they can become distracting. If you are using handouts, make sure you have enough for everyone in the audience. It is important to have an accurate idea of how many audience members will be present. It is better to overestimate than underestimate.

IN REVIEW
When creating presentation aids, be sure to use aids that...

- Contribute to the message (no decorations)
- Are not overloaded
- Are formatted consistently
- Are large enough
- Are in color
- Are professional
- Are simple

Questions:

Reflections:

Do not ask your audience to look at something and then pass it around. By the time it is to the third person, you will most likely be on a new topic. If you are passing something around because it is too small to be seen by the whole room, enlarge it or find a larger version. A small photograph is easily copied onto transparency paper or scanned into your computer to make a slide.

Once your aid has been displayed, make sure you explain its purpose. While the purpose of some aids may be obvious, more than often they are not. It will be your job, then, as the speaker to interpret and relate the information you are providing.

Finally, practice your speech with your aids. Too often, students will prepare a wonderful aid to accompany a very good presentation, but they haven't practiced delivering the two together. An otherwise fluent delivery can be hindered by awkwardness in uncovering a poster, uncertainty in when exactly to refer to the aid, or inexperience in using the chosen technology. Occasionally, students who practice their delivery without using their aid will forget to use it during their actual presentation. Using your props or slides in practice will help you appear more prepared, as well as ease your level of nervousness.

When you have prepared, planned, and practiced with your visual aids, you will decrease the likelihood of problems. However, some things are beyond your control when it comes to presentation aids, and sometimes they don't always work out as planned. You may unveil a poster that is upside down. You may discover a misspelled word on your slide as you are giving your speech. If the problem is something you can easily fix, fix it. Don't stop your speech. Don't become upset. Audiences will not condemn a speaker for a small error or mishap; they will judge you by how you handle it. If you become upset, it may affect credibility. But if you remain calm, or even lighthearted, it may boost credibility, leaving the audience with the impression that you, the speaker, are unflappable and in control of the situation.

If the problem is something you cannot fix, likewise, continue your speech. Point out the error if it contains misinformation or will confuse the audience. Otherwise, you will need to decide how important it is to acknowledge something the audience may not have noticed.

Sometimes the problem is one that completely disables you from using an aid in your speech. It is possible that you are using a person to help you demonstrate a process and that person has a flat tire on their way to your presentation. They don't show up. The VCR may destroy your tape, the computer holding your slide presentation may crash, and the rain may destroy your posters as you are running into the building. But your speech must continue. Presentation aids are meant to enhance your message. As a speaker, you must be knowledgeable on your topic and prepared enough to continue without them. Always have a "Plan B." Decide in advance how you plan to give your presentation without the aids.

While the point of this chapter has been to enable you to effectively use presentation aids, remember the message itself is of ultimate importance. When an audience sees an unprepared message with great visual aids, they will still see the unprepared, unorganized, or illogical nature of the message. Know that your message is sound and convincing. Know how you will relate the message to your audience. Then, consider how to improve that message with the use of presentation aids.

In order to be effective, you must practice with your visual aids. What do you think are some of the issues you are likely to encounter?

How can you use your practice time to prepare to deal with those issues?

IN REVIEW
When using presentation aids, remember to…

- Give careful consideration to where they are placed
- Only display them when being used
- Minimize the chance they can distract the audience
- Explain the purpose of the aid
- Practice with your aid
- Prepare for problems
- Have a "Plan B"

Questions:

Reflections:

BEYOND THE FUNDAMENTALS ━━━

USING AUDIO AIDS

Throughout this chapter we have generally used the term "presentation aids," and have discussed the concept to include both audio and visual aids. However, you may have noticed that much of the chapter material, particularly the chapter introduction, has focused on visual aids, and that is intentional. The basic reason for adding presentation aids to a speech is to add clarity to your presentation in ways that oral delivery won't allow. Because a speech is an oral exercise, presentation aids that stimulate a different sense (like seeing) have more of a chance to reach the audience in unique ways. Therefore, there is just less need for audio aids.

However, sometimes audio aids are necessary. For example, if you are presenting a speech on the difference between major and minor chords in music, it would certainly be helpful for the audience to hear what a major chord and a minor chord sound like and that is not something done with a speaking voice. In that case, and similar situations, an audio aid makes sense. However, as with any presentation aid, audio aids must add to, and not detract from, the primary message. Further, audio aids present some additional unique challenges when trying to keep your aids from becoming a distraction.

First, if the audience needs to hear an audio aid then you need to stop talking. That will shift the audience's focus from you to the aid (as opposed to a visual aid where the audience can use different senses to process both messages simultaneously). That means that after you use the aid, you will need to get the audience's attention back on you. As discussed in Chapter 9, it is difficult to get the audience's attention in the first place, so you want to be careful how willingly you give that up. Related to this issue is another one: the longer an audio aid is, the more the attention of the audience shifts from you and the more difficult it is to get their attention back. So, first you should think careful about whether an audio aid adds enough to the speech to deal with this loss of focus and then, if you decide that it is, you still want to keep the audio aid as short as possible (like playing a single minor chord, not a whole song in a minor key) to minimize these issues.

Finally, there is an issue of respect for your audience. They came to hear your speech, not listen to music or watch a video. As discussed in several sections of this text, being aware of, and properly responding to, the rhetorical context of the speech is a critical component for a successful speech, and here is another place where this becomes an issue. You don't want the audience leaving your speech wondering why they needed to come to your presentation as opposed to just playing a couple of songs on their MP3 player or watching a YouTube video. If they are thinking things like that, they are essentially questioning your ethos and that is likely to make the speech less effective.

The key issue with audio aids is that, like any presentation aid, they must be used carefully, but because they compete with, rather than complement, the primary mode of presentation of the message, there are more things to consider when trying to use them effectively.

SUMMARY

Because we can be so strongly impacted by what we see, it can benefit you as a speaker to incorporate visual aids into your presentation (and sometimes audio aids can aid information not accessible through basic speech). When properly prepared and delivered, presentation aids offer several important advantages, including increased audience interest, understanding, and memory, as well as increased comfort, credibility, and message effectiveness for the speaker. There are many types of presentation aids from which to choose. You can bring objects, models, pictures, diagrams, charts, overheads, or even people. You can use computer slideshows, VCR or DVD technology, as well as a stereo to play music, spoken words, or some other audio element. Whatever you decide to use, make sure it is something that is interesting, simple, clear, and professional, so it actually contributes to your message, rather than serving as a decoration or detracting from the effectiveness of the message. Plan out where in your speech you will use the aid, where in the room you will set it up, and make sure to practice not only delivering the words, but practice using your presentation aids. Even with the maximum amount of preparation, you must be prepared to deal with the unexpected. Have a plan for recovering from an error or a technology problem, and absolutely be prepared to continue without your presentation aid. As speakers, we incorporate aids to create more effective messages, but, ultimately, we hold the responsibility of being able to deliver a message without the presentation aid.

Is it better to use high-tech or low-tech visual aids in your speech?

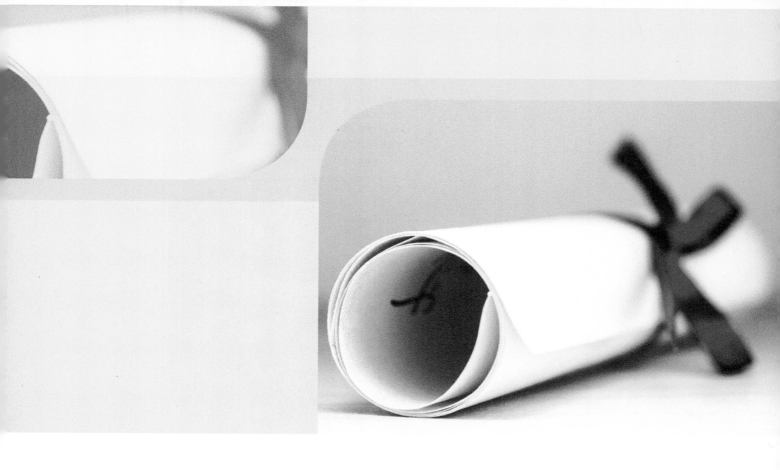

CHAPTER 14

OTHER SPEAKING CONTEXTS AND FORMATS

A special occasion speech must respond effectively to the situation to be successful.

© Cartoon Stock Ltd.

*Being rhetorically sensitive to the unique nature of the context
is very important when speaking for special occasions.*

Sometimes finding the right words for a speech can be a difficult thing to do. Like the cow in the cartoon, our sentiments may not be effectively expressed because we do not use the most appropriate words. So far in this text, we have focused on two of the common general purposes, persuading and informing, where that is perhaps a bit less of an issue. Remember, in Chapter 10, we said that many speeches are delivered extemporaneously and that delivery style does not rely as heavily on the exact words recorded in a script. While that delivery style often works well for informative and persuasive speeches, not all public speaking involves those types of speeches. In this chapter, we will turn our attention to other speaking contexts and styles, speech settings where word choice, style, and speech construction need to be even more rhetorically sensitive. We will first look at some forms of speaking other than persuasive and informative. Then we will examine some group presentation formats.

SPECIAL OCCASION SPEECHES

Today we tend to refer to many of the speeches that are not truly informative or persuasive in nature (the speeches to inspire, first mentioned in Chapter 5) as special occasion speeches. This is a good label, because it highlights the nature of most of these speeches. These are, in fact, speeches that respond to unique or special occasions. Some of these speeches are classified by the situation in which they occur: commencement speeches, inaugural addresses, and eulogies are examples of these kinds of speeches. Other speeches are classified by their function. These speeches would include anniversary speeches, farewell speeches, and dedication speeches, as well as the speech of introduction, speech of presentation, speech of acceptance, speech of praise and nominations, to name just a few.

SPEECHES DEFINED BY SITUATION

The first group of speeches attempt to respond to the particular situation in which they occur. Each of these situations is characterized by a particular and unique context and an effective speech will properly respond to that context.

COMMENCEMENT SPEECHES

Commencement speeches, for example, logically occur at a commencement or graduation. At these ceremonies, graduates are being honored for their accomplishments. We are also celebrating a transition in the graduates' lives, so a good commencement speech will mention the graduates' accomplishments and praise them for their efforts and their results. These speeches should also mention those who helped the graduates achieve those results. The speech may mention significant events that occurred during the students' studies, but it should not dwell on negatives; this is a day for celebration. Because this speech also marks a transition in the graduates' lives, it should include advice for the future and wisdom for life.

Commencement speeches are one example of a speech that demand a particular response due to the context of the speech.

INAUGURAL ADDRESSES

Inaugural addresses are another example of a speech that responds to a unique situation. These are speeches given when someone begins a new job and lays out, in broad terms, their agenda for the new position. Today in the United States, these speeches have come to be specifically associated with the inauguration of a new president (or re-elected president). In these speeches our new president will discuss in general terms what will be the tenor of the new administration. The themes the new president chooses to highlight may give some hints to new policies, but specific detail will probably be presented in other speeches, like a state of the union address. So, for example, President Kennedy hinted at a partnership between government and the people when he said, "Ask not what your country can do for you, ask what you can do for your country," but the specific details of programs like VISTA would be laid out in other forums. New presidents may also choose to inspire or calm the people of this country by responding to particular situations. A good example of this is Franklin Roosevelt's "We have nothing to fear but fear itself" comment, designed to ease Americans concerns about the Great Depression.

Have you experienced a eulogy that you thought was particularly effective? What do you think made it so effective?

EULOGIES

Eulogies are perhaps the best example of a speech defined by the situation. Eulogies are speeches that praise a specific individual (or group) and are most commonly presented at funerals and memorial services. The praise in these speeches is generally thematic. Instead of presenting a chronological review of the person's life, the speaker will pick particular themes to develop and draw on events from the subject's life to exemplify those themes. For example, Ronald Reagan's Eulogy for the Challenger Astronauts discussed the difficulty of opening any new frontier, noting "(t)he sacrifice of your loved ones has stirred the soul of our nation and, through the pain, our hearts have been opened to a profound truth—the future is not free, the story of all human progress is one of a struggle against all odds." He then compared the sacrifice of the Challenger Astronauts to the sacrifices of the early pioneers. He talked about the fact that Commander Dick Scobee had noted that no disaster should stop the shuttle program, and how the families of the astronauts had agreed, again tying to the theme that the United States has grown thanks to the sacrifice of brave men and women.

A good eulogy will make the basis of praise seem reasonable—the subject should not seem larger than life. So, do not exaggerate the person's accomplishment; do not embellish or lie. Draw on the subject's own experiences as the basis of celebrating that life. Reagan does this masterfully in the Challenger eulogy. As he praises each of the astronauts, he relies on very ordinary accomplishments: the piano playing of Judith Resnik, Ronald McNair's desire to play his saxophone on the space station, and the fact that Ellison Onizuka was an Eagle Scout.

Also, while it is often difficult for the speaker, eulogies should also not be overly emotional. As the speech is designed to dwell on the positive aspects of the subject's life, it should not dwell on the specific circumstances that have given rise to the speech (usually the subject's death). Obviously, that was difficult in the case of Reagan's eulogy, but in the entire speech, only one sentence refers directly to the actual event—and even that sentence referred more to how the people of this country had responded to the disaster.

SPEECHES DEFINED BY FUNCTION

Other examples of special occasion speeches respond to more generic situations, and are classified more by the functions they serve. These types of speeches would include, but not be limited to, speeches of welcome, speeches of farewell, speeches of presentation and acceptance, introductions, nominations, and commemorative speeches (like speeches for anniversaries).

SPEECHES OF WELCOME AND SPEECHES OF INTRODUCTION

A speech of welcome would tell why the person being welcomed has come to that situation, and tell a bit about the person, the occasion, and the correlation between the two. A speech of welcome could also serve some of the functions of a speech of introduction, which, quite simply, is to introduce the person to the audience. The key thing to remember in a speech of introduction is that the person being introduced and what he or she has to say is the focus of the occasion. The speech of introduction should be brief, highlighting a few key accomplishments, particularly focusing on the ones that explain the person's presence at that occasion. In short, a speech of introduction should be brief and not detract from the primary purpose of the occasion.

SPEECHES OF PRESENTATION

Typically, in speeches of welcome and introduction, the subject will be introduced in the opening sentence of the presentation. This is done because the focus is on the person. On the other hand, in a speech of presentation, the name of the subject is generally withheld until the end of the speech, as is any information or language structures (like gender specific pronouns) which could identify the specific individual. This is because the focus in these speeches is on what is being presented, generally some kind of award. So, by withholding the name of the recipient until the end of the speech, the speaker forces the audience to focus on the presentation rather than the recipient. The speaker should also place the focus on the award being presented by telling something about the award, perhaps some of the history of the award, the criteria for selection, and other pertinent details about the award.

SPEECHES OF ACCEPTANCE

The speech one gives when accepting an award is another example of a speech defined by function. In this case, the key is for the speaker to be humble. If you are receiving an award, do not act like you deserve it. Thank the people who presented you with the award. Thank the people who helped you win the award. If the award includes some kind of monetary award, you may want to express how you will use the award, making sure that use is consistent with the standards for the award. High school and college students often make this kind of speech when they are presented with a scholarship to aid their college studies. In this case, you can tell the audience how you will use the scholarship, mentioning things like what college you will attend (if that is not clear from the award) and what your major will be. You could also discuss your life goals and explain how the scholarship helps you pursue those goals.

APPLYING THE FUNDAMENTALS

VIOLATING EXPECTATIONS AT THE OSCARS

Generally a teacher will advise students to find their own style in developing their speeches, but, even in those classroom assignments, there are limits to how far students can go to make the speech uniquely their own. Professors will have expectations for length, style, and purpose, for example. Outside of the classroom, as we have previously discussed, those constraints also exist and are often defined by a rhetorical analysis. In most cases, those limits still leave the speaker with lots of choices and opportunities, but in the case of special occasion speeches, the bounds of what is acceptable, born of audience expectations, are rather restrictive and if a speaker violates those norms he or she is likely to not be very effective as a speaker. Perhaps there are no better examples of this than the reactions to Academy Award acceptance speeches that do not conform to standard expectations. While there are many cases of this happening over the years, three specific cases can highlight the common negative reaction to what is perceived to be an inappropriate speech.

In 1973, amidst tensions at Wounded Knee, South Dakota, where militant Oglala Sioux had taken over the Pine Ridge Indian Reservation, Marlon Brando won an Oscar for *The Godfather*. Rather than showing up in person, he sent Sacheen Littlefeather in his place. The Apache actress read a prepared statement rejecting the award, condemning this country's treatment of the native people, and how they were portrayed in films. The speech was met mostly with silence and disapproval, and several other actors, including Raquel Welch and Clint Eastwood, made pointed comments about the inappropriateness of Brando's actions later in the ceremony. The audience reacted similarly to Vanessa Redgrave's 1977 acceptance speech for her Oscar for her role in *Julia*. Redgrave's speech was largely anti-Zionist and went so far as to compliment the academy for voting for her despite threats from "Zionist hoodlums." More recently, in 2003, Michael Moore used his acceptance speech for the movie *Bowling for Columbine* to speak against the recent United States' invasion of Iraq. While reaction to Moore's speech was more mixed than the others, many seemed to agree with Cliff Robertson that the Oscars should not be a place for political statements. Even a supporter, like Gail Dolgin, admitted that Moore "broke the rules."

In all three cases, the presentations were not humble. These speeches were not about thanking the academy or those that helped the person win the award (while Redgrave did "thank" the academy, the purpose of the statement was to advance her political agenda, and not really to thank the academy). Because the speeches violated common norms and expectations for acceptance speeches, they were generally not well received. This reminds us again that public speaking is not about us as the speaker and our agenda or views, *per se*. Rather, we need to look at public speaking as an opportunity to reach out to the people in our audience and work with them and their expectations to develop an acceptable message for that time and place.

SPEECHES THAT NOMINATE AND SPEECHES THAT ACCEPT NOMINATIONS

A nominating speech is one of the most specific of these types of speeches. Often when an organization holds elections for various positions, candidates are nominated without much fanfare. However, in some cases, nominations are much more involved. The best examples of this are our country's political conventions, where the parties select their candidates for president. At these conventions, when a candidate is nominated, there are generally one or more speeches of nomination. Like eulogies, these speeches should also praise the individual, but not as a larger-than-life figure. For example, in his speech nominating Robert Dole to be the Republican candidate for President in 1996, John McCain referred to Dole as "the modest man who does his duty without complaint or expectation of praise."

Unlike eulogies, in this case the praise and celebration is not of a life completed, but of a task yet to be fulfilled. So, the speaker should focus the speech on why the subject is uniquely qualified to take on the task for which the subject is being nominated, as when McCain discusses Dole's life during and after World War II and how that experience made him qualified to lead this country at the end of the twentieth century.

The person making the nomination should also discuss what personal qualities would make a person well suited for the particular position and then show how the subject's life and character demonstrate that he or she has those particular qualities. McCain does this when he refers to Dole "as a man of honor, a man of firm purpose and deep commitment to his country's cause."

A speech accepting a nomination should be similar to a speech accepting an award—humble and grateful. Dole does this when he accepts the Republican nomination, noting

> but this is not my moment, it is yours. It is yours, Elizabeth. It is yours, Robin. It is yours, Jack and Joanne Kemp. And do not think that I have forgotten whose moment this is above all. It is for the people of America that I stand here tonight, and by their generous leave. And as my voice echoes across darkness and desert, as it is heard over car radios on coastal roads, and as it travels above farmland and suburb, deep into the heart of cities that, from space look tonight like strings of sparkling diamonds, I can tell you that I know whose moment this is: It is yours. It is yours entirely.

He then goes on to present himself as a simple man from Russell, Kansas. In addition, in a speech accepting a nomination, a speaker should also lay out what he or she will do if elected to the position for which they have been nominated. In this way, the speech accepting a nomination would resemble an inaugural speech.

There are many other types of special occasion speeches. However, what should become clear from the previous discussion is that all of these speeches must respond well to the particular situation in which they are presented, and, in order to be effective, must respond to the expectations of the occasion. So, whenever you find yourself needing to make a presentation of this type, be sure to carefully evaluate the context and audience as discussed in Chapter 4, and be sure you respond appropriately to the situation.

Do you agree that special occasion speeches are more context-dependent than other types of speeches?

IN REVIEW

Examples of special occasion speeches which are defined by the situation are...

- Commencement speeches
- Inaugural addresses
- Eulogies

Examples of special occasion speeches which are defined by function are...

- Speeches of welcome
- Speeches of introduction
- Speeches of presentation
- Speeches of nomination
- Speeches of acceptance (both for award presentations and nominations)

Questions:

Reflections:

BEYOND OUR PERSPECTIVE ▬▬▬

SPECIAL OCCASION SPEECHES IN OTHER CULTURES—STORYTELLING

As defined in this chapter, special occasion speeches include any speech designed to respond to a special occasion or fulfill a particular function. In this chapter, we have looked at some of the most common special occasion speeches in our society. However, different societies and cultures have their own unique forms of oral communication. For example, many native tribes, like other groups around the world, rely heavily on storytelling as a way of transmitting history and culture. Early in the history of these tribes, the storytellers were some of the most important and influential members of the tribe. It was their job to maintain the cultural history of the tribe, and these stories were often told to only members of the tribe and often in special ceremonies. For example, under traditional Cherokee law their stories could be told only to other Cherokee and perhaps members of other tribes. Even people who could hear the stories had to be invited to hear the stories and had to go through a significant ritual before hearing the stories. In other tribes there were different types of stories and the telling of those stories served different purposes. Today, in an age defined by a number of different media, the stories are not as essential as the primary way to transmit culture. But, the traditions and rituals still are significant to the tribes and so many native people maintain the traditions of storytelling.

All cultures, even our own, rely to some extent on stories to maintain history and transmit ideas and values. The telling of those stories is just not as ritualistic as it is in other cultures. For them, these stories do indeed respond, and respond appropriately, to a special occasion.

OTHER SPEAKING FORMATS

The other types of unique speeches we will look at in this chapter are formats that involve more than one person in the presentation. These formats can include situations where more than one person participates in the presentation or situations where the audience, or some part of the audience, is involved in the presentation.

SPEECHES INVOLVING MORE THAN ONE PRESENTER

PANEL DISCUSSION

The most common forms of multiple speaker formats are the panel discussion, the symposium, and the debate. A panel discussion involves several people talking about an issue. These presentations more resemble a conversation than a speech. Generally, there are no pre-prepared presentations (although individuals on the panel may have particular points they hope to raise somewhere in the course of the conversation). In a panel discussion, a leader or moderator will introduce the topic of the discussion and the panelists and then, for the most part, allow the conversation to unfold. If the conversation appears to be getting off track, the moderator may intervene and move the conversation back to an appropriate focus. While these conversations may appear to the audience to be free-flowing and there are no prepared scripts, in some cases the discussions will be very controlled and planned, allowing the panel to be sure to make very particular points. An example of this is the discussions by sports panelists at half-time of a basketball or football game. Generally, during the first half, the panelists will have noticed particular issues they want to discuss, and they will plan the discussion so certain people have the opportunity to raise those issues during the discussion of the first half of the game.

THE SYMPOSIUM

The symposium also involves multiple speakers discussing a broad topic area. The difference between a symposium and a panel discussion is that in a symposium each participant presents, uninterrupted, a complete speech with its own introduction, body, and conclusion. Each speech will be about some facet of the symposium topic and the speeches will likely be presented in an overall order that is easy for the audience to follow, so there is a lot of unity among the presentations. However, each speech should also be independent enough that it could stand on its own, if need be. That is the biggest difference between a symposium and a panel discussion. While both benefit from the presentation of multiple viewpoints and ideas, the participants in a panel discussion are much more dependent on the other people in the group.

DEBATES

While a speaker in a symposium may be less dependent on the other members of the group, both a panel discussion and a symposium are marked by a high degree of cooperation among the participants. That is not always true in a debate. In a debate, one or more speakers who have a particular outlook on an issue engage the other speakers who have a very different outlook on that issue. For example, a debate about abortion would probably have people with a pro-life perspective on one side of the issue and people with a pro-choice perspective on the other. A debate has a very specific format that has been agreed to by the participants prior to the event. The format can be as simple as the three-speech format utilized in the famous Lincoln–Douglas debates where one speaker presented a case, then the other speaker had a longer speech to both present his own case and refute the case of the other speaker, then the first speaker had a shorter speech in which to refute the case of the second speaker. Other formats can be more complex. For example, typical intercollegiate policy debates involve competition between two 2-person teams. The side that advocates for a policy change is called the affirmative (and the speakers are referred to as the First Affirmative Speaker and Second Affirmative Speaker). The side that argues against a policy change is referred to as the negative team (again, there is a First Negative Speaker and a Second Negative Speaker). The debate starts with the First Affirmative Speaker presenting the case for change. Then, the First Negative Speaker refutes that case for change and the Second Affirmative Speaker counters the negative position. The Second Negative Speaker then presents a more general reason why no change is needed or why the specific change the affirmative team is supporting is a bad idea. All four speakers then have one last opportunity to strengthen the arguments for their position.

This discussion of debates makes them appear highly competitive, and they often are. However, it should be noted that debates can also be more cooperative. Sometimes debates are used as a forum for presenting multiple outlooks on an issue. In this case, the speeches, and even some of the refutation, may be carefully planned to ensure that particular issues are raised. In this way, debates can more closely resemble symposiums and panel discussions.

If you were planning an event, would you be more likely to utilize a panel discussion or a symposium? Why?

Is a presidential debate really a presidential debate?

Which type of group presentation do you think would be most effective? Why?

In a forum, should a speaker try to answer every question asked by the audience? Would you answer differently if the context were a more traditional public speaking setting? Why or why not?

Can questions from the audience negate the effectiveness of a speech?

IN REVIEW

Speech formats that include more than one speaker include...

• Panel discussions

• Symposiums

• Debates

Speech formats that involve the audience include...

• Forums

• Interviews

FORMATS THAT ALLOW FOR AUDIENCE INVOLVEMENT

FORUMS

Other formats allow a single speaker to interact with the audience. These formats include the forum and the interview. The forum is defined by a particular relationship between the speaker and the audience. In any speech setting, a speaker is always free to take questions from the audience and usually the speaker will dictate when questions should be asked, either at the end of the speech or at particular times during the speech. However, in most of these cases, the speaker is still very much in control of the speech situation, both in terms of content and the degree and placement of audience participation. In a true forum, the speaker would not have as much control. In a forum, audience members are allowed to ask questions more freely and those questions may lead the speaker to address issues he or she did not originally intend to address.

INTERVIEWS

If we consider a traditional speech as one end of a continuum representing how much control a speaker has of the situation and the forum as somewhere in the middle, the other end of the continuum is the interview. In an interview format, the audience, or perhaps some panel representing the audience, asks the speaker questions to which he or she must respond (although the response may be rather evasive). While there may be some discussion or negotiation before the interview, the person being interviewed does not exercise much control over what questions may be asked. In addition, in an interview, the speaker does not generally get to give an opening statement that could steer the presentation in a particular direction. Those opening statements are more common in forums. In sum, in the interview, the audience (or some facet of the audience) controls the situation much more than the speaker does.

SUMMARY

In this chapter, we have looked at a number of speech settings and styles that vary in some way from the speeches we have looked at in the other chapters in this text. We have not gone into much depth about any of the formats discussed in this chapter because all of them represent some level of departure from the traditional public speech that is more than likely the focus of your class. It is important to note, however, that the skills you develop for traditional speaking formats will also help you in these formats as well. If you are interested in learning more about some of these formats, chances are your school provides other classes that focus on some of these particular formats, particularly debates and interviews.

CHAPTER 15

GROUP COMMUNICATION

The key to group success is effective communication.

Being able to communicate effectively in groups will be an important key to your long-term effectiveness as a communicator.

As the United States Secretary of Labor, a Supreme Court Justice, and U.S. Ambassador to the United Nations, Arthur Goldberg had an opportunity to observe many examples of group communication and decision making. He once suggested that if Columbus had consulted an advisory committee about his voyages, he never would have left the dock. That comment reflects many people's frustration when dealing with groups: they feel much time is wasted and few decisions are made. However, groups, teams, and committees are bound to be a significant part of your adult life. In fact, Ernest Benn, who died in 1967, thought the time in history when he lived may come to be known as the age of committees, and over the last half century, groups and committees have become even more prevalent. So, in this chapter we turn our attention from one particular setting or context—the public presentation—and focus, instead, on another context you are likely to encounter in the future: group communication. As with public speaking, the measure of effectiveness in group communication is whether that communication helps the communicators accomplish their goal. In the case of groups, however, the goal is not the goal of one individual speaker, but rather it should be a goal shared by all members of the group. It is that collective nature of group communication that makes it unique. In this chapter, we look at not only that uniqueness, but at some practical tips for improving your communication in group settings. We will then finish the chapter by looking briefly at the concept of leadership in groups.

DEFINING GROUPS

In order to understand how to communicate effectively in groups, we first must clearly understand what a group is. Many of us have a sense of what a group is; we use the term all the time. We use it to refer to a crowd of people waiting for a bus, a design team in our office, and a collection of volunteers responding to a national disaster. But, when used by communication scholars, the term "group" has a very specific meaning, and having a clear sense of that meaning and its implications is important if we are to understand the assumptions we make about what are effective communication behaviors in groups. We can define a group as a collection of three or more people who have some goal in common. They must work together to accomplish that goal. Therefore, they will interact, mostly directly, to develop a structure and will use that structure to accomplish that goal. Each element of this definition highlights some important idea that scholars have about groups.

SIZE OF GROUPS

There has been a lot of theoretic discussion about whether or not two people can constitute a group. For a more advanced class in group theory, those discussions are important. For the sake of offering you a brief introduction to groups, it is more important to clearly distinguish groups from other kinds of relationships, like friendships. So, for the sake of that simplicity, we will consider a group as being made up of at least three people.

Do you think that two people really can be considered a group?

GOALS AND INTERDEPENDENCE

Another assumption we make about groups is that they have something in common. Just as we assume that public speaking is purposeful, meaning that speeches are given to respond to some particular purpose, we also assume that groups come together to address some purpose. However, the something that a group has in common must require a group response. Not only do we say that a group will have something in common, but, further, they are interdependent in terms of their response to the situation. So, a collection of people standing on a corner waiting for a bus would not be considered a group because, while they have something in common (they want to get on the bus), they are not interdependent in terms of accomplishing that goal. If the bus is late and some people decide to walk to their destination instead, the others can still get on the bus; they are not interdependent. On the other hand, imagine that the bus drivers go on strike and all the people waiting there discover they are all going to about the same place and if they share their money they have just enough money to hire a taxi. Now they are interdependent because if anyone decides not to join in, the remaining people do not have enough money to hire the taxi. Often it is this kind of resource sharing that makes a group interdependent, although rarely is the resource money, as we will see in the next section.

GROUP STRUCTURE

Finally, we also assume the group will develop some kind of internal structure that helps them accomplish their task. Common elements of this structure can include roles, norms, and rules. Roles define what certain tasks each member of the group is expected to accomplish for the benefit of the whole group (for example, researcher, note taker, etc.). Norms define what acceptable and unacceptable behaviors in groups are and how the group will respond to violations of those norms. Often, the norms can be codified into a specific set of rules. For example, within a group one person may take on the role of note taker, while another will be the researcher and yet another will write the reports for the group. A norm can develop that at the start of each meeting the note taker will briefly summarize what happened at the last meeting, the report writer will present a summary of the information discussed, and the researcher will present the information for the group to move forward to the next task. The group may formally discuss what they are doing, and therefore come to expect that these things will happen at each meeting—a norm (or series of norms) has been established. The group could choose to formalize these norms through adoption of a formal agenda—that would be a type of rule: we will always follow this particular agenda. On the other hand, the emergence of the group structure could be more informal. Sometimes when groups get started on a project people just drift into particular roles and norms develop without being discussed. As long as the roles and norms help the group accomplish its task, it really does not matter if the process of role and norm development is more explicit (clearly discussed) or implicit (informal).

The one potential problem with implicit norms is that, since they happen without much discussion, group members can see them as "natural," and assume that is the way the group has to be. Particularly if someone is uncomfortable with their role, that can be a problem (as we will see later in this chapter). For example, you attend the first meeting of a group and are asked to take notes, and while you don't like being a note taker, you agree for the good of the group. At other group meetings, people just assume that you will take the notes. Implicitly, you have been assigned a role and a norm has developed, but you never had the chance to express your dissatisfaction with the setup because the group never actually discussed this emerging structure. In those situations, be willing to request a more explicit discussion of group structure.

Are these collections of people groups? The business people seem to be working together on a project, so they are probably a group. The firefighters may or may not be. If they are discussing how to fight a fire, they probably are, but if they are talking about their individual plans for the upcoming weekend, then they are probably not a group. Remember, groups must have something in common and must be working together on that project.

WHY WORK IN GROUPS

This definition of a group paints a picture of a rather complex entity. With the development of structure, the risk involved in acknowledging and accepting interdependence, and simply the complex interaction that dealing with many more people entails, it is hard not to wonder why anyone would want to join a group in the first place. The answer to that is found in the interdependence. People *need* to accomplish something and cannot do it alone; therefore they seek (or are required to work with) other people with different resources who can help accomplish the task.

As noted earlier, interdependence often develops over resources people can and do bring to a group discussion. In some cases, that resource is knowledge. Different people know different things, so each person in a group can contribute to a collective knowledge base that is broader than any one member's. With that greater base of knowledge, the group can address whatever issue it is trying to address in a more appropriate and effective way than any one individual can.

At a more abstract level, the resource may be more an issue of perspective, not simply knowledge. Here we are talking about how each individual person looks at the problem to be addressed, and we assume that each person will look at the problem slightly differently. For example, a group may be looking at ways to address the cost of textbooks. From a student's perspective, the problem may be cost. For a professor's, the issue may be availability of appropriate material. From a publisher's outlook, the issue may be protection of copyright or cost of production. The best recommendation about what to do would probably respond to all of those issues. With more people in the group, more perspectives will be presented and the group will be able to suggest a high quality solution to the problem.

The point is people join groups because they can better respond to a situation than individuals can. However, that also tells us when groups would be less appropriate. When a situation does not benefit from multiple perspectives or a wider knowledge base (or the sharing of some other resource), a group probably isn't necessary. For example, we probably do not need to form a group to add 1 and 3. Most people have that knowledge, and perspective is really not an issue (it does not matter if we add the 1 to the 3 or the 3 to the 1; the answer is still 4). In some similar cases, the advantage of the group is limited. For example, a group may be better than an individual when working on a calculus problem, because among a group of people you are more likely to find one who knows how to do calculus. However, once you have identified that person, it is probably reasonable to let them work on the problem individually. At the back end of the process, the advantage of perspective might be to have someone else check the problem, because by looking at it from a different perspective they might discover something the first person missed. In either case, the advantage of the group is rather narrow and limited.

On the other hand, there certainly are occasions when a group is ideal and necessary. In those situations, in order to achieve the best group decision, the members of the group must be willing to share the resources that have brought them together. In situations where those resources are more intangible (meaning things like knowledge or perspective that cannot be held in your hand), communication becomes the mechanism by which the resources are shared. In simple terms, you cannot know the perspective of someone else in the group unless they share it with you. That is why we study group interactions in a communication context. Effective communication is the key to effective group operation.

COHESION: THE KEY TO COMMUNICATING EFFECTIVELY IN GROUPS

Quite simply, the key to group success is effective communication. Group members must be willing to share their thoughts and ideas and they must do so in a way that encourages others to share as well. However, for that to happen, a particular environment must develop in the group. People must feel it is okay to share with others, they must feel their ideas will be valued, they must feel respected as people, and they must support the ultimate goals of the group. In short, all group members must feel a commitment to the goals of the group, they must sense a personal stake in the success of the group, and they must be willing to place the needs of the group ahead of any particular individual goal. The degree to which a group fosters those feelings is measured by the degree of what we call cohesion in the group. Cohesion has been

Rate how important it would be to form a group to address each of the following tasks:

Design a new library for your college

Pick the color of the cover for a report

Count the number of seats in an auditorium

Pick an essay contest winner

The commonly accepted tradeoff for working in groups is less efficiency (more input of time) for better decisions. Do you think that is a good tradeoff?

defined by communication scholars Aubrey Fisher and Donald Ellis as "the ability of group members to get along, the feeling of loyalty, pride and commitment of members towards the group." The communication behavior group members engage in will greatly impact the level of cohesion in the group and by extension the success of the group.

DETERMINANTS OF COHESION

So how do we develop a high degree of cohesion in groups? In order to answer that question we must first identify the key determinants of cohesion. Most group scholars agree that there are three primary determinants of cohesion: attraction, member satisfaction and identification. **Attraction** is the degree to which members of the group are drawn to other members of the group. Essentially, it is a measure of how well the members of the group like each other. **Member satisfaction** is the degree to which the members are happy in the group. This will generally be determined by whether or not members like their role in a group, are comfortable with the group norms and are satisfied with the outcomes of the group process. Finally, **identification** refers to how much group members see themselves as an integral part of the group. Most successful groups develop as a single entity, not as a collection of parts. Therefore, in order for a group to be successful the members of the group must see the group in that way, which means seeing themselves as one functioning part in a large organism, not as an individual who happens to be a member of a group.

FOSTERING COHESION

There are several ways you as a member of a group can help develop these characteristics in a group. In this section, we look at some of the best methods for building cohesion in groups.

PARTICIPATE ACTIVELY

First and foremost, be sure you are an active participant in the group. As previously noted, the resources that tend to most help groups accomplish their goal are intangible resources that cannot just be handed over to the group. They are knowledge and perspective that must be shared, so be willing to do that. Communicate with other group members. Tell them what you know and what you think, but also be ready to listen. Just as the group needs to hear your ideas, they also need to hear everyone else's. Do not dominate the discussion; let others express their ideas as well. Active participation involves three key skills: communicating ideas, encouraging others to communicate their ideas, and listening carefully to the ideas expressed.

BE OPEN TO CRITIQUE OF YOUR IDEAS

Closely related to this first skill is a second that has to do with what happens after the ideas are shared. Those ideas must be examined and analyzed. In many ways, groups are the epitome of Aristotle's approach to rhetoric. Aristotle believed that through open discussion truth would emerge. If ideas were wrong or manipulative, they would be revealed as such through discussion and dialogue. In much the same way, the group arrives at the best outcome when ideas are discussed and the best ideas are allowed to emerge from the discussion. No one is ever always right, so we have to be willing to have our ideas examined and critiqued. This is particularly true because of the different perspectives that people bring to groups. We may see an idea as very solid because of the way we look at the situation, but someone else looking at our idea from a different perspective might see a flaw we did not see— and that is okay. If we are open to that analysis, ultimately the group will be successful, and that is what we want.

In order to have this happen in groups, we must remember two things: do not take criticism personally and do not make criticism personal. When evaluating the ideas of others, do just that: evaluate the ideas, not the person. Beware of comments like, "I would expect an idea like that from you," or worse, "Only a moron would present such a thought." Believe it or not, group interaction sometimes does get that personal. However, even if a comment is not that directly insulting, any comment that is focused more on the person than at the idea is likely to engender defensiveness. When people get defensive, they are not likely to share their ideas with the group, so always check yourself and make sure your comments are focused on the idea. On the other hand, when someone does evaluate or analyze your ideas, do not take it personally. In a good group, no one is out to win individual points—this is not a competition within the group. Recognize that the free exchange of ideas is what is likely to bring the group success.

AVOID PERSONAL AGENDAS

The third key to ensuring that groups have good dialogue is to remember that personal agendas are irrelevant. The goal of a group is to make the best decision it can. So, your goal should always be a good discussion process and a good outcome. You do not need to win every argument, and you do not need to show that you are always right. In fact, your personal success is irrelevant. If the fact that you presented these positions fostered positive discussion, even if the group eventually went off in another direction, then you have done your job. That should be your focus in a group. Beyond issues of discussion, always remember to focus on the group goal—never pursue any individual agenda in a group. Group members must work together. They must trust each other. They must believe they are all working for a common goal and a common good. If group members become suspicious of other group members, that is not likely to occur. Appearing to work for an individual agenda, rather than the group agenda, is one of the fastest ways to create suspicion in groups.

BALANCE GROUP ACTIVITIES

There are also things a group can do as a whole to maintain and improve cohesion. One is to maintain an appropriate balance in group activities. Many people believe that the best groups are the ones that just get down to work and "get it done." Most research indicates this is not true. There are actually three dimensions that need to be developed in group processes: task, social, and procedural. The **task dimension** is the easiest to recognize. Obviously, the group needs to get the job done—complete their task. Closely related to that effort is the **procedural dimension**: the way the group gets the task done. Groups must be willing to talk about that because, remember, one of the key factors in member satisfaction is whether or not group members are comfortable with the roles and norms in the group. Therefore, the procedures that a group uses to accomplish a task are as important to the success of the group as the task itself.

The last dimension is the **social dimension**. The social dimension has to do with the interpersonal attraction among members. Many people see this dimension as unimportant. They will tell you that they are there to get a job done, not to make friends. While that may be true, the social dimension is, in fact, important for several reasons. First, if people are going to be willing to share ideas and risk how the group will respond to those ideas, they need to trust the other members of the group. Developing the social dimension allows for the development of the

Why do you suppose trust is so important in groups?

Which of the three dimensions of the group process do you think is most important? Why?

interpersonal relationships that are necessary to foster that kind of trust. Second, the development of attraction requires that people get to know each other. Again, that is a function of the social dimension. Finally, while a group does everything it can to reduce defensiveness among its members, sometimes discussions will get heated and a group may need a break. Basic social topics like hobbies, interests, or even the weather can provide a safe haven for the group to cool down before continuing their discussions.

FOSTER A SENSE OF ACCOMPLISHMENT

In addition to maintaining a good balance among the three dimensions in a group, another way to build cohesion is to develop a sense of accomplishment. Given the nature of the tasks a group undertakes, it is easy to get discouraged. As noted previously, groups tend to work on large and complex tasks, which can seem daunting to individual group members. If members do not see progress toward their goal, they may get discouraged. To combat that, groups need to focus on their successes and remind themselves that they are getting things done. One of the easiest ways to do that is to break the large task into several smaller ones and establish a timeline for the completion of each task—then be sure to stick to the schedule. And, as the group reaches each milestone, recognize the progress that is being made.

MANAGE CONFLICT

Finally, groups need to manage conflict. Note that the term here is "manage," not "eliminate." Groups that never argue tend to make bad decisions. Remember we work in groups to get multiple perspectives on the issue. If we are not getting those perspectives, we will not make a good decision. In fact, complete agreement in a group is referred to as groupthink, which is one of the most serious problems that can occur in a group. Groupthink happens when groups stop engaging in critical analysis.

Can you think of a time when you avoided expressing an idea in a group, just to avoid conflict? What was the outcome? Do you think the group might have made a better decision if you had expressed your opinion?

One common mistake groups make is to try to eliminate conflict. They will do this either by limiting discussion of issues to avoid having to deal with conflicting viewpoints or they will adopt a decision system that avoids discussion like majority rule or simple compromise. Neither of these approaches is likely to lead a group to a satisfactory decision. The only way to avoid conflict between ideas and viewpoints is not to express those ideas and viewpoints and we have already seen that is not a good idea. As previously discussed, the key is to conduct the discussions in a positive, non-threatening way. People need to be comfortable expressing their ideas so that they are also comfortable with the outcome of the project, even if the group decides on a course of action other than the one they originally supported.

Conflict avoidance limits the effectiveness of the group process. Sometimes groups will just vote and go with the majority decision. There are three problems with this approach. First, just because more people agree with an idea does not make it the best idea. Again, the only way to know what is the best idea is to talk it out. Second, using voting techniques can put too much emphasis on the process and not the decision. Members of groups start "counting votes," thinking about how to get people to vote for their position rather than actually evaluating outlooks and alternatives and determining the best course of action. This is one of the fundamental failures of many government systems. Finally, as some people do better at building coalitions and collecting votes, the minority will begin to feel disenfranchised. That will undermine cohesion and the group will no longer operate as a unit. As we have already seen, that tends to lead to poorer decisions.

Another conflict avoidance decision-making technique is the uncritical compromise. This occurs when groups try to find a middle ground, when, in fact, none exists. For example, consider a group that is thinking about a daycare center. Let's say state law requires one caregiver for every four children (or fraction thereof) in daycare. Part of the group thinks the daycare should start with four children and one caregiver, so the operation is very simple until they have a good sense of how to run the business. Other members think there should be at least eight children and two caregivers to keep the business economically viable. When the group cannot reach a decision, they "compromise." They decide to take six children, averaging four and eight. The problems are they still need a second caregiver because they have more than four children, the operation is not as simple as it could be, and the economic picture is weaker because they have to hire the second caregiver and are not getting the revenue from the additional two children. Everyone loses. The group would be better off talking about the issues and finding a solution they all can agree with.

In sum, groups need to be willing to work through complex problems to reach shared solutions. They should not take shortcuts or work to avoid conflict. As previously noted, avoiding conflict can lead to groupthink and that is bad for groups. Groupthink occurs when groups are so concerned about avoiding conflict that they do not critically evaluate the decisions they make. Because critical evaluation is so important for groups to make good decisions, the results of groupthink are generally quite disastrous for groups. When a group is victimized by groupthink, they tend to make poor decisions.

IN REVIEW
You can build a climate that promotes discussion and effective decision making in groups if you...

• Participate actively

• Accept criticism of your ideas

• Avoid personal agendas

• Balance group activities

  • task

  • procedural

  • social

• Foster a sense of accomplishment

• Manage conflict (not eliminate)

Questions:

Reflections:

BEYOND THE FUNDAMENTALS

DRINKING THE KOOL-AID

In 1972, Irving Janis first identified the phenomenon he called groupthink, a situation where a group becomes more concerned with getting along than with making a quality decision. In those situations, the group avoids discussing different ideas and perspectives because they are not willing to risk the conflict such discussions could engender—they want to maintain harmony in the group. Recently, another phrase has been used to describe the phenomenon: drinking the Kool-Aid. The phrase is a reference to events that occurred six years after Janis first published his work, when more than 900 followers of cult leader Jim Jones committed suicide in Jonestown, Guyana by drinking cyanide-laced Kool-Aid. Since then, according to the Urban Dictionary, an online slang dictionary, the phrase "Drinking the Kool-Aid" has been used to refer to situations where people suspend critical thinking. Initially, the reference was to the fact that many cult members voluntarily committed suicide, seemingly without giving the decision much thought. The concept has morphed over the years to refer to any situation where people act without the appearance of careful thought, and the metaphor of collectively "drinking the Kool-Aid" has been used to identify situations where groups of people act communally, usually based on an outlook that is seen as inconsistent with a careful analysis of the situation. That is essentially what groupthink is. For example, the *Chronicle of Higher Education* in a January 2006 article noted that some people are using the phrase to identify collective misperceptions regarding United States' policy in Iraq. Likewise, *The Houston Chronicle* used the phrase in a 2002 article discussing the culture at Enron that permitted the actions that resulted in the financial crisis there. The same analysis could have been made about many other companies and their actions at the start of this century.

Out of context, the metaphor seems cute, raising visions of young children drinking Kool-Aid on a summer day. When one understands the origin of the phrase, 900 people drinking tainted Kool-Aid in the South American jungle, it certainly isn't cute. It is this second vision we should keep in mind when discussing groupthink. Groupthink is dangerous. When groups fail to examine issues carefully, and thus make poor decisions, people can get hurt. The space shuttle Challenger disaster is another example. Engineers were deeply concerned about the cold temperatures on the day of the launch and the negative consequences those temperatures could have on a critical component, the O-rings. However, ultimately they gave into pressure from others involved in the launch process and chose harmony in the launch team over careful analysis. In hindsight, we know that was a bad choice. While the consequences of groupthink don't always involve the loss of life, the poor quality decisions that groups make when affected by groupthink will generally have some kind of negative consequence. So, remember: the benefits of groups extend from the multiple perspectives and resources people bring to the groups. You must be willing to share your perspectives and outlook and you must be willing to allow others to share their views as well. Not everyone in a group should enjoy the same Kool-Aid. While the conflict and debate this interaction may create will make the group process more cumbersome, it will also lead to the best quality decisions.

BEYOND OUR PERSPECTIVE

©Corbis

WE MUST SHARE THE KOOL-AID

The prior discussion looks at the impact groupthink has on groups and their decisions, but groupthink has another impact that has not been as readily recognized. One of the results of groupthink is an increasing stridency in group opinions. Where groupthink is occurring, groups will come to see the dominant position as right and every other position as wrong, whether that position comes from inside the group or outside. That rejection of outside views can lead to another phenomenon known as polarization, where group positions become more extreme the more the group interacts with outsiders. The more polarized a group becomes, the more isolated it gets from other groups and the external context generally. So, one of the dangers of groupthink is that it can make a group more extreme and isolated.

However, polarization (and to a larger extent groupthink) has been studied as mostly an intra-group phenomenon. In other words, the focus has been on how these phenomena affect the group itself. But Dittus, in his master thesis, notes that there are inter-group impacts as well, and those impacts can be quite significant, particularly in a diverse world.

There will always be competing viewpoints in society, especially on significant social issues like abortion and police/citizen relations. Not surprisingly, within these debates people are likely to gravitate toward people who share their views. Because it is likely that group interaction will strengthen existing opinions, as people associate with "their own," those views will become even stronger. In fact, many people have noted that groupthink is most common when, among other things, there is a strong shared worldview. Additionally, the increased stridency on each side will become a justification for great insulation and more groupthink. It becomes a self-perpetuating cycle. Over time, each side moves farther from the other; dialogue and compromise become more difficult. We see this all the time: in discussions about events in the Middle East, abortion, and other social issues; and in interactions between Israelis and Palestinians, Shiites and Sunnis, Catholics and Protestants in Northern Ireland, and warring tribes in Africa.

Dittus' work focuses on developing better public input processes for government decision making, so his suggestion is to avoid the problem before it starts. However, there are situations where that is no longer possible. In those cases, people need to make the effort to come together, to drink the other side's Kool-Aid, and to share their own (metaphorically speaking, of course!). We need to engage in the critical thinking that is so important to effectively communicating with others. As we have seen throughout this text, from Aristotle's approach to rhetoric, to the need to build effective arguments in persuasive speeches, to the guidelines for effective group decision making in this chapter, open-minded critical analysis is an absolutely essential component of effective communication, and, it is equally critical to have harmony among people and groups. Watch for groupthink in groups you work with because it will not only affect the quality of your decisions, but it can, and does, affect your group's relationship with other groups.

Can you think of a time when a group you were working with was victimized by groupthink? Did you notice it at the time? If not, why not? If so, why do you think you couldn't stop it?

203

LEADERSHIP IN GROUPS

The last concept we should examine in groups is the idea of leaders and leadership. Clearly, someone has to help groups move through the process. Over the years, the analysis of who that person may be and how groups identify him or her have changed, but the fundamental goal of leadership in groups has not: to help the group make an effective decision.

APPROACHES TO LEADERSHIP

EARLY APPROACH

Early approaches to leadership focused on trying to identify one person who would lead the group. Some of these approaches focused on physical and psychological traits while others looked at people's leadership styles. All of them had one thing in common: they sought to identify people who would be leaders regardless of how the group developed.

THE FUNCTIONAL APPROACH TO LEADERSHIP

More modern approaches to leadership, sometime called the functional approach to leadership, focus more on the roles leaders serve in groups. The functional approach to leadership assumes leaders will help groups make good decisions and looks at what roles most likely will make that happen. Thus, the functions of leadership are behaviors that are likely to support an effective group process. These functions include encouraging all members to participate; controlling disruptive members; maintaining an appropriate focus on the task, while still managing the social dimension; and managing the procedural dimension to ensure effective meetings. No one person is likely to do all of these things well, so different people may serve as leaders at different times in groups. The functional approach understands that and, therefore, it does not seek to find a single person who can always lead the group. As with everything about group processes, the functional approach suggests that everyone in the group should make their best effort to guarantee a successful outcome. That includes offering their unique skills to help guide the group when those skills are necessary.

One of the potential practical problems with the functional approach is that frequently someone is put in charge of the group, often by an external agent (a supervisor or teacher who is not part of the group). That person is given the responsibility of making sure the group does its job and does it well. It is not surprising when that person wants to be the leader and guide of the group. However, when we are put in a situation like that, we should recognize our goal is still to have the group operate as effectively as possible to develop the best possible outcome. That is most likely to happen if we let everyone in the group share their talents. When someone is made the head of a group, they can still use the functional approach to leadership by allowing others to lead when appropriate. Remember, leaders will be most respected by the group and help the group accomplish its goals if they act from a perspective focused on helping the group, not one based on maintaining authority.

Can you think of a time when there was a "power struggle" in a group you were working with? Does the functional approach help you to see why that might have occurred? Does the functional approach also suggest a way you could have managed the conflict?

Is it necessary to have an official group leader for a project to be successful?

SUMMARY

This chapter has provided a very brief overview of the group process. We have seen that the group process is highly complex, but if a group can work through that process they are likely to make high quality decisions. We have suggested some ways you can help groups be more effective. Group communication is one of the most heavily studied areas of communication and whole classes are dedicated to effective group communication, so there is obviously much more to say. However, hopefully this introduction to the group process has at least provided you with some ideas and skills that you will be able to practice and develop. Those skills will help you be a part of, and even lead, an effective group. They will help you do your part to facilitate quality decisions within your own groups.

APPENDIX I

SAMPLE OUTLINES

Following are two sample preparation outlines that reflect different philosophies for presenting your plan for your speech. They are presented here to allow you to reflect on the strengths and weaknesses of the various approaches. Your professor will tell you exactly what form and level of detail your outline should have. There is also a sample of speaking notes so you can see how different speaking notes are from a preparation outline, as noted in Chapter 8.

SAMPLE OUTLINE

INFORMATIVE SPEECH

INTRODUCTION

Did you ever wonder why so many people have a fear of public speaking? Or why your parents warned you not to talk to strangers? The reason is simple: fear. Although the reasons behind these common questions may seem personal, like I fear public speaking because my face gets red, or universal, such as I didn't talk to strangers because I didn't want to get kidnapped, the actual reasons why humans have fear is much more subconscious than that. For my psychology final last semester, I wrote a research paper on fear from an evolutionary perspective. It was actually really interesting to discover the roots of some common fears, and learning about the most fundamental reasons people fear certain things can help lessen anxiety and fear. So, for the next few minutes, I will briefly explain why humans today have this universal reaction to fear, the difference between biological and conditioned fears, and the most primal biological fear and some of the conditioned fears that have derived from it—which includes the fear of public speaking.

BODY

I. This universal reaction to fear is called the "fight-or-flight response," but humans did not always have this. Instead, this reaction is a product of evolution.

    A. For our ancestors, who faced life-threatening and unavoidable perils on a daily basis, fear was vital for survival.

        1. Those that were quicker to respond to fear survived and passed this trait on.

        2. Throughout the following generations, this trait was perfected and continued to be passed down, which inevitably led to the instinctual "fight-or-flight response" that all humans have today.

    B. This reaction produces the same physiological responses in all humans.

        1. According to Don and Sandra Hockenbury, authors of *Psychology*, a psych textbook, stress hormones are released almost immediately, and a number of reactions happen simultaneously; a few examples would be pupils dilating to focus on the perceived threat, digestion stopping to reroute blood to the muscles and brain, heart rate increasing, and breaking into a cold sweat.

        2. These processes result in an instinctive response to either flee or fight the threat. Only after the threat is gone do body processes return to normal.

II. According to a History Channel documentary called *Primal Fear*, the main threats that instigate fear in humans are classified into two main categories:

    A. Biological Fears

        1. Those fears instilled by evolution because they are directly related to death; in other words, the fears our ancestors had.

        2. A few examples of these types of fears are animal attacks, fire, and darkness.

B. Conditioned Fears

1. Our ancestors didn't have these fears, but they are directly related to a specific biological fear. These are the fears that are unique to each person because they develop either from personal or indirect experience.

2. For example, the biological fear of fire was exploited in the Middle Ages when people would be publicly burned at the stake. Those who witnessed the burnings then developed a conditioned fear of being burned alive.

III. The most basic and primal of all fears is that of animal attacks, because our fight-or-flight response derived specifically from it.

A. Roughly 10,000 years ago, humans were hunted by the Smilodon (saber tooth tiger). Even with spears and other primitive weapons, humans were no match for it, so an intense fear of Smilodons and other big animals developed.

B. Because humans discovered just how physically unequipped we are to deal with our environment alone, a fear of being vulnerable in our environment developed. For this reason, humans banded together in order to hunt in groups for protection. Rush W. Dozier, Jr., author of *Fear Itself*, interprets, "early humans survived only through cooperation...several [conditioned] fears seem to relate to the dangers of either wandering off alone or finding oneself alone in a threatening situation."

1. Conditioned fear of isolation stems from the biological fear of animal attacks. The issue here is that someone might be trapped along with predators lurking.

2. Fear of strangers also relates to the social behavior of humans caused by animal attacks. According to Dozier, early human interaction was "probably limited to their immediate tribal band...[which] can breed a potent fear of strangers, who may have hostile intentions and represent a real threat...[this] might have led to a[conditioned fear of]strangers."

3. Coupled with this fear of strangers is that of speaking in public. Obviously because sometimes speeches are given to strangers, the reasons for fear of public speaking and fear of strangers are the same in that sense. Also, anxiety about failing in a social situation may have led our ancestors to be outcasts and alone in their environment, making them extremely vulnerable. One of the main issues of public speaking today, according to our textbook, is feeling different or feeling judged, both of which can make the speaker feel alienated and vulnerable— the same fear our ancestors had.

CONCLUSION

Although it may not seem like it with the cushy lives we lead today, the fight-or-flight response is indispensable for humans. Whether it is reacting to biological or conditioned fears, especially the most primal of all fears—the animal attack—our fear response was and is vital for human survival. It might not seem helpful when we get the same symptoms for seeing a tiger ten feet from us as we do for giving speeches, but understanding this reaction is key to using it to our benefit. So instead of dreading the scary act of public speaking, we can do what our ancestors did and get ready to fight the fear.

Written by Jamieson Credille, Used with Permission

What are the strengths and weaknesses of this outline?

SAMPLE OUTLINE
PERSUASION OF POLICY

INTRODUCTION

Attention-getter: Steve and Pat meet for dinner and compare notes on what they think has been a horrible day. Steve is upset because he has heard this great new song, and he wants to add it to his MP3 player, but he can't afford the cost of the download. He's really upset because he doesn't think people should even have to pay for music. Pat's day seems even worse. After years of hard work, her band has finally found a producer who is willing to market their music, but some of his other acts aren't making much money so he can't afford studio time for Pat's band, so they can't record their music.

Introduce Topic: What Steve and Pat don't realize is their concerns are related. Music piracy is threatening the music industry and our broader economy. If people like Steve don't pay for music, people like Pat won't be able to make music. We need to stop that.

Relate to the Audience: Like many of you, I never thought I would be saying that. I was more than willing to side with Steve.

Establish Credibility: In fact, I started working on this speech to argue that piracy should be allowed, but, after doing my research, I feel differently, and now I want to share with you what I have found.

Thesis and Preview: So, in order to demonstrate that we need to take a stand against music piracy, I will first show that music piracy does have negative impacts on the music industry and our economy as a whole and then I will tell you how we can personally take a stand against music piracy?

BODY

Transition: So what did I discover that made me "change my tune" about music piracy?

I.   There is a serious problem with people pirating music from the internet

    A.   60 million people have downloaded music

    B.   Many of those downloads are illegal

        1.   30% of people admitted to illegal file sharing (and how many more weren't willing to admit it)

        2.   About 1/3 of music in this county is actually paid for

    C.   They're only files; what's the big deal? The "big deal" is that stealing is wrong, and like any kind of theft, this activity has major consequences.

        1.   Stealing is wrong.

        2.   Internet piracy significantly hurts our economy.

What are the strengths and weaknesses of this outline?

    a. According to the Institute for Policy Innovation (IFPI), over 70,000 jobs and almost $3 billion in wages are lost due to internet piracy.

    b. This hurts our already fragile economy for people (unemployed and governments)

    c. Based on IRS data, this represents a loss of $300 million dollars in tax revenue for the Federal Government

    d. There would also be a loss for state governments

3. For those who feel this isn't really lost money because music should be free, there is another problem: the potential death of the music industry

    a. Artists have expenses

    b. They cannot make music if they can't cover those expenses.

    c. Andrew Lloyd Webber (noted theater musician and producer) recently stated he doesn't think there may be a viable music industry in Britain within 10 years—no more Beatles, no more Rolling Stones, no more Coldplay.

Transition: So, not only is piracy wrong and devastating to our economy, in the end, it is also self-defeating. People pirate music because they want to hear the music, but ultimately, piracy may kill the music industry. Given that, what should we do?

II. The solution rests in our hands.

    A. Legislative solutions are not likely to work—internet is too big

    B. A recent Canadian study found piracy is the worst in places where media costs are the highest. That shows companies need to develop pricing structures which minimize the sense of a need for piracy.

    C. But, most simply, we need to stop doing it.

        1. If we saw a really cool shirt at Old Navy, but we didn't have the money, we would save for it, not steal it—why should music be any different.

        2. Consumer can "vote with their click" by support services like iTunes or Moog which are providing reasonable cost music.

Which sample outline do you think would help you better prepare to present an effective speech? Why?

CONCLUSION

Review: So now you know: music can't be free and treating it like it is causes significant problems which only we can solve

Reinforce the Central Message: Based on what I have found, I would like you to join me in singing this different tune. I want you to be a part of a movement which rejects internet music piracy.

Logical Conclusion: I like music; I like hearing new music; I like discovering new bands. I'd love to hear what Pat's band is up to, and, if that means Steve and I and you have to pay a reasonable price for music, well, then, we should be willing to do that. I can accept that; will you?

Why do you think speaking notes need to be so brief to be effective?

SAMPLE SPEAKING NOTES

INTRODUCTION

Attention-getter: Steve (download) and Pat (band) meet for dinner

Introduce Topic: Concerns related = need to stop piracy.

Relate to the Audience: I used to side with Steve

Establish Credibility: After research I see things differently

Thesis: need to take a stand against music piracy

Preview: 1. Problem 2. Solution

BODY

Transition: why "change my tune"

I.   Problem

      People download (60M)

      People download illegally (30%+) (1/3 paid for)

      Problem

          It's wrong

          Hurts our economy (70k jobs/$3B wages/$300M taxes)

          Hurts industry (no money/no music, Webber's concern)

Transition: Save the industry, take these actions

II.   Solution

      Can't legislate

      Control costs (Canadian study)

      We take control (don't pirate, support reasonable priced options)

CONCLUSION

Review: Problem/Solution

Reinforce the Central Message: Sing my tune/stop pirating.

Logical Conclusion: Like music/willing to pay to save/challenge audience

What are some things you can do to make yourself comfortable working with notes that are this brief?

APPENDIX II

SAMPLE SPEECH EVALUATION FORMS

INFORMATIVE SPEECH

GRADING STANDARDS	GRADE	COMMENTS
Introduction		
C – Gains attention and states topic		
B – Meets "C" and establishes personal credibility		
A – Meets "B" and has a clear thesis developed, discusses importance of topic to audience		
Organization/Invention		
C – Pattern is easy to follow		
B – Meets "C," has relevant main ideas, and organization is appropriate for topic		
A – Meets "B," uses structural elements to aid audience, and logical ending to each main idea		
Analysis		
C – Main ideas are somewhat developed (i.e., not just a list of info), outside sources used and cited		
B – Meets "C," uses new and original info in main ideas, gives support to back up info used		
A – Meets "B," relates ideas to audience expertise, analysis is easily understood by audience		
Conclusion		
C – Brings speech to logical end		
B – Meets "C," reviews main ideas of speech		
A – Meets "B," summarizes importance of speech		
Delivery		
C – Uses a conversational manner without reading, rate and volume easy to hear and follow, has eye contact, uses appropriate posture, uses effective hand gestures		
B – Meets "C," uses appropriate pauses and inflection, has few verbal fillers, has near constant eye contact		
A – Meets "B," fillers don't distract from message, delivery fluent and articulate, has constant eye contact, fluently responds to questions		

In addition to using the criteria listed above, your speech is also evaluated in the context of the specific assignment given by your instructor. A student who develops a good speech may thus receive a low grade if he or she fails to do the assignment in part or in full (your instructor may provide specific information on various reductions and penalties). Also, your final grade (recorded to the right) is not a mere summary of your performance in each area but expresses the speech's overall effectiveness. Because a lack of skill in one major area often severely limits a speech's effectiveness, a speech that fails in any one area will likely earn an overall grade less than the average of the area grades.	GRADE

APPENDIX II

PERSUASIVE SPEECH

GRADING STANDARDS	GRADE	COMMENTS
Introduction		
C – Gains attention and states topic		
B – Meets "C" and establishes personal credibility		
A – Meets "B" and has a clear thesis developed, discusses importance of topic to audience		
Organization/Invention		
C – Pattern is easy to follow		
B – Meets "C," has relevant main ideas, and organization is appropriate for topic		
A – Meets "B," uses structural elements to aid audience, and logical ending to each main idea		
Analysis		
C – Main ideas are somewhat developed (i.e., not just a list of info), outside sources used and cited		
B – Meets "C," uses new and original info in main ideas, gives support to back up info used		
A – Meets "B," relates ideas to audience expertise, analysis is easily understood by audience		
Argument		
C – Takes a stand, position not completely clear, supports proposition, acknowledges existence of counterarguments but doesn't refute, neglects at least one form of rhetorical proof (source, emotional, logical), uses little or no fallacies		
B – Meets "C," clearly states position, uses support for position, refutes some counterarguments but not major ones, uses a combo of appeals, but not balanced, logical message that can be improved		
A – Meets "B," clearly states position and relates it to audience and situation, uses support that makes a strong impact, refutes significant counterarguments, balance of appeals, uses evidence and critical thought		
Conclusion		
C – Brings speech to logical end		
B – Meets "C," reviews main ideas of speech		
A – Meets "B," summarizes importance of speech		
Delivery		
C – Uses a conversational manner without reading, rate and volume easy to hear and follow, has eye contact, uses appropriate posture, uses effective hand gestures		
B – Meets "C," uses appropriate pauses and inflection, has few verbal fillers, has near constant eye contact		
A – Meets "B," fillers don't distract from message, delivery fluent and articulate, has constant eye contact, fluently responds to questions		

In addition to using the criteria listed above, your speech is also evaluated in the context of the specific assignment given by your instructor. A student who develops a good speech may thus receive a low grade if he or she fails to do the assignment in part or in full (your instructor may provide specific information on various reductions and penalties). Also, your final grade (recorded to the right) is not a mere summary of your performance in each area but expresses the speech's overall effectiveness. Because a lack of skill in one major area often severely limits a speech's effectiveness, a speech that fails in any one area will likely earn an overall grade less than the average of the area grades.

GRADE

APPENDIX II

INDEX

practice, 32, 111, 130

rate, 127

speaking notes, 110–111, 212

vocal delivery, 127–128

volume, 127

demonstration speeches, 52

denotations, 9

dependent arguments, 103

derived credibility, 119

descriptive speeches, 51

direct questions, 117

DiResta, Diane, 138

discriminative listening, 137

Dole, Robert, 189

domino effect, 161

doubtful authority fallacy, 160

"drinking the Kool-Aid," 202

E

Eisenhower, Dwight, 50

Ellis, Donald, 198

emotional appeals, 45, 46, 147

empathic listening, 137

ethical codes, 17–19

ethics

 audience and, 22–24

 definition of, 16

 ethical codes, 17–19

 ethical speakers, 17–22

ethnicity, 41–42

ethos, 20–21, 62–63, 71, 146–147, 173

eulogies, 186

evaluation forms, 215, 217

evidence

 evaluation of, 11

 purpose and, 58–59

Toulmin's model and, 149

 See also data

example reasoning, 155, 159

examples, 65

expectancy, 30–31

exposition speeches, 52

extemporaneous delivery, 110–111, 132, 184

eye contact, 128

F

fallacies, 157–161

false analogy, 159

false dilemma, 160

favorable audiences, 45, 50

feedback, 5, 23–24, 29

Field of Empty Chairs Memorial, 166

field-specific analysis, 151

First Amendment, 18

Fisher, Aubrey, 198

flags, 7–8

forums, 192

freedom of speech, 18–19

G

gestures, 129

global plagiarism, 22

goal setting, 28–29

goals. *See* purpose; thesis

goals-criteria persuasion speech, 105–106

Goldberg, Arthur, 194

Google. *See* Internet

groups

 attraction, 198

 cohesion and, 197–201

 communication and, 197–198